At Your Own Pace

At Your Own Pace

Traveling Your *Way*
in *Your Motorhome*

BERNICE BEARD

ARBOR HOUSE PUBLISHING
WESTMINSTER, MARYLAND

Arbor House Publishing
P.O. Box 2173
Westminster, MD 21158-3649
Tel: (410) 857-4146 Fax: (410) 857-3835

Ordering Information

Quantity sales. Special discounts are available on quantity purchases by corporations, associations, and others. For details, contact the "Special Sales Department" at the Arbor House Publishing address above.

Printed in the United States of America

Library of Congress Cataloging-in-Publication Data

Beard, Bernice, 1927-
  At your own pace: traveling *your* way in your motorhome / by Bernice
  Beard
1st ed.   p. cm.
Includes appendix and index.
International Standard Book Number: 0-9653063-9-9
    1. United States—Description and travel.
    2. Recreational vehicles—United States.
    3. Voyages and travels—Anecdotes.
917.304928-dc21 1997
Library of Congress Catalog Card Number: 96-95017
CIP First Edition

Editing: PeopleSpeak
Indexing: Rachel Rice
Interior Design: Joel Friedlander Publishing Services
Cover Design: Lightbourne Images
Cover Photograph: Susan Ruddick Bloom
Cover Talent: Sandra P. and Edward A. Tenney
Cover Motorhome: Holiday Rambler Endeavor, courtesy Endless Summer RV's,
    Frederick, MD

Every effort has been made to properly identify and capitalize trademark names used in this book.

The author and publisher assume neither liability nor responsibility to any person or entity with respect to any direct or indirect loss or damage caused, or alleged to be caused, by the information contained herein, or for errors, omissions, inaccuracies, or any other inconsistency within these pages, or for unintentional slights against people or organizations. The author and publisher are not associated with any manufacturers of motorhomes (or other products) and are not guaranteeing the safety of these homes.

*To Betty June Beaver, friend, who had no idea
her sincere questions about motorhoming
would lead to this book.*

*Jeff and Nancy, son and daughter-in-law,
who constantly inspire me with their creativity and
sense of what is important in life.*

*Paul, husband, who patiently unveiled the mysteries of
motorhoming to me and who continues to be my favorite
traveling companion.*

Contents

Preface

WELCOME TO THE WORLD of motorhoming! Whether you're an armchair traveler, perhaps thinking about renting or buying a motorhome for the first time, or an expert RVer, you're sure to have a wonderful experience when you travel *your* way in your own motorhome.

I remember vividly how bewildered I felt when my husband first began to talk about a motorhome, which was a mystery to me. I hardly knew what questions to ask. I wanted to read intimate details about what it was like to own and use a motorhome.

Actually, a friend who did not own a motorhome innocently and initially motivated me to write this book, even before our dream journey took place, when she asked probing questions about motorhoming. I realized her questions were the same ones I once had and that you the reader may have them as well.

We had owned a motorhome only three years before we took off on an exploratory journey to find a warm place to stay for a few months each winter. When we first bought our coach, my husband was retired but I still worked full time. We did, however, take a summer trip to the West Coast, which is when I decided to retire the following September on my 62nd birthday. Shortly after I retired, we spent two weeks motorhoming in New England, admiring the fall foliage. We had also used the coach on summer weekends spent with our church camping group.

So when we set out on our journey the following January to seek an escape from snowy Maryland winters, we had traveled enough to get the "bugs" out of our motorhome, but we still had to adjust to being retired—or at least I did. This was the first time in our 41-year marriage that we were together all day, every day. By the time I retired, Paul had been enjoying the peace and quiet of being at home and working uninterrupted on his projects. He had to adjust to my being there. As a former college administrator, I had to adjust to life without office associates and goals and motivations and challenges and schedules. I had to learn what retirement was and was not.

In thinking about where to go on our great adventure, we knew we wanted to explore new territory. We had visited Florida earlier so we decided to answer the call of the West.

Perhaps you, like Paul and me, have a background in tenting. Before motorhoming, our "RV" was a nine-by-nine-foot wall tent. We pitched it with enthusiasm when our son, Jeffrey, was young—and so were we. How well I remember air mattresses, sleeping bags, and getting cold during the night. After Jeff's days in Boy Scouts were over, we stayed in motels when traveling and only intermittently pitched the tent at a campground.

Eventually, we put away the tent and opted entirely for motels. We wrestled with carrying suitcases in and out and often left something in the car that we wanted in the room. No wonder we now enjoy the comfort and convenience of the motorhome, where our belongings ride with us and our suitcases stay at home in the attic. No wonder I want to share our experiences with you.

These pages take you along with us—letting you see what motorhoming is like and some of the ways people adjust while they enjoy the ride. In the appendix are questions that will help you build upon the experience of others, and the index refers you to useful tips and examples. I hope the photographs give you a better "picture" of our journey.

You may ask how I remembered all the details presented in this book. A journal keeper by nature, I was aided by notes I made both before and during our travels. Contributing to these pages were personal journals that were both hand-written and keyed into a laptop computer, transcription from a hand-held tape recorder, entries in a logbook, a daily calendar, a notebook of campground receipts and leaflets, slides, and a photographic log, as well as AAA maps and booklets, the *Trailer Life Campground/RV Park & Services Directory*, and local brochures and newspapers gathered along the way.

In addition, Paul gave me valuable technical information. As a retired central office technician who worked with long-distance and specialized circuits for the Chesapeake and Potomac Telephone Company of Maryland (later Bell Atlantic-MD), he has both passionate interest and proven experience in electronics, mechanics, and other technical subjects.

My background includes freelance writing, two college degrees, and 27 years at Western Maryland College as an admissions counselor, then assistant director of admissions, and lastly executive assistant to the president.

Many people brought this book into being, and I owe each one my acknowledgment and appreciation.

First of all, I thank wholeheartedly the members of the Westminster Church of the Brethren Camping Group for their part in my introduction to and continuing education and enthusiasm for motorhoming.

My heartfelt thanks go also to the following: Nancy Godwin, who encouraged me in the very beginning to try motorhoming; Dr. Pamela Regis, who said, "You can do it, Bernice. You can do it!" about publishing this book; Joyce Muller and Carol Wetherson for professional publication expertise; Jane Sharpe for expert library cataloging copy; Jan Hurst and Shirley Lippy, who enthusiastically laid the groundwork for my understanding of graphic design; Nancy Beard for designing the delightful drawings in the page headings; Thom Beckley, of Endless Summer RV's, for generously providing the latest model Holiday Rambler motorhome for our cover photograph; fellow campers Sandy and Ed Tenney for so graciously providing talent for the cover photograph early on a Saturday morning; Sue Bloom, art and art history professor and fine arts photographer, who included us so willingly in her very busy schedule; Lightbourne Images for the beautiful, enchanting design of the book cover; Joel Friedlander for the superb interior design of the book; and Sharon Goldinger, of PeopleSpeak, for her excellent, enthusiastic editorial expertise in bringing out the humanity and detail in these pages and for being a joy to work with.

A very special thank you to Nell Young, Betty Scott, and Nancy Godwin, who were the first readers of the manuscript and gave invaluable guidance. For believing in me and my writing, I thank sincerely all of those friends who have at one time or another encouraged me to write. I started to list your names, but I realized that I might miss someone, so please know that your words did not go unheard or unappreciated. And an all-inclusive thank you to the members of the Westminster Church of the Brethren; to the Western Maryland College community; and to the Nusbaums, Talbotts, and Beards for their continuing fellowship, friendship, and family warmth.

In closing, I thank you for opening this book and hope that our story will come alive for you so that you may build upon my experience in the captivating world of motorhoming. Now, sit back and enjoy the ride.

About the Author

Bernice Beard is a published writer of essays, articles, and short stories. In addition to writing, she is an active member of the Church of the Brethren. In 1989 she retired after a 27-year career in administration at Western Maryland College, a private liberal arts college, as executive assistant to the president emerita. She holds a bachelor of arts and master of liberal arts degrees from that same institution. Her favorite activities include oil painting, walking in the mall, and, of course, traveling in her motorhome.

She lives near Westminster, Maryland, with her husband, Paul. They have a son, Jeffrey, and a daughter-in-law, Nancy. In the seven years following her retirement, the author and her husband have taken 12 major trips in their motorhome, including a 44-day RV caravan tour of Alaska.

Chapter 8 in this book was the basis for the article "Mind If My Wife Drove This?" that appeared in the October 1995 issue of *Family Motor Coaching Magazine*. She is listed in the 20th edition of *Who's Who of American Women*.

· 1 ·

Getting Ready

MY MIND WAS GOING in all directions—
only 36 hours until Paul and I would set out on our dream journey;
36 hours to finish getting ready. In 36 hours, the gleaming, cream-
colored, 34-foot, Class A motorhome in our driveway would be both
condo and conveyor of my husband and me for at least two months.
We had only that Tuesday afternoon and Wednesday to finish loading, try out the tow car hitch, get last-minute groceries, do final laundry, clean the house, and do whatever else might pop into our heads
before we left.

We had developed a handful of "to-do" lists, of course, and followed them to the letter. But almost every last-minute duty accomplished had seemed to lead to another absolutely essential errand or
phone call. We had traveled in the motorhome before but never for
two months at a stretch. Before this dream journey, I was working
and our travel time was limited; however, now I would be retired.
Paul had retired four years earlier; I was new at it.

Breathless from trips between the house and the motorhome on
that wintry January afternoon to load supplies into oak cupboards, I
dropped into my favorite mint green, velvety recliner in the den for
my usual short nap. I raised the footrest and stretched out to relax,
breathing deeply and closing my eyes. I soon discovered that, unlike
my body, my mind kept going. It sought out an image it loved to dwell
upon—our dream journey that would begin on Thursday. From
scenes of our past travels as well as from brochures, magazines, and

books, it had created a delightful fantasy. That fantasy entailed finding a fabulous, ideal campsite somewhere out there, away from snowy winters in Maryland, that radiated warm sunshine—a place where we might return to in future years. In my mind I saw our motorhome nestled among forested foothills where we can look out beyond a deep blue lake toward distant mountain peaks. Around us friendly people are enjoying activities like oil painting and woodworking. A realistic question squeezed itself through my fantasy—Would we really find such a splendid campsite?

My mind lingered on that idyllic scene until other questions muscled in as if they were waiting for this relaxing moment to grab my full attention. While we're away, will I continue to feel connected to friends and loved ones? Will my friends think I'm running away from church involvements and responsibilities? What happenings at home will I miss? Will my English ivy in its ceramic planter survive in the well pit of the basement? Will the post office forward our mail to our son as requested? Will I grow lethargic as I ride along on the road all day?

On that Tuesday afternoon as my body continued to rest, my mind pushed ahead. I pictured Paul and me riding, eating, and relaxing inside the motorhome—day in, day out. What will happen to us as a couple during this long trip? Will we get on one another's nerves or will we develop a closer, more intimate relationship in that narrow space? Will Paul continue to "let nature take its course" or will he somehow learn to plan? Will I change? How? Will I overcome feeling guilty because I'm not "working"? Will I continue to write in my journal? Will I utilize my new laptop computer bought specifically for this motorhome trip? Will close quarters, constant companionship, and inevitable interruptions frustrate me when I want to write? With our intriguing motorhome itself a monument to mechanical and electrical engineering, will I master more of its operation, something I had postponed purposely until this leisurely trip? Will Mother Beard, my elderly mother-in-law who is in a nursing home, stay well?

With that last question, my mind leaped back to the evening before last. We had visited my one-in-a-million, selfless mother-in-law to say goodbye before our dream journey. She lived in a nearby nursing home, a caring place called Carroll Lutheran Village Health Care Center. As we talked, I couldn't help wondering if she'd be alive when we got back. Surely such a family death wouldn't happen again, as it had with Dad Beard the last time we went across the country on vacation in our car.

That trip was four years ago. We were 2,700 miles away from home when Paul got the midnight telephone call in our motel room in British Columbia. His father had died in the same nursing care facility in which Mother Beard now lived. He was 89. Although he had had a stroke a few years earlier that left him partially paralyzed, we hadn't expected his death. Distressed and saddened, we left for home immediately, driving night and day back to Maryland in our tan, two-door Lincoln Continental. Other than for gasoline, we stopped only once for a six-hour respite at a motel. In between my driving turns, I sat in the passenger seat reading the map or looking at scenery rushing past, or I lay napping on the back seat, unable to stretch my legs. We arrived home bone tired but in time to say goodbye symbolically to Dad and receive the sympathy of family and many friends during various memorial events.

Since that sad time, our lives have gone on, as they must. Not long after Dad Beard's death Mother Beard had moved into the health care center, where we visited her on Sunday evening. At 94 and with crippling arthritis, she lay in bed in front of us under a lightweight bedspread. She wore a pink sweater; its delicate color enhanced her softly curled hair, which now showed only tints of its former red color. She spent her days either resting in bed or sitting in a cushioned wheelchair beside it. When mobile, she used a walker or leaned on someone's arm. She had once told me apologetically that she never thought her hands and feet would get so twisted and painful.

Toward the end of our visit, she asked pleasantly how long we would be away. Paul joked, "We're not sure, probably six to eight weeks or until the money runs out!" I wondered if she, too, questioned whether she'd be alive when we returned. Outwardly unworried, she wished us a good time and a safe trip as she spoke slowly, with the familiar twinkle in her eye.

After we stepped into the hall away from her room to head home, I had mentioned my doubts to Paul. He had thought of that, too, he said, but he knew his mother would not want to keep us from going. And we had proceeded with our to-do lists that evening, all day Monday, and Tuesday morning.

My body lay glued to the recliner while my mind continued to roam. Paul retired a little over four years ago; I retired only four months prior to our big dream trip. We bought the Holiday Rambler motorhome while I was still working and had taken shorter "practice" trips in it. This vacation, however, was going to be different—we would be away from home longer, see many more new sights, and test the livability of the motorhome on an extended trip as well as how the two of us would get along being together day and night in a space much smaller than our house. The trip would be an opportunity for me to learn. I already knew how to drive the motorhome; I wanted to learn more about its operations and features—not exactly exciting adventures but experiences I thought would be valuable.

Many things motivated us to take *the trip*. We wanted to escape Maryland's blustery, snowbound winters and experience two months in a warm climate. We had enjoyed previous motorhome ventures—no suitcases to carry in and out of motels, the economical lifestyle, the chance to meet easygoing people from all over the country at campgrounds, and the convenience of daily activities in our own homelike travel facilities while going down the road. I must also admit that we wanted to see if we were really retired—if we fully accepted our freedom and knew what to do with it. It would be the "big trip" that many new retirees took.

In only 36 hours, it would be Thursday, the day of departure. I had no idea what time of day Paul wanted to leave, although I thought it would be in the morning. I would be ready in any case.

With my mind batting out its barrage of questions surrounding our upcoming trip, I remembered something especially valuable from psychology classes during my college days: the closer one got to carrying out a decision, the more uncertainty one would encounter about that decision. With our actual leaving so near, I realized my sudden questions were part of making a major decision; they were typical of the doubting phase, and I knew I should accept them as such and go forward with our plans. Moreover, I thought about Paul's earnest work in preparing our motorhome and tow car for the journey. He certainly wouldn't *not* want to go. As I thought about our detailed preparations and Paul's confidence in both himself and in me, my apprehensions quieted down. After all, we'd decided together to buy the motorhome and take this extended trip. Together, we'd work out any problems that might arise.

Instead of doubts, I began to picture us riding high above the road in the motorhome, adventuring toward a sunny paradise—just the two of us at our own pace. I thanked God for the way our lives had evolved and for the exciting journey ahead and then slipped off into a siesta.

·2·

Leave-Taking in Question

MY TUESDAY AFTERNOON SIESTA in the recliner lasted less than a half-hour. I awoke ready to tackle last-minute preparations. For weeks, both Paul and I had jotted down what we needed to do before leaving and what we wanted to take along. Now those to-do lists were almost completed.

When Paul and I had set our departure date, we didn't specify a certain hour in the day to leave. It was too early then, and as time went on I put off discussing the matter. Paul became consumed with getting his projects completed, even working into the night on preparing the tow car. I hesitated to put additional pressure on him by discussing a precise starting time, but by not doing so I had created a dilemma for myself. People had been asking me what time we planned to leave on Thursday. It was merely a social question for them. For me, however, knowing what my schedule would be had been very important in my career as an executive assistant to the president of a liberal arts college. Since retiring, I had felt a little lost when I didn't know what time I would do this or that. I had a strong desire to work by a schedule. Paul told friends and former coworkers that it only took him five minutes to adjust to retirement living. I wrestled with the notion of whether I was being wimpish by not discussing a starting time with my husband or whether I was showing loving consideration.

I let the quandary go unsolved, continuing to repress the urge to pin down a starting time. Instead, I concentrated on the next task, which was driving the Lincoln into Westminster to buy final groceries for the trip. Because of cloudy skies, the afternoon temperature had not risen much above freezing. As I rode along hoping the car heater would soon blow warm air, I pulled my soft wool scarf closer around my chin. I could hardly wait for the warm weather of the South and Southwest.

While I was in town getting groceries, Paul drove the motorhome with our old Toyota in tow about 30 miles north over the Blue Ridge Mountains to Waynesboro, Pennsylvania. He wanted to test how the tow car tracked behind the motorhome.

For this journey, we'd decided to pull a small car behind the motorhome—something new for us. We thought it would be useful for short trips and sightseeing. The most economical option turned out to be our faithful Toyota Corona with more than 200,000 miles on its odometer. That car had crisscrossed the country so often when our son used it to attend the University of Idaho that it would have known its way alone. Its former shiny, gold-flecked bronze finish, however, had become rusty, cracked, and pock marked. Paul riveted new metal where the old had worn or rusted and spray-painted areas needing a touch-up. Because of the Toyota's faithfulness over many years and the way it looked after Paul's repairs, we affectionately named it Patches.

To hitch Patches to the motorhome, we needed a tow bar that we could attach to the front of the car. After much thought and research, Paul bought and installed a Stowmaster.

We also had to be sure that the combined weight of the Toyota and motorhome did not exceed 19,000 pounds, which was the gross combined vehicle weight (GCVW) recommended by the Holiday Rambler Corporation. Earlier that Tuesday, Paul and I had driven the motorhome containing all but last-minute items onto the truck scales at Southern States Cooperative, Inc., a feed and fertilizer sales and service company in Westminster. While Paul was inside the office getting our vehicle weighed, a friendly woman stopped by my passenger window to ask for a handout. Unbeknownst to her and to me, she stood on the scale. When Paul came out of the office and saw her standing there, he may as well have seen an elephant. Seldom had I seen him as irritated as he was then. He had expected an accurate reading, something dear to his psyche, but that unsuspecting woman had caused an inaccurate one—and he had just paid $2 for it.

The poor woman had no inkling what frustration she caused my conscientious, overworked husband. Her weight, of course, made no difference in the overall picture. For even with her standing on the scales, the total weight was only 15,000 pounds. Since the Toyota weighed about 2,600 pounds, this added up to 17,600 pounds, still less than the maximum. This calculation assured us that the motorhome's engine, power train, brakes, front and rear axles, and tires could handle pulling the weight of Patches behind us.

It was late Tuesday afternoon when I returned from Westminster with the groceries. Paul had already come back from his test drive over the mountains. He was quite satisfied not only with the way in which the tow car tracked behind the motorhome but also with the auxiliary transmission fluid cooler that he had recently installed himself. The cooler's purpose was to keep the transmission fluid from overheating when we drive over mountains in the Southwest in anticipated hot temperatures.

As I transferred bananas from the brown paper shopping bag into one of two vegetable bins of the motorhome's refrigerator, I felt focused and good about what I was doing to make the trip enjoyable. I had put much more organization into this longer journey than into earlier, shorter ones. A natural organizer, I had labeled manila file folders for greeting cards, credit cards, paperwork for the Stowmaster tow bar, and other papers and lined up the folders in an oak overhead cabinet in the motorhome. Also, I had attended to details for this trip—things I didn't take time to do when I was working—like hanging small framed oil paintings on the dinette and bedroom walls of the coach and sewing Velcro strips on six pairs of draperies to keep them closed.

Through it all, I had followed my to-do lists, which helped reassure me that I had not forgotten something important. But all the while, my mind raced, coming up with more items to do. That morning, for instance, I had used toll-free 800 numbers to call Arizona camping resorts for cost and facilities comparisons. Then at lunch, I thought of making a list of credit card numbers with their applicable telephone numbers in case of loss or theft. Although we planned to use a debit card to obtain cash along the way, we were taking credit cards as backup. As I worked on tasks, I consciously tried to stay focused and relaxed, and to move in an unhurried manner, occasionally reminding myself that "slow and steady wins the race." Travel could be tiring, and I didn't want to start our dream journey frazzled and exhausted.

I did worry about Paul's health and energy level. I didn't want to tell him to slow down for that would have only added to his mostly self-imposed heavy load. I thought back to how, in finger-freezing wind, he had installed the auxiliary transmission fluid cooler. He had worked late at night in our garage preparing Patches to tow behind the motorhome. He seemed driven because he wanted everything done right and working well for the trip; he labored methodically and carefully on each detail of a task for as long as it took. Some motorhome owners would have had a dealer do these jobs, but Paul wanted to do them himself so that he could learn and understand as much as possible about the motorhome. "What if we're on the road and something breaks down? I want to know all I can about this coach," he told me repeatedly.

In addition to taking care of the mechanical projects for our dream journey, Paul also paid as many household bills as possible ahead of schedule. He decided what tools to take along, drove the motorhome to a local dealer for liquefied propane (LP) gas, called the *Baltimore Sun* carrier to stop the newspaper temporarily, and filled out a card at the post office that would authorize it to forward our mail to Jeff.

Wednesday morning came quickly. I finished the final loads of laundry and cleaned our one-and-a-half story Cape Cod home, which

I wanted to leave shipshape for possible houseguests like Jeff and Nancy. We had also invited Hazel and Elsie, Paul's sisters, to use the house while we were away. Both of them lived in Pennsylvania and traveled over mountains to visit Mother Beard at the health care center, which is about five miles from us; they might need either a rest stop or an overnight haven.

At 1:30 on Wednesday afternoon, I climbed into the cushioned chair at the Esquire Salon in Westminster for my weekly shampoo and blow-dry. I'm one of those people who thrives on "good hair days." Knowing that I'd need to get another permanent while on the trip, I asked my very competent hair stylist for detailed, written instructions so that I could pass them along to whoever did my hair en route.

That evening at the dinner table in our cheerful, yellow kitchen, I asked Paul if he was excited about our leaving tomorrow. Black grease splotched his tan work shirt; his sleeves were rolled up to his elbows. Strands of graying hair lay plastered to his forehead, indicating that he had been wearing his work cap. "I'm too tired to be excited," he said and then revealed that he was glad to be going but still had some things to do before we could leave.

His words sent a pang of uncertainty through me. What did he mean by "some things to do before we could leave," I asked. He stated emphatically that he would not leave town without stopping by the Nationwide Insurance office in the morning to drop off the license plates from a car he had sold recently and get the insurance straightened out on that and our remaining three vehicles. I had not realized he carried that obligation and wondered whether it would cause some major snag that would demand a delay and if we would really take off the next day after all.

With that new uncertainty and my husband's fatigue, my desire to have a definite starting time for the next morning faded. Visualizing Paul's all-out effort to get everything done, I asked myself whether it really mattered to have a set departure time. After all, we *were* retired and could leave whenever we were ready.

· 3 ·

The Lure of Motorhoming

ON THURSDAY MORNING, departure day for our dream journey, I hurried from the house through the cold drizzle, carrying last-minute items to the motorhome: my Bible and shower cap, our bathrobes, the brown crocheted afghan for the sofa, and the goose-down comforter just in case we had a chilly night.

"I think I'm ready when you are," Paul called from the garage through the adjoining hall doorway. "If you'll drive the Toyota to Nationwide, we can hook up down there after we're sure everything's okay with the car tags and insurance. Hooking up will be easier to do in the parking lot of the shopping center across from Nationwide. I think it's fairly level."

"Oh, okay," I yelled back trying to act matter-of-fact but feeling excited inside.

Nationwide Insurance Agency was a few miles east of Westminster in Finksburg. Paul had recently sold the 1964 Cadillac de Ville that he had restored. I continued to feel unsettled about whether the insurance matter would go smoothly. I knew that Paul wanted everything to be just right before we left town.

I shouted to Paul that I wanted to walk around in the house and give it one last check. I knew that if I didn't, I would feel uneasy, wondering if I'd forgotten or overlooked something. I paused in the doorway of each room, letting my eyes sweep the area for anything left behind that we would need, seeing if the room was ready for guests, and checking whether something remained plugged into a wall outlet that needed to be disconnected. Then I walked around in each room, looking at places I couldn't see from the doorway, and closed the door as I left. In the hallway leading to the garage, I switched off the light and bid a cautious but exhilarated farewell. "Bye, house! See you in two months—I hope." I locked the house and garage doors behind me. If I had missed anything, it would have to stay missed.

Wearing my tan, insulated, hooded full-length coat over lined navy blue pants and a long-sleeved red knit top, I slid into the cold vinyl seat of Patches, started the motor, and turned on the windshield wipers. I looked across the lawn toward the other driveway where Paul waited behind the steering wheel of the motorhome. He always warmed up an engine before starting out, whether it was one of the cars or the motorhome. As I watched, waiting for him to make eye contact before he pulled out, I thought about how this incredible moment had evolved—how the dream of a journey with a motorhome had started and then seemed to take on a life of its own.

Sometime, somewhere, during the early part of our 41-year marriage, Paul had seen a motorhome that charmed him. He had kept the image in the back of his mind until he thought we could afford one, which turned out to be just about the time he retired. I realize now that I had been oblivious to the degree of his motorhome fascination.

For me, even the word "motorhome" had been foreign. I had paid little attention to recreational vehicles except for unfavorably associating them with run-down trailer parks. I suppose I had seen small trailers, fifth-wheel trailers (those in the know just say "fifth wheels"), and motorhomes on the road, but they passed by invisibly as I dwelt instead on wildflowers and mountain peaks. And so when Paul began talking about these behemoths of the road, I only half-listened. He could have been discussing a strange mammal from the dinosaur age; those odd vehicles seemed so distant and foreign to me. (And I say that with only the utmost respect.)

When Paul finished restoring our Cadillac, he began to visualize a new hobby—some type of recreational vehicle (or RV). He began to point out people we knew who owned a trailer or a motorhome, some of whom had organized a camping group at our church. He lingered at newsstands looking at trailer and motorhome magazines and bought a few because he had a lot to learn, too. Occasionally, he showed an article to me. I politely indulged his curiosity, but I had no feeling about the "objects."

One evening as I sat at my desk at home, Paul marched in with his latest find, the March 1987 issue of *Trailer Life*. It contained a 15-page special section with articles entitled "Follow the Open Road," "Selecting a Rig," "The Cost," and "The Basics." Rarely did he go out of his way to bring an article in a magazine to my attention, and feeling rather flattered by his wanting to share it with me, I forced myself to read and to learn. The vocabulary was different, like that in a textbook on a new subject. "Full-timers" were people who had rented out or sold their real property and lived in their RVs year-round. A tow vehicle was the car or truck used to pull a trailer or fifth wheel. "Motorhomers" often towed a small car behind them.

The articles told how to handle banking, insurance, medical matters, and mail as well as how to keep in touch with one's family en route. I discovered that when traveling in an RV, there was usually more than one solution to a problem, just as there was at the office. Since I had found solutions to dilemmas there, perhaps I could do the same for predicaments that developed with an RV.

By the end of that reading session, my first serious interest in RVs had been kindled. I began to understand what RVs were, how people used them, and why they attracted travelers.

Ever so gently, almost offhandedly, Paul suggested that we go to RV shows in our area—"just to look." Attending these annual exhibits, which took place in enormous, high-raftered, warehouse-type structures at state fairgrounds and convention centers, was a phenomenon itself.

With a throng of other browsers in a great hubbub of movement, Paul and I traipsed in and out of hundreds of apartments on wheels—

Bounders, Southwinds, Pace Arrows, Airstreams, Winnebagos, Holiday Ramblers, Allegros, Prowlers, Itascas, Country Coaches, Jaycos, Monte Carlos, Newmars, Excels, Carriages, Georgie Boys, Foretravels, Tiogas, Terrys, Komforts, Tauruses, and Shastas. Like colleagues at a huge company picnic, we struck up conversations with RV owners and potential owners, picking up facts and opinions. We discovered that RV manufacturers had reputations for different things: prices, innovations, standing behind their products, giving customers their money's worth, quality of materials, and skill of construction in their vehicles.

As we wandered inside the mammoth buildings, we gawked, amassed brochures, chatted with other visitors, and sometimes waited in line to enter a vehicle. There was so much to absorb. Breaks were a necessity for both mental and physical needs.

We got caught up in comparisons—Paul would mention a feature that attracted him while I did my best to relate to it and keep in mind what I liked. We learned that motorhomes, those vehicles that contained both the living quarters and engine in the same unit on wheels, could be Class A (buslike), Class B (van type), or Class C (with a bed or storage area over the cab). Trailers were units pulled behind cars and included fifth wheels that hooked to pickup trucks. With that knowledge, we felt more competent to compare categories—conversion vans, conversion buses, pop-up tent trailers, trailers, and motorhomes—and categories within categories.

We compared sizes from 15 to 40 feet long and prices, which ranged from $2,800 for pop-up trailers to more than $200,000 for Class A motorhomes. We explored similarities and differences in floor plans, accessories, options, color schemes, and gas or diesel engines.

We met dealers and manufacturers' representatives. Though friendly, smiling, and not pushy, they could not always provide answers to Paul's probing questions. What is the rear axle ratio on this motorhome? Does it have an auxiliary transmission fluid cooler?

While Paul asked more technical questions about the electrical and mechanical systems, I soaked up information on colors, fabrics, and floor plans. Sometimes I browsed alone among the vehicles and exhibit booths, many of which publicized campgrounds (more auxiliary information to gather and absorb). Too green to ask questions, I hoped the friendly looking strangers behind their tables would not pressure me as I paused to look, and surprisingly, they did not.

On the way home from each show, I purposely repressed any attraction I felt toward a specific RV because I was not yet sure if this was the right direction for us. Simultaneously, I tried to be open to talking with Paul about what I liked or definitely would not want in an RV. Yet even as I walked this tightrope, without recognizing it, I was bonding with Paul on his motorhome vision.

Away from RV shows, Paul questioned members of our church's camping group about their vehicles and experiences. In the winter, a few months after we first expressed an interest in RVs, they invited us to an ice cream social where they made plans for the upcoming camping season. They used familiar words in a new way. A "wagon master" contacted campgrounds to reserve sites, and the members spoke of "hooking up" and "dumping." At least I was able to understand their lingo when they relived sensational potluck suppers and hilarious tales of campfire follies.

In his usual meticulous, independent, take-charge manner, Paul continued his research, including following up leads on used (or "previously owned") RVs for sale. He began subscribing to trailer and motorhome magazines. He thought he would prefer driving a motorhome to pulling a trailer. As a young man, even while still in high school, he had driven a school bus part-time and later, when he was 20, a truck that hauled apples. He thought a motorhome would handle similarly. When he visualized our car pulling a trailer, he pictured high cross winds buffeting them about, causing him to feel anxious about properly handling the two linked units. He liked the stability of handling, backing, and parking one larger vehicle. But he still wasn't sure. So with a week of vacation ahead, we rented a 27-foot Allegro motorhome from a local dealer, Metro RV of Finksburg. It cost $625 a week plus ten cents a mile.

We set off in this great carriage with Paul beaming behind the wheel and me feeling courageous for accompanying him, a novice motorhome operator, on this unconventional adventure as we traveled south from our home in central Maryland into Virginia. The spare tire cover said it well: "Roughing It Smoothly." As former tent campers, we thought this motorhome was incredibly luxurious.

After sightseeing a few days, we parked on a roadside site in the Peaks of Otter Park Campground in Jefferson National Forest. Early the next morning, with no other campers in sight, I sat with my journal at a picnic table on the woodsy slope adjacent to our unit. I wanted to hear the sounds, breathe in the fresh air, and soak up the beauty of the forest. Tall trees surrounded me; birds trilled as if announcing the new day. Once as I paused from scribbling, I saw a fawn observe me and deftly disappear in the underbrush. Breathing deeply, I looked around at the green hues and intricate patterns of the woods then toward the cloudless sky. I couldn't help but thank God for creating all that I saw and for renewing and refreshing my spirit.

Meanwhile, Paul had gotten up and made the beds. We had twin beds at home and had purposely asked for them in this rental. Paul climbed the low bank toward me and said, "I know one thing."

"Early the next morning, with no other campers in sight, I sat with my journal at a picnic table on the woodsy slope adjacent to our unit."

"What's that?"

"If we ever buy one of these things, we're not going to have twin beds!"

"Why not?"

"They're too hard to make! You can't get to the other side. You have to get on the bed to make it right!" That settled the bed question. From then on, we would look for floor plans with a queen-sized bed that could be made from both sides.

After Paul shuffled back down the bank to the motorhome, I confided to my journal:

> I think we may be on a roll toward a motorhome. It could be exciting, something new and different in my world. I like to do new things and go new places. Yet I feel conscience-stricken about spending $60-80,000 for a second home. It's probably my Church of the Brethren upbringing. I think about people who have no home and who are starving as well. Growing up during the Great Depression may also be part of my hesitancy.
>
> Would a purchase later weigh on us as an outdated monster whose market value had depreciated drastically, thus causing us to take a tremendous loss during our retirement years? Are we foolish to consider this size of an expenditure? Where would we park it? Would we enjoy it, or would it bring its own problems like a swimming pool that draws "friends" you never knew you had?
>
> My biggest hurdle is spending so much money on something for ourselves that we do not really need. Is that a sin, Lord? I have no problem spending smaller amounts of money for bowling or movies, or even a trip abroad. Is this merely the equivalent of combining many smaller recreational expenditures?

The rented motorhome came with a sofa located across the aisle from the dinette. By the end of the week, we knew that if we could afford it, we wanted a separate living room area in which to relax. We also knew that we liked having a separate bedroom rather than converting a sofa to a bed every night. Those choices would require a longer coach—ergo more dollars—but for comfort Paul was usually willing to pay the price.

As we discovered these preferences, I wondered if they would lead toward an actual purchase, and if so, what would we buy? At the Virginia campground, we had talked with an enthusiastic motorhoming couple who served as hosts for the park. They were living in a spacious 34-foot Class A Imperial Holiday Rambler, which they liked tremendously and came with all the options—even an ice-maker. They insisted on showing us the inside and then gave us printed materials on how to join the Family Motor Coach Association if we did buy a motorhome. I was impressed and happy for them but dared not think that someday a similar grand vehicle might be ours.

· 4 ·

Motorhome Shopping

WHEN WE RETURNED home from Virginia, Paul was eager to visit more RV showrooms—his vision of ownership became clearer due to our rental motorhome experience. Wasn't it too soon? We had not yet explored the preowned market. We decided to find out more and investigate a less-expensive unit. Paul subscribed to *FMC Motor Coach Mart*, a publication of *Family Motor Coaching* magazine, which advertised preowned vehicles. Together we watched for listings of preowned Class A models in other motorhome magazines and on dealer lots. For me, our casting about was an enjoyable game because it gave us a fun focus, like people hunting for antiques.

We were having problems finding a used motorhome that was right for us. If we liked the floor plan, I didn't like the orange, plush fabric on the upholstery; if I liked the fabric, Paul didn't like the type of engine in the motorhome. And so as we continued to visit dealers, we began to look at *new* motorhomes. We took test rides in one or two of our top choices.

At one dealership, we were walking around the lot with its endless lineup of RVs when an energetic salesman joined us. After talking a few minutes, we accepted his invitation to try out a brand new motorhome.

Inside, I perched on the sofa's edge behind Paul in the driver's seat as we left the dealer's property and drove onto the highway. Paul and the salesman talked about engine size, gas mileage, and maneuverability of the 33-foot vehicle. Suddenly Paul asked, "Would you mind if my wife drove this?"

The salesman looked back at me and I gulped. "Sure, that'd be fine," he said. Paul pulled over.

I transferred myself and my astonishment to the driver's seat. I could not believe the salesman was letting me drive that big, strange box on wheels, fresh from the factory. (How could he trust a novice like me?)

From the chair behind the passenger seat, Paul leaned toward me and calmly told me that driving a motorhome was like driving our Lincoln. He said it had automatic shifting, power brakes, and power steering.

"Just put it in 'D' for Drive and step on the accelerator," he said in a calm, deliberate voice.

As I pressed the gas pedal and clenched the steering wheel, the motor revved louder and the enormous vehicle moved ahead. The two men directed me out onto a winding country road where the mailboxes seemed to leap out from both sides.

I remembered the salesman saying earlier to Paul, "Most new drivers stay too close to the edge of the road." I, too, wanted to hug the edge—it was surely safer than being too near the center of this narrow road with oncoming traffic.

My peripheral vision sensed dark objects whizzing past. From behind me, I heard Paul comment that I barely missed that mailbox. His voice sounded carefully controlled. By that time, although brief in actual minutes, I was more than ready to terminate my test drive.

"Where shall I pull over?" I asked. Amazingly, we all survived—and not one mark on the vehicle. (I was thrown into the ocean and somehow controlled a whale!)

I think this test drive was what finally convinced me that Paul was serious about buying a motorhome. As I went about my days at the office, I got a secret thrill when I thought about my test drive. From then on, I wholeheartedly accepted the idea of RV ownership.

I realized that the motorhome vision had hooked me, too. There was no turning back.

I was still working full time at Western Maryland College, but Paul had time to scout around on weekdays, taking his time, seeing what was new, and discussing with salespeople the questions that he had. And so it was that on one special Saturday, Paul invited me to Beckley's Camping Center near Thurmont, Maryland, where he had seen a coach that he liked on one of his solo exploratory trips.

"It's sold, but I'd like to get your opinion on it. I've talked with people who started with a 21-foot motorhome and then traded up to a 24-footer, then a 27-footer, and then a 33-footer. Each time they lost money due to depreciation. I think we'd be smart, at our stage of life and perhaps wanting to live in this vehicle for a couple of months at a time, to buy what we'd ultimately like to have," Paul reasoned.

As we approached Beckley's Camping Center, which was about 26 miles from our home, I saw that its three-acre lot abounded with trailers and motorhomes. We walked among parked motorhomes in the outdoor showroom until Paul said, "I believe this is the one."

"This one?"

I stood facing the front of a vehicle towering high and extending beyond my view—a 34-foot Holiday Rambler Class A motorhome. It looked like a Greyhound bus! I drew in my breath and dared not think this behemoth could be in the running for us. The others we had tested were not this gargantuan. Paul had really surprised me. I never dreamed he would be interested in one like this! He would never spend that much money, would he? He's usually conservative, even to the point of wearing his clothes to shreds. Yet I must say when he decides to do something, he does it right. He's fond of the saying "It only costs a quarter more to go first class." But wouldn't this kind of monster be overdoing it for us (and anyone else who dared to be on the road at the same time we were)?

"Let's see if it's open," he said.

Paul unlatched the side entry door, located more toward the front of the motorhome than the back. As I stepped up into it, I immediately fell in love with the soft blue tapestry fabric on the upholstery of the dinette seats and sofa. I explored from back to front, left to right, ceiling to floor, getting a feel for what the coach offered and how the various living areas were arranged. In the rear was a queen-sized bed with aisles on both sides. The adjacent bathroom contained ample elbow room in the shower. Off the hallway, I opened lots of closet doors, including a tall one for robes and full-length coats. Midship, opposite the dual stainless steel sink, counter, and range top, the refrigerator/freezer loomed larger than I thought possible in an RV. Forward, I sat in the driver's seat and in the passenger's seat and tried out the two beige upholstered swivel chairs across from the sofa in the living room area.

Eventually, Paul and I sat on the sofa and talked, taking our time, getting up to examine specific features as questions came to us. Paul's voice sounded serious and objective—I could tell that although he was thrilled inside, he didn't want to show any emotion and unduly influence me. I knew he liked this motorhome and that it was his carefully considered choice. Then he asked me, point blank, what I thought about this particular motorhome—for us. Well, could Cinderella refuse the beautiful coach transformed from a poor pumpkin? Could she refuse to try on the glass slipper offered by Prince Charming? We both finally had a passion for the same vehicle—this Holiday Rambler motorhome.

Paul was ready to make a deal and so was I. After talking with the salesman, Max Bowker, about costs and specifics of ordering options, we went home to discuss it further. Having forgotten to ask during our visit, Paul called the salesman to find out what amount of deposit would be required should we decide to order the motorhome.

A week later, we sat across the desk from Max in his small but adequate, wood-paneled, glassed-in office at Beckley's. I could hardly contain my excitement, but Paul seemed very much under control. We ordered a Class A, 34-foot Holiday Rambler Presidential motorhome—complete with a kitchen on the curbside of the vehicle, a queen-sized bed, and light oak interior—and paid the deposit.

We each had our own reasons for choosing the Presidential model over the Imperial. The long, wide silver stripe on the sides of the Presidential model appealed to me more than the gold one of the Imperial. As a fair-skinned brunette who was an adherent of the *Color Me Beautiful* principles, I knew silver was a better hue than gold for me and had come to prefer it.

Paul wanted the Presidential for other reasons. While it was the same basic coach as the Imperial that came with "everything," the Presidential offered a choice of options, thus allowing us to save money by not ordering some of the items that didn't seem worth the expense, such as the icemaker and power/heated/remote aerodynamic exterior mirrors (which we later wished we had).

Working from a list we brought with us and talking with Max, we ordered as options a microwave/convection oven; central vacuum cleaner; cable television hookup; Intec television monitor (in place of a rear view mirror); a Citizens Band (CB) radio hookup and antenna; two power seats for the driver and passenger; a 12-volt, dual-disconnect switch; a 4.0-kilowatt Onan auxiliary generator; HWH (the corporation's name) hydraulic leveling jacks; LP gas detector; smooth sides (instead of corrugated); a rear hitch; the Captain's package (an oak beverage and article holder located between the driver and passenger seats); and a Coleman roof air conditioner. Oh yes, I nearly forgot—and blue and white A&E Elite 9000 awnings!

Ecstatically, I selected Jefferson County fabric for the sofa and dinette cushions; it was the same material that I had seen in the coach Paul showed me the week before—a tapestry design with a soft blue background, large white and pinkish-peach flowers, and occasional narrow stripes in the same white and pinkish-peach color. Beige carpeting came with the Jefferson County fabric selection. On the way home, we animatedly (as much as possible for Paul) reviewed what we had ordered. It felt like all my childhood Christmases at once— only we were our own Santa Claus!

While we waited to receive our new vehicle, we decided to visit the Holiday Rambler manufacturing plant in Wakarusa, Indiana. Perhaps we could see our very own motorhome in the making. It turned out that the motorhome plant itself was not open to visitors, but we joined a tour visiting other buildings of the Holiday Rambler complex in which trailers and fifth wheels were manufactured. We gained an appreciation for the complicated process and the dedication of the people on the assembly lines. Then we went home to continue waiting.

· 5 ·

Our New Motorhome

TWO MONTHS AFTER we ordered it, our Holiday Rambler arrived at Beckley's! Max Bowker called to tell us that it had been driven east from the factory in Indiana. Although the dealer had to check it out before we could bring it home, Max offered us visiting privileges. I was still working but excitedly arranged to visit it with Paul during an extended lunch hour.

When we arrived at Beckley's, we quickly singled out our new motorhome in the parking area in front of the showroom—it looked like a newborn because it needed washing from its travel east and its black tires were not yet dressed with shiny chrome wheel covers. A huge hulk, it embodied enormous energy as it seemingly strained for the highway. Although disappointed by its outward state of nudeness, I could hardly wait to see the inside.

Sure enough, Jefferson County fabric greeted me from the sofa and dinette. I *liked* it! Breathing in its newness, I sat on the sofa. I tried the electric seats up front, opened oak cupboards and closets, stroked its real wood, stood in the shower to check out elbow room, and admired the white and blue floral draperies in the bedroom. I walked on each side of the queen-sized bed.

When Paul came inside after looking over the exterior of the vehicle, I was trying out a beige swivel chair in the living room area. One of two, it was bolted to the floor flanking a small table fastened to the wall beneath the curbside window. Both swivel chairs faced the sofa as did the small table between them. Delirious with realization, we left Beckley's and I returned to the office where I could not help but share my excitement.

A few days later, again at the dealership, we handed Max a check for the motorhome. We had driven the Lincoln to Beckley's and planned to drive the new vehicle home together, and then return later in the day in the Toyota to pick up the Lincoln. Outside the showroom, I took a picture of Thom Beckley, the service manager (and later, owner of Endless Summer RV's near Frederick, Maryland), handing the keys of our brand new coach to a grinning Paul, who kept any elation under his usual careful control.

"Are they really the keys to this?" I asked Paul as Thom walked away and we headed for our freshly washed and prepped coach with its shiny chrome wheel covers.

"They'd better be! We paid enough for them!" Paul said. As he held open the motorhome door, I walked up the steps and into the coach, carrying my journal and tote bag, feeling as excited as

"Thom Beckley . . . handing the keys of our brand new coach to a grinning Paul . . ."

Cinderella must have been when she was going to the ball. Paul followed and closed the door, and I heard the electric, outside metal steps folding underneath the frame.

"I guess I'll drive this time?" Paul offered.

"Please!" My knees felt weak. Also I had something else in mind. I told Paul that I wanted to ask him something.

"Shoot," he said.

"I brought along a bottle of sparkling juice and two mugs. I was wondering if we could have a kind of little dedication service. Maybe somewhere between here and home. You know, like we did for our house when we first moved in—when Dorothy LeFevre sang 'Bless This House.' Do you think you might be willing to do something like that?"

"Okay. But let's move out of here. Maybe we can find a place to pull off the road on the way home or even do it at home," agreed Paul. I secretly hoped we would dedicate the motorhome en route—the sooner the better.

A few minutes later, in a lovely, peaceful wooded area on a wide shoulder of US 15, Paul parked our RV and turned off the motor. He asked that the ceremony not be too touching as he gets sentimental and emotional rather easily. With our heads bowed, I thanked God for that extraordinary moment in our lives and for all the people who had made it possible, and I prayed for God's blessing upon both the vehicle and us, asking that we would be safe drivers and good stewards in the use of the motorhome. I ended with a benediction from Numbers 6:24–26 (Revised Standard Version): "The Lord bless you and keep you: The Lord make his face to shine upon you, and be gracious to you: The Lord lift up his countenance upon you, and give you peace."

After the prayer, Paul opened the bottle of Sundance Sparkling Cranberry Juice Cocktail, poured some into a mug for each of us, and then raised his mug and said, "To you," and I raised mine to his, clinking them together. Laughing, we decided not to go outside and smash the bottle against the vehicle as people do when launching ships. I could have stayed longer, enjoying the moment, but Paul was anxious to get our new one home.

As we settled in for the rest of the drive, Paul immediately took to handling the machine well, as if he had rehearsed in his mind those moments of being behind the steering wheel and gliding down the road. His dream, his vision of ownership, had come true and he was more than ready for it! I was still feeling a bit wary about totally accepting the unit. In a short time, however, I would come to love the motorhome and the idea of going away in it. When we got home, we parked the new rig on one side of our driveway and then drove back to the dealer's lot in the Toyota to pick up the Lincoln. Later Paul would prepare a separate driveway and concrete pad for the motorhome on the opposite side of the house and lawn from the existing driveway.

We had become owners of a motorhome. As a teenager, Paul had yearned to own an airplane; he hung around the local airport and exchanged labor for lessons until he got his solo license. When we got married, he postponed his dream. I, in turn, had dreamed of a new home on a wood lot we owned. An architect drew exciting plans for it. Then Paul became ill and we put the construction on hold. Eventually, we expanded and remodeled our present house instead. I knew that my early reluctance to fall in love with a motorhome that might never materialize was based on the earlier disappointment. But now, this offspring of Moby Dick had turned out to be Paul's airplane and my home in the woods, our dreams-come-true in a way neither of us had expected. No wonder I had wanted to thank God for his generous provision in a ceremonious way as soon as possible.

I struggled to bring my thoughts back to the present as I waited in Patches for Paul to finish warming up the motorhome in the driveway across the lawn from me. We've closed up the house and we're starting on our trip today. It was no wonder either that I now smiled as I looked at Paul sitting high inside the motorhome and heard the engine as he revved it. His vision had brought us to this exhilarating moment. From my place behind the steering wheel of the tow car in the main driveway, I nodded my head to show him that I was ready.

As Paul pulled out, I wondered what time it was so that I could write it in the motorhome logbook that I had decided to keep whenever we traveled. Alas, my wrist watch had stopped working just before I retired, and I thought it would be fun to see if I could get along without one. Now I wished I had one. In the motorhome, I would have looked at the wall clock in the dinette and jotted down the time.

Nevertheless, I steered Patches behind the motorhome and down the long hill of the paved country road that ran in front of our house. Once on the highway, I tried to be the first car following Paul yet allow enough space between the motorhome and Patches for traffic to pass around me.

As we curved around the outskirts of Westminster on Route 140 headed toward Finksburg and the insurance office, I glanced at the Vermont Federal Bank sign: 44°, 10:27 A.M. You did it again, Lord! I chuckled to myself. You provided that humongous clock so I could know what time it was. Thank you!

A few miles farther, at Finksburg Plaza shopping center, Paul parked the motorhome and joined me inside Patches. We then drove in the cold, steady rain across the highway to the Nationwide Insurance office. Our business there took only a few minutes, thanks to its staff's efficiency. Afterward, outside the office, I asked Paul if he was satisfied with the insurance arrangements.

"Yes," he said. "Now I can leave town feeling that's all taken care of." Now that all had worked out with the insurance, I started wondering where we would be spending the first night of our dream journey.

· 6 ·

Heading Out

SATISFIED WITH THE insurance situation, Paul and I returned through steady rain to the shopping center parking lot where I positioned Patches behind the motorhome. Juggling my red umbrella over his head, Paul began the simple process of attaching the tow car to the motorhome. I stayed in the driver's seat so that I could inch the car forward when Paul signaled that he was ready. How relieved I was that the insurance business had gone smoothly. We could leave shortly and make our way south toward New Orleans before heading west to Arizona and California. Our next uncertainty, albeit an expected one, was where we would find our first campground that night.

In front of me, Paul had unfolded the tow bar from the front of Patches and beckoned me to slowly drive the car toward him as he stood behind the motorhome. Then he lowered the socket of the tow bar tongue onto the ball of the hitch at the rear of the motorhome. Clunk! He made an across-the-throat motion indicating that I could turn off the motor.

After Paul fastened safety chains between the two vehicles, he pushed a heavy black electrical plug from the tow car into an electrical outlet at the rear of the motorhome so that the brake, turn signal, and other outside lights on the two vehicles lit at the same time, which is an essential safety measure when towing a car. It was as easy as plugging in a lamp at home. I had always wondered how others had done this when driving behind them on the highway.

Even though it was raining, Paul wanted to be sure that the electrical connection worked. To check it, I dashed through the rain to the driver's seat of the motorhome. Paul stood behind Patches, red umbrella and all, giving hand signals to me. As I looked into the side-view mirror on my left, I responded to his hand motions by turning on the left turn signal, then the right turn signal, and finally pushing in the brake pedal. Each time, Paul glanced to see that the pertinent lights came on for both the motorhome and the tow car. Already, I saw that participating in the hookup and checking steps was making me feel a part of our journey.

After the test, I stepped around the carpeted engine hump to the passenger seat while Paul settled behind the steering wheel and turned on the ignition. Soon he shifted into Drive and pulled away slowly from our parking place while watching the rear view monitor and the side view mirrors to be sure the wheels on Patches didn't lock sideways and drag on the asphalt. He appeared nonchalant, as if we were off on just a weekend of camping.

While we now took the rear view monitor for granted, it was a very important "window" to what happened behind us. Its television-like screen to the driver's upper right worked with a video camera perched on the roof at the rear of the motorhome that sent a picture of everything from the rear bumper to about 20 feet backward, making a rear view mirror obsolete. Whenever we slipped the gearshift into Reverse, this small black-and-white screen switched on automatically, or we could operate it manually. At that moment, we were driving with the monitor turned on to check that Patches remained linked behind us.

Buckled into the passenger seat, I sat up straight and looked around. Were we actually leaving? I wanted to savor the moment. Just for the fun of it, I asked Paul if he saw a brass band anywhere and a great crowd of people giving us a rollicking send-off. It was fun to think of all our friends and relatives who had so enthusiastically wished us Godspeed during the last few months. Bless them! In the end—the beginning for us—it was Paul and I, in our own time, setting forth.

Paul maneuvered us around in the Finksburg Plaza parking lot until we reached the exit stop sign, paused, turned the front wheels to the right, and accelerated onto Route 91 South at 11:05 A.M. with the odometer registering 16,172 miles (from our two practice trips) and rain christening our two vehicles.

As we drove toward 70 West with its higher elevations, Paul announced, "I thought we'd stop for lunch at South Mountain." I glanced over at him. He seemed into the trip and comfortable about the Cadillac tags and our vehicle insurance. Now that we had actually left the parking lot and were on our way, I began to relax, too.

At the South Mountain Rest Area, we settled across from each other at our beige Formica-topped dinette table to eat lunch. Four place settings would fit on its surface, and two people would fit easily on each side on the cushioned seats. From where I sat facing the front of the motorhome, I could easily reach across the 23-inch-wide aisle to kitchen drawers and the counter without getting up. That was the narrowest passage in the coach, and we often laughed as we both wanted to negotiate it at the same time. The true test for dealing with it would certainly come on this longer trip.

Outside, rain washed the mountain while fog swathed it. I mused, "I suppose we can stop early if the weather gets worse."

"That's what I've been looking forward to—being free to stop early, not having a time frame," Paul affirmed.

We had turned on the furnace when we first parked, which made the coach cozy and warm. As we lingered over lunch, we had no idea where we would stay that night. Paul gazed through the large, black-metal-framed window at the end of the dinette table. I noted that its ivory venetian blind was folded up inside the oak-trimmed, beige vinyl valance, and beige draperies were tied back on each side. Paul leaned against a rectangular cushion covered with the soft blue tapestry material that matched the sofa behind it. The cushion fastened by snaps on all four corners to an oak backboard. An L-shaped, upright panel of solid oak between the dinette seat and the sofa sported a small oil painting of a vase and some fruit.

As I looked upward, I saw the oak cupboards, which were 12 inches high by 14 inches deep and lined the coach on both sides near the ceiling. Toward the front above the windshield, a cupboard on the left with a roll-top door hid Paul's flashlight, fuses, tire pressure gauge, and other items. On the right was a matching cupboard that contained my collection of maps, directories, tour books, and audio tapes. Round, black-metal-screened speakers for the AM/FM radio nestled near the corners beside the overhead cupboards. A walnut-veneered television set was mounted on the carpeted engine hump between the driver's and passenger's high-backed, beige plush seats.

Above the 69-inch-long sofa that converted into a double bed was another large black-metal-framed window with the same window treatment as that at the dinette table. On the right, opposite the sofa, two beige, plushly upholstered swivel chairs were bolted to the floor and an oak console with a beige Formica top was between them. Behind and above the chairs and console was a large window that matched the one across the coach.

Also on my right, between the swivel chair and the end of the kitchen counter, was the entry door and screen door. The stairwell

"I could easily reach across the 23-inch-wide aisle to kitchen drawers and the counter without getting up."

just inside the door contained a level area and one step to reach the main floor level of the coach. Coming into the motorhome from outside, one would come up the two black metal steps that automatically folded under the coach when on the road, going up one step to the stairwell and then another step to reach the floor level. The steps were not steep and were easy to use. Paul had installed a fire extinguisher on the wall adjacent to the steps.

Overhead, fastened to the off-white, plush, fabric-covered ceiling were the air conditioner unit, a round taupe smoke detector, the television antenna control knob and handle, and two fluorescent lights. Above the dinette table was our touch of glamour, a three-bulb brass and glass chandelier.

Above the entry door were monitoring panels that indicated whether the coach and chassis batteries needed to be charged and also the fullness of the tanks for fresh water, gray water, black water, and LP gas. Alongside were switches for the water pump and water heater. A courtesy light was just above the doorframe.

After dawdling, we finished our lunch and continued west on Interstate 70 (I-70) toward I-81 at Hagerstown. The fog closed in. In spite of my apprehension about the weather, I lay down on the sofa behind Paul's driving seat for a nap that turned out to be two hours long.

As I climbed back into the passenger seat at 2:15 P.M., I asked Paul how far he thought we should go that day.

"Well, I'm ready to find something any time. See what you can find somewhere in northern Virginia," meaning that I should look in the campground directory.

So began the first of our almost daily searches in the *Trailer Life Campground/RV Park & Services Directory*, which I kept handy on the floor to the right of my feet. Picking it up, I looked first in the map section, finding Virginia, then I-81 on which we were traveling. Along I-81 on the map, I saw roads with red or black dots that indicated campgrounds and other services. The red dots indicated those places offering the Good Sam Club discount for members who pay cash and show their membership card; the black dots indicated locations not offering the discount.

Then I looked in the main section of that large directory for campground listings. This section showed states, towns, and campgrounds all in alphabetical order.

As I studied the possibilities, one emerged—Rancho Campground, New Market, Virginia, in the Shenandoah Valley. We decided to try it.

Our windshield wipers kept up their rhythm in the rain as we sloshed southward.

At 3:17 P.M., Paul turned into the entrance of Rancho Campground and went into the office to register for a campsite. Soon he emerged with a tall, gray-haired man who strode ahead of our moving motorhome in the rain without an umbrella and led us to a site. His high-spirited, fun-loving, gracious manner reminded me of a friend who had grown up in this area.

"Now if you folks need anything, you just come on down to the office, and we'll fix you right up. You have a good evening now!" he said as he gave a friendly salute and hurried back to the office.

In the evening of this first day on the road, at a homespun campground in the Shenandoah Valley of Virginia, I closeted myself with my journal and wrote:

> You cannot imagine how cozy I feel in this motorhome. I am sitting on the thermal blanketed bed in the bedroom at the rear of the coach as rain patters on the roof. As soon as I closed the folding oak door, the sounds in the front of the coach faded away. Only Paul's footsteps shake the vehicle, which sits on its wheels, not its jacks. With the soggy ground, Paul thought the metal jacks that we use to level the coach would sink in deeper than the tire treads.

> What a difference my being retired makes on a trip like this. What a difference it made in preparing. I took time to do tasks right and to dream up ways of making living here easier.

I went on to describe how I had installed custom-made, clear Plexiglas strips across the front of the shelves in the bathroom closets, which kept the items visible and accessible and yet they didn't fall out when someone opened a door while on the road. Although he usually doesn't say much about my projects, Paul commented several times that day, "I sure do like those clear plastic strips."

I wrote about how the excursion felt open-ended, free, and without the tension of allotted vacation time. We could go at our own pace. I mentioned how, earlier in the evening, I had taken time to consult the motorhome's microwave/convection cookbook in order to fix baked potatoes, which turned out to be cooked to perfection as our forks broke them apart.

At 9:10 P.M., I finished writing and laid the journal on the bedside cabinet. Beside it, I settled Mary and her Little Lamb, which were two stuffed fabric dolls that romped on the bed by day and slept on the cabinet top at night. Nancy Godwin, an enthusiastic RVer as well as a friend and coworker, had made and given them to us expressly for the motorhome.

After turning down the bedcovers, I joined Paul up front at the dinette table for a snack. The rain continued. I could hear its pace quicken, then slacken, its quantity heavy, then light; it became a chorale from nature. I asked Paul what he thought the weather would be like in the morning. Warmer and drier, he hoped.

It had been a full first day for our dream journey. Thanks to the directory, we had easily found a comfortable campground and were on our way toward our Shangri-la.

· 7 ·

Second Day Out

OVERNIGHT, the temperature dipped to a chilly 35 degrees. We were astonished to see that during the darkness, yesterday's rain had turned into snow and sleet. But at least the precipitation had stopped and the clouds didn't look quite so ominous.

At breakfast on that Friday morning, Paul chuckled good-naturedly, saying it would take him about three days to get rested from having pushed himself preparing for the trip. I, however, already felt well rested because I had taken my usual afternoon naps, though brief, and had not pushed myself. In any case, we were both in high spirits and enjoying the easygoing lifestyle in our coach.

Around 9:30 A.M., we left Rancho Campground, continuing our odyssey toward a milder climate. Having started out in cold rain when we left home and seeing snow and sleet on the hills beginning this day, I hoped for bright sunshine as we traveled south. After all, our dream was to escape Maryland's wintry chill.

I almost cheered when the sun broke through the clouds soon after we drove onto I-81. Even so, we could not yet shed our sweaters or turn off the dashboard heat.

Thinking ahead, Paul informed me, "When we get farther along and our gas tank gets down to one-quarter full, we'll stop and fill up."

I asked if that were a rule.

"No, it's not exactly a rule. It's just that I try not to let the tank get below one-fourth full in case we need to use the auxiliary generator."

"Why's that?"

"You want the long answer or the short one?"

"The short," I laughed.

His answer brought to light that the gasoline tank on our motorhome held 60 gallons. It stored fuel for both the motorhome engine and an auxiliary generator located to the rear of the driver's side door. According to Paul, our coach came equipped with a safety feature whereby the flow of gasoline to the generator stopped automatically whenever the gasoline tank was down to one-quarter full, thus preventing the motorhome engine from running out of gasoline. As the name implies, the auxiliary generator supplied electricity for our overhead air conditioner, microwave oven, television set, and wall outlets when we didn't have a campground electrical outlet available. When the generator ran, it did so on gasoline. In other words, the first priority for the gasoline supply was to start and run the engine of the coach. How responsible of the designer!

Paul usually continued thinking until he was satisfied that he had fully covered a subject, and so he added to his comments about the gasoline tank, "Now if we were out West where I wasn't sure how many miles it would be to the next gas station, I wouldn't let the tank get below *half* full. I sure wouldn't want to run out of gas!"

Nor would I.

"Is the furnace turned off?" Paul asked. We had turned it on the night before, of course, after we parked at Rancho Campground. When riding on the highway, we always used dash heat instead of the furnace. Speaking of riding, I planned to be as active as possible when in the passenger seat; otherwise, I noticed from earlier trips that I became stodgy after miles and miles without getting up from the seat. I'd learned in freshman biology that inactivity causes lactic acid to accumulate in the body, which in turn causes fatigue, so on this trip I intended to act as energized as possible when I was the passenger. I hoped to respond immediately to requests from Paul or any ideas I had that required physical activity, even though I was "retired" and "deserved" to recline. Paul's question about the furnace was the first test of my resolution.

Forcing myself to overcome inertia, I immediately unbuckled my seat belt and swiveled the passenger chair. Touching sides of tables, counters, and closets for balance, I teetertottered back to the bedroom at the rear of the coach. Looking closely, I saw that the thermostat mounted on the oak-paneled wall indicated that the furnace was indeed on. I pushed its tiny lever to Off. During earlier travels, I had learned that the furnace, unlike the auxiliary generator and the motorhome engine, ran on LP gas. Some filling stations and most campgrounds sell LP gas. Although our LP gas tank held 21.8 gallons, it was never filled more than 80 percent because the liquefied gas required space to vaporize before leaving the tank. The furnace, stovetop range, refrigerator, and water heater all were designed to use LP gas as vapor; liquefied LP gas reaching an appliance would be a fire hazard.

We had ordered an LP gas detector as an option with the motorhome. Located on the inside wall behind the swivel chair nearest the stairwell, the detector had a tiny flashing light, indicating that it was sniffing for LP gas leaks. If a leak developed, the detector would automatically shut off the LP gas. It more than paid for itself as a safety device because of the peace of mind it gave us.

When I returned to the passenger seat, I realized that it had taken only a speck of extra effort to go back and turn off the furnace. Had I resisted the impulse to act, I knew I would have found it harder to move the next time.

"See the snow on the Allegheny Mountains?" Paul asked. We often pointed out sights and commented to one another on what we saw, as I'm sure most travelers do. It's part of the exhilaration of the journey—seeing, discovering, sharing, laughing, discussing, understanding, misunderstanding, comparing, correcting, kidding, and learning together.

A little farther on, he announced like a train conductor, "Bridgewater College. Exit 61." We named some of our best friends who had attended this liberal arts college, related to the Church of the Brethren, and reminisced convivially about youth and young adult conferences that we had attended on its campus.

Later at Staunton, Virginia, we stopped for gasoline—our first fill-up this trip. Without realizing it, we began a pattern of individual duties. Paul pumped the gasoline and paid for it; while staying inside, I logged information into a six-by-nine-inch, three-ringed notebook. In it, I wrote information that would help me figure how many miles we traveled on a gallon of gasoline, which is a statistic most RVers are fond of comparing. My first entry on the road read: Odometer 16,378; 89 octane; Citgo; $1.099 per gallon; 40 gallons; $43.96; off I-81 south of Staunton, VA.

As he climbed back into the driver's seat, Paul asked humorously, "How far did we go on that last 40 gallons of petrol?" He was fond of good-naturedly substituting the word "petrol" for gas.

Using information from Wednesday, the day before we started this trip when Paul last filled the gasoline tank in Westminster, along with a solar calculator that we kept in the motorhome dash compartment, I began figuring. We had traveled 222 miles since the Westminster fill-up. I divided 40 gallons, the amount we had just purchased, into 222 and got 5.55 miles per gallon—not so great. But a truck driver had told Paul that he started to get maximum mileage when his vehicle's odometer read 30,000 miles. We were only about halfway there.

We rolled down I-81. "Not that I'm looking forward to it, but do you think I should practice driving with the tow car? Maybe on a stretch of road like this?" I asked tentatively, referring to the dual-lane interstate highway ahead of us.

"I definitely want that to happen, but I think it might be better to practice when there's less cross wind." I felt the coach shift as Paul kept it straight on the road and was quite content to postpone my rehearsal. Instead, I enjoyed the scenery in Shenandoah Valley.

A tractor trailer bearing an AT&T logo and pulling a long flatbed passed us, going the same direction. After it moved into the lane ahead, Paul reached for the microphone of the CB radio. Having worked for the Chesapeake and Potomac Telephone Company (later Bell Atlantic-MD) in the Westminster area for 38 years, Paul felt a camaraderie with all telephone people. In addition, he had known AT&T workers in his job as a central office technician concentrating on long distance and specialty circuits.

"Break 19 for Mr. AT&T with the empty reels," Paul called over the CB.

Paul knew that the scratchy garble of voices on the CB gave me a headache so he used earphones. As they talked about their work experiences and got acquainted, Paul learned that Mr. AT&T was headed for his home terminal in Phoenix, Arizona, where his wife last night had said that the weather was beautiful! Promising news!

"That's a 10-4. Have a good, safe trip!" Paul hung the CB microphone in its cradle beside the rear view monitor suspended from the underside of the overhead storage cabinets.

A little after 11:00 A.M., Paul suddenly realized that he had forgotten to put in eye drops for his glaucoma after breakfast and pulled into a rest area, parking along the curb. Rest areas are located conveniently along major highways, and the legends on maps give their symbols so that travelers may plan for them. Such areas may simply be a parking area with no facilities or parking areas with all kinds of convenient facilities for travelers, such as bathrooms, drinking fountains, telephones, snack machines, and an information desk. A few even have overnight hookup sites for RVers. Nonchalantly, as he had done for many years, he leaned his head back and squeezed a drop from the plastic bottle into one eye and then the other.

When he steered away from the curb, he detected a slight jerk on the motorhome and knew instinctively that the front wheels of the tow car had locked sideways.

"Would you go back and turn the steering wheel so that it straightens those front wheels?" he asked me.

With my charged attitude about physical activity, I soon reached Patches and opened the driver's door. Standing alongside the open car, I leaned in and turned the steering wheel until the front tires pointed straight ahead and then closed the door.

To test that the front wheels on Patches tracked in alignment behind the motorhome, Paul slowly drove forward and out into the through traffic lane of the rest area and around a huge tractor trailer that was parked in front of us. As I walked behind Patches, he kept going about 150 feet and pulled into a front parking space being vacated by another motorhome pulling a tow car. I locked the door of the tow car and walked ahead to the motorhome. Meanwhile, Paul strode back to Patches to see if the tires had been damaged by their brief sideways travel. They seemed fine. Paul couldn't figure out what had caused the wheels to lock sideways but would watch for future occurrences.

After we regained the highway, Paul said, "You did a professional job back there, you know."

"Thanks. I felt like a shepherdess bringing in her sheep when you pulled ahead and I walked behind Patches," I laughed and added, "You were rather unruffled yourself."

By 4:10 P.M., we were cruising south of Bristol, Tennessee, enjoying the sunshine instead of coping with yesterday's rain and fog. We had decided to try for a Kampground of America (KOA) in Knoxville, Tennessee, which meant we had many miles yet to go on the ribbon of highway ahead.

As we neared Knoxville, Paul asked me to look at the map. "What is the next big town beyond Knoxville on our route south? It might help us as we go through Knoxville to know a further destination."

"Chattanooga and then Birmingham, Alabama," I soon replied, looking up from the map and wondering how he would use that information. Then as we navigated the city and looked at road signs, I realized that it helped us find our way more easily when we knew whether we were headed for Chattanooga (south on I-75) or for Nashville (west on I-40).

At 7:00, in the dark, we pulled into a hilly campsite at KOA Knoxville West. After a full day's travel and with the uneven terrain of the campground, we were grateful for another option we ordered for the motorhome—the hydraulic leveling system! Instead of placing blocks of wood by hand under the tires to level the motorhome,

Paul simply reached down from the driver's seat to four levers on the floor at his left. Each lever hydraulically raised or lowered a metal jack beneath a corner of the coach.

As Paul worked the levers up front, I checked the leveler disk, a silver-dollar-size, clear plastic, circular object that we kept inside the freezer compartment above the refrigerator. The wafer-like object contained an air bubble that indicated how level the refrigerator/freezer was—being on a level plane for parking was essential in order to prevent damage to its cooling system. When at least two-thirds of the bubble floated inside a center circle on top of the wafer, the refrigerator/freezer was safely level. When it was level, the motorhome was too. It seemed laughable to me that such a tiny and inexpensive object could be so important.

On this second day out, we had driven 387 miles, despite a leisurely start. Settling for the night in Knoxville, we realized we had made a good decision in buying a motorhome that was comfortable at the end of a long day's travel, one that had a separate living room for relaxing with television and a waiting bed where we had only to turn down the covers.

Earlier, at the Staunton gas stop in Virginia, I had bought a postcard showing a beautiful panoramic view of the Shenandoah Valley from Skyline Drive. I wrote on it:

Dear Mother,

We got off in the rain yesterday at 11:05 A.M. We stayed at a campground in New Market, VA, last night. Today we drove south on I-81. Sunny and cold, with snow in higher elevations. Beautiful scenery, however. Enjoying this lifestyle so far. Thinking of you.

Love,

Paul & Bernice

P.S. Tonight we are in Knoxville, TN.

Paul's battle with headstrong winds buffeting our vehicles and this second day's long drive sent him to bed early for a nap. Having written to Mother Beard, I snuggled into the corner pillows of the sofa, pulled the afghan over my lap and legs, and turned on the television with the sound off. My eyelids felt heavy and I half-dozed. It had been a long day on the road, longer than we normally like to drive. The night would be short. I had been glad to postpone practicing driving with the tow car, but tomorrow could well be the day. I did want to do it before something happened that made it necessary.

I wondered, too, about the cold weather, how far south we would have to go before summer temperatures warmed our goose flesh. So far, I continued to wear my long coat when outside and a sweater inside, just as I would have at home in Maryland. My shorts and summer tops hung unused in the motorhome closet.

· 8 ·

Driving Lessons

ON THE THIRD MORNING of our long-awaited journey, frost covered everything at the Knoxville KOA, creating glistening picnic tables, silvery-brown leaves scattered on stiff icy grass, and white-veiled railroad ties used to bank the edges of campsites. Each cold day we encountered made us even more impatient to reach what we northerners assumed would be warmer weather in the southern latitudes.

The winds had died, thankfully, so driving would be easier for Paul that day. I thought I might even get to practice driving the motorhome with the car in tow. Like learning to ride a bicycle, it was something I wanted to do but didn't particularly look forward to. Yet I knew that when it was over, I'd be glad I had done it.

After breakfast at the dinette table, Paul went outside. I heard his steps crunching leaves and then the engine of the Toyota running as he let it idle to be sure it would run after two days of towing. It remained secured to the motorhome in this "pull-through" campsite, where we could simply drive in one end of the site and out the other without unhooking the car. Many campgrounds offered these convenient sites.

A few minutes later, Paul opened the motorhome door, his cheeks and nose red from the cold. "Okay if I disconnect water and electricity?"

"Yep," I answered. "I'm all finished." I had just washed a few dishes.

As we prepared to leave this campground, I knew Paul would simply unplug our heavy, black electric cord from the outlet on the campground post, then methodically coil and store it in a rear outside compartment of the motorhome, just as easily as I would have unplugged an iron at home, coiled its cord, and stored it in a cupboard. Then he would unscrew the water hose from both the campground spigot and the motorhome itself and place the hose into an outside compartment of the coach, just as I would do with the garden hose after watering flower beds or grass at home.

While I waited for Paul, I saw that the sun had begun to melt the frost crystals, which sent a wave of hope through me for warmer weather today.

"I knew Paul would simply unplug our heavy, black electric cord from the outlet on the campground post."

At 9:05 A.M., we unhurriedly pulled away from the Knoxville KOA with Patches in tow and soon merged with other traffic as we headed south toward New Orleans where we would then turn toward the Southwest.

"My, it's nice being able to take our time in the mornings and not having to drive extra long in the evening so we can get home by a certain time," I said as we glided along.

"It's what I've been waiting for," Paul agreed in his reserved way.

At 9:50 A.M., Paul pulled over to the wide highway shoulder and said, "Since the winds have died down, and with this straight highway and level area, this would be a good time for you to drive."

Once again, Paul simply expected me to drive the motorhome with the car in tow. I felt good about his confidence in my driving skills.

Thinking back to when I had first learned to drive the motorhome itself, I could hear Paul's voice preparing me shortly after we had brought it home from the dealer's. "What if we're on the road and I can't drive for some reason? I'd hesitate to start on a long trip if I were the only driver," Paul had said. On long trips in the car, we had often shared the driving.

Yet I held back from learning to drive the leviathan. I saw images of cramped tunnels without much leeway for passing either oncoming vehicles or side walls, narrow high bridges, and tight highway construction areas, all with fast-moving traffic. What if I scraped the sides of the motorhome or someone else's vehicle? What if I suddenly panicked and caused a pileup. As I lay down to take my naps on the living room sofa, I imagined all sorts of dreadful things happening until I made myself stop thinking about the negative possibilities. But it was a constant struggle to overcome those thoughts. I knew I had to think positively or else I would never get behind the wheel.

Well, if I must, I must, I thought as Paul suggested a dry run in our own driveway. Sitting behind the wheel, I felt apprehensive and yet excited.

Following Paul's gentle and simple beginner's suggestions, I practiced turning on the ignition, moving the gear shift lever from one position to another, turning off the ignition, and getting the feel of the driver's seat, moving it electrically up and down, back and forth, until it seemed right. That part was fun—I had control! I also tried to get a feel for placing the vehicle on the road.

"There are some differences between this and our car. One is that this motorhome is much wider," Paul instructed.

"How much?"

"About a foot and a half."

"Is that all?" I pictured at least three feet.

"Well, our Lincoln is about six-and-a-half feet wide and this is eight feet wide. You use the sideview mirrors to see where you are on the road." While still in the driver's seat, I practiced looking right and left into them. Then I asked how I would have time to look at the mirrors when I was looking straight ahead at the road.

"You'll get used to it. Just check them every now and then. Also, because this vehicle is much longer than our car, you need to allow more room to turn corners. And you have to allow room for the tail end to swing in the opposite direction of the turn." He paused and then added, enunciating his words clearly, "And remember, since there is a lot of weight behind you, it takes longer to slow down and stop."

A few days after my initial driveway lesson, I summoned courage from somewhere and, with Paul as my coach, drove six miles on US 15, a dual-lane highway with wide shoulders, and continued 17 miles more, right down Main Street of Littlestown, Pennsylvania, where cars and trucks were parked on both sides. I felt like an aerialist performing a new routine on a tightrope—without a net! Each mile added know-how, but learning was hard work. I sat high above the road behind the steering wheel, a dutiful, unsure student. Paul tutored me calmly, saying he knew I could do it. Had he not been so sure, I might have given up. I was 61 years old; he was 62. (And you know what they say about "old dogs.")

Operating the motorhome with its automatic transmission was actually as easy as driving a car with the same type of transmission. But the big bugaboo for me was placing the motorhome in the center of my lane. I learned to look in both side view mirrors, checking that the coach was inside the painted lines. From where I sat, the motorhome seemed too near the centerline, but not so. It was an optical illusion.

I practiced on country roads, once coming to a place hardly wider than the motorhome itself with a tree on one side and a rocky bank on the other. Slowly, I crept through with Paul looking at the passenger side and me watching the driver's side. "I told you you could do it," Paul praised.

"Don't turn too short," Paul cautioned as I slowed to turn right onto another narrow country lane. "Go a little farther before you turn and then swing around. You don't want your tail end to hit that electric pole as you turn. Great! You're clearing the pole. Now straighten up your wheels and you've got it made." I felt both relieved and exhilarated.

Yet after each driving session ended, I continued to dread getting behind the wheel. The motorhome was Paul's pet. What if I dented or scratched it? Or damaged the transmission or something worse? I envisioned all sorts of terrible occurrences, but I noticed that once I got into the driver's seat, rather than focusing on the fears, my mind focused on the job at hand.

Not long after my lessons, when we started on a three-week trip from Maryland to Oregon (a test run for our dream journey), it turned out that Paul had bursitis in his right shoulder joint. Having had that malady several times myself, I knew the excruciating pain involved and had no doubts that he should not drive. He was brave to even want to start out. So I pulled out of our driveway behind the wheel with Paul as passenger, navigator, and encourager.

The next day, almost before I knew what was happening, we entered the freeway on the south side of Chicago at evening rush

"So I pulled out of our driveway behind the wheel with Paul as passenger, navigator, and encourager."

hour, with thundering trucks on both sides and all of us going the maximum speed. I hung onto the wheel and focused straight ahead. I heard Paul say, "You're doing fine. Just stay in your lane."

On that same trip, I maneuvered through miles of road construction that diverted traffic through narrow lanes created by portable concrete walls on one side and movable orange cones on the other. Paul started a lighthearted, mind-conditioning banter when we came upon road work: "Oh, goody! You get to drive through a construction area!" It eased my self-doubts and relaxed me.

After Paul's bursitis calmed down, he resumed his role as chief driver. Whenever he needed a break, however, he would drive into a rest area where we exchanged seats.

"Before pulling onto the main highway, I would always review in my mind how the cruise control worked and what the dials and meters on the dash told me."

Before pulling onto the main highway, I would always review in my mind how the cruise control worked and what the dials and meters on the dash told me. I looked in the side view mirrors and the rear view monitor to see that all was clear.

Moving the gearshift lever to "D," I kept my right foot on the brake while I looked in the left side view mirror to make sure no traffic was coming from behind us. Then, taking my foot from the brake, I pushed it gently onto the accelerator and eased into the right lane of traffic.

Gradually increasing speed to 55 miles per hour, I looked ahead four or five car lengths and focused on the center of the lane in which I was driving. I had learned this technique from reading an article in an RV magazine; it miraculously and effortlessly helped me center our motorhome on the road without having to continually check the road lines in the side view mirrors.

When the speed reached 55, I would set the cruise control and then lift my right foot from the accelerator. Also I checked the side-view mirrors for vehicles coming from behind or passing. Intermittently, I monitored the gauges for fuel supply, oil temperature, and water temperature.

After those days on the road to Oregon, logging hours and hours of driving time, I felt my confidence building. I found myself looking forward to getting into the driver's seat. Sitting up high, with my hands on the steering wheel, lifted my spirits. I liked the power of the vehicle, the secure feeling I got from the sheer bulk of the motorhome, and how well I could see from my lofty seat. I enjoyed the waving hands and surprised looks of passersby and pedestrians on city streets when they saw a woman at the wheel. I was an old dog who had learned a new trick!

"After those days on the road to Oregon, logging hours and hours of driving time, I felt my confidence building."

Paul, my teacher-husband, not only knew the subject of motorhome driving well but also had been an effective instructor. If he had felt nervous about my driving, he did not let it show. Rather, he had always shown his confidence in me by simply expecting me to drive.

I brought my thoughts back to the stopped motorhome on our dream journey to New Orleans and the Southwest. Paul had pulled over onto the wide shoulder of the road and expected me to drive with the car in tow. Without hesitation of body, only mental reservations, I moved from the passenger's seat to the driver's seat. I had felt anxious about this moment, but once behind the wheel, I took on the challenge with gusto.

As I had done before, I looked at the locations of the various cruise control buttons on the steering wheel, the dash dials and meters, the side view mirrors, and at the rear view monitor where I saw Patches waiting behind us.

Soon we were on the road again. Other than noticing more stability for the motorhome, I found no difference in the feel of driving with a tow car behind.

"The main things to remember," Paul said, "are to slow down sooner because there's more weight behind you and not turn too short on corners, which locks the front wheels of Patches."

I drove along on I-75 toward Chattanooga for three-quarters of an hour, dauntlessly passing a slow-moving pickup truck. I felt thankful to Paul. I could not have had a better teacher.

Driving made me an integral part of the whole venture of motorhome travel. We were a couple who traveled together rather than one person who drove and the other who rode along. We shared the driving part of the RV experience as well as the sights along the way. Knowing that two drivers were available gave us security. In addition, driving gave me a personal feeling of accomplishment while making me empathetic toward other RV drivers.

Had Paul not encouraged me to drive, had he not coached gently yet determinedly, had he not gone against the myth that a spouse should not teach a spouse, he would have had the full responsibility for driving our motorhome. But because of his steady confidence and reassuring coaching, he had a partner, and that had made it more fun for us both.

A sign alongside the highway announced a scenic view area ahead. I pulled in, getting the feel of turning and stopping with the tow car behind. Paul walked around outside, looking at the tires on both vehicles. Moving to the passenger seat, I told myself that now I knew I could do it—I could drive the motorhome with a tow car behind. I had a sense of what it felt like, which was really not that different. When he returned, Paul congratulated me with a handshake, and then he stepped into the driver's domain. We both laughed as he took over.

After lunch, I drove again. The radio played beautiful music, "Somewhere My Love" from *Dr. Zhivago*. The sun shone and the Alabama road proved a smooth ride.

"This is what retirement is all about," I said as I looked over at Paul leaning back in the passenger seat, his cap cocked sideways to shield his eyes from the sun. "Just traveling along, listening to good music, and being happy together."

"This is why I've been waiting for you to retire," he said with his eyes closed.

Inwardly, I thanked God for his love and abundant blessings. My hands moved the steering wheel slightly as I focused ahead on the center of the lane leading us through Alabama. Beyond lay Mississippi, where we planned to camp tonight. What weather would we find there?

· 9 ·

Flood Worries

LATE SATURDAY AFTERNOON, when Paul pulled into a Texaco gas station in Livingston, Alabama, he felt a jerk on the motorhome—the front wheels of the tow car had locked up again. After getting gasoline, he drove to an open area of the station, dragging Patches behind. I wondered how in the world he would fix the predicament.

To solve the problem for the rest of the trip, Paul turned on the ignition switch in Patches to the "run" position, which unlocked the front wheels and allowed them to pivot under all circumstances. But set in that ignition position without running the engine would have drained the battery, so Paul disconnected the positive clamp from the battery just while towing. He would reconnect it when we wanted to take Patches for a spin. Many later model cars come equipped with an electrical and steering system arrangement that makes disconnecting the battery unnecessary.

As we turned away from the station with Patches now smoothly following, Paul told me that a customer inside the store had mentioned possible flooding in Mississippi, whose border was only 15 miles away. Paul didn't know whether it would affect us on our route, but he thought we should continue. At home, we didn't have to cope with floods because we lived on a hill and only one small creek lay between us and the nearest town, Westminster. In our home area, we had seen only small streams and creeks, not rivers, that overflowed briefly into adjacent meadows and woods. But in unfamiliar territory such as that in which we drove, I stayed alert for possible floodwaters.

We pushed on. It was getting dark and we were more than ready to stop for the day as we pulled into a level grove of trees with spacious campsites at Nanabe Creek Campground near Meridian, Mississippi. After hooking up and returning inside the coach, Paul summed things up: "The thing I like about motorhoming is, when you pull into a campground and you hook up to water and electricity, you're all set—no carrying suitcases in and out."

Since it was already past our usual dinner hour and we wanted to do something special on a Saturday night, we unhooked the tow car for the first time this trip and took ourselves out to Morrison Cafeteria in a nearby mall. I tasted fresh, fried catfish for the first time—delectable in spite of its name! Afterward, at a public telephone off the main concourse, we called Jeff and Nancy. How I loved hearing their voices, even though we had only been on the road three days. I told them about the snow in Virginia and gave them our whereabouts. They didn't have a lot of news except that their work at their individual companies was going well and Nancy's horse, Moonshine, and 31-year-old pony, Redsy, were fine and eating their winter hay and "num-nums," as Nancy labeled the pellets of prepared horse feed. Redsy just loved his num-nums. It was just good to be on the line with them.

Back at the campground in the cozy, warm coach, I wrote another postcard to Mother Beard, this one sending "Greetings from Mississippi, The Hospitality State." I told her that we could actually hear the frogs "holler" at this campground, that Knoxville had a heavy frost that morning, that the temperature that evening was in the forties, and that we sent our love, of course.

Since the next morning was Sunday, a day for rest and worship, we took it easy and stayed at the campground. Sunshine danced through the slender, towering pine trees surrounding our campsite, dappling the area with lacy shadows. Five wild turkeys, punctuating the tranquility of the outdoor scene with their gobbling, strutted stiff-legged over long pine needles that covered the level glade around us. A father watched his two small boys bounce on a trampoline and then played ball with them, using a fat orange plastic bat. I pushed open the motorhome door and let it hook itself against the outside wall, leaving the screen door in place to keep unwanted insects at bay. For the first time this trip, warm air touched my face— air that had been warmed naturally by the sun, not the heaters in the motorhome.

Wearing my red sweater (not my long coat) and jeans, I sauntered over to the campground office. I wanted a closer look at an inviting wood-slatted porch swing. Nobody stirred inside the office. Assuming it was okay to use the swing, I sat down and enjoyed the rhythm and exercise of pushing back and forth as the weathered wooden seat cradled my body. I listened to birds calling to one another and to children's voices as they played at a distant campsite. How pleasant it was to just sit and swing—it reminded me of the porch swing on the farm where I grew up.

As a young girl, I used to write poetry while reclining on the sturdy wooden swing that hung suspended from the ceiling of our front porch. With my back against a bed pillow to protect my bony

"Sunshine danced through the slender, towering pine trees surrounding our campsite, dappling the area with lacy shadows."

spine from the hard wooden frame of the swing, I could look out across the meadow and watch the cows and horses graze, hear the pigs snuffle in the hogpen down the hill beside the meadow and an occasional hen cluck as she pecked at the ground around the corner near the chicken house, and breathe in the wonderful fragrance of the purple lilac blossoms that grew where the front yard met the meadow fence. No neighboring houses were within eyesight. My parents and three sisters were all somewhere else doing their own things. Only Fannie, our brown and white, mixed-breed collie, lay nearby in her shady spot under the porch. I had these wonderful moments to myself, back there on the farm (as Garrison Keillor might say).

Coming reluctantly out of my reverie, I stopped the swing and stood up, inhaling deeply the fresh pine aroma. Then I strolled back to the motorhome, moving quietly in my black soft-soled shoes over the pine needles. At home, Paul and I would have been in church at this hour. Instead, I hoped to find a religious program on television. I saw Paul behind the motorhome checking the air in the tires on Patches. When I told him my plans, he said he was going to take the tow car to a nearby truck stop to put air in the front tires and learn about possible flood detours on our route to New Orleans.

Settling into the swivel chair near the door with the remote control in hand, I roamed the channels until I saw a group of vivacious men and women singing sacred music on the *Day of Discovery*. Their voices harmonized soulfully as I listened in the milieu of the tranquil, sunlit campground. Fresh air drifted through the screen door. I let myself be open to those worshipful moments. When the program was over, I turned off the television and bowed my head to talk silently with God.

Following my time of worship, I prepared lunch after which we unhooked and left the campground. Checkout time was 12:00 noon; I logged our departure time as 12:05 P.M., a few minutes late. We always tried to honor the checkout times, but this one occurred at an unusually awkward hour for us. I could see that no one was waiting for a vacant campsite and no one was in the office. The temperature was 60 degrees.

As we headed south toward Hattiesburg, we indeed watched for high water in the rivers because Paul had heard from a person at the Meridian truck stop that he had to detour around flooded areas as he drove from Jackson, Mississippi. The map showed that the Pearl River lay between Jackson and Meridian and that the same Pearl River flowed southeast so that near New Orleans it would cross under the highway (I-59) on which we would be traveling.

That afternoon as we rolled southward, I searched the campground directory for a place to stay that night, intentionally looking for a description that included "rolling hills" instead of "grassy flatlands."

We chose the rolling hills of Paul B. Johnson State Park in Hattiesburg and at 5:25 P.M. drove into a spacious 50-foot-wide, pullthrough campsite that sat high above Geiger Lake. The 805-acre park in rolling hills seemed like a haven with its tall, long-leaf and lob lolly pines, great oak trees, and smaller shrubs. Its Visitor's Center, a short walk downhill from our site, also overlooked the lake and housed a souvenir area, a game room, rest rooms, fast-food service, and park offices. After we ate in the motorhome, we walked down to the water's edge. With a cloudy nightfall coming on, the water looked gray but calm. The wind turned chilly and we headed back up the hill to our warm motorhome. On a warmer evening, we would have lingered and watched people who could have rented paddle boats, canoes, and fishing boats. The enormous lake was stocked with bass, crappie, catfish, and bream. In spite of the cloudy weather, our first impression of the park was enthusiastic—the layout, services, facilities, and grounds maintenance—it seemed to offer everything! We could have stayed there much longer than one day.

After a rainy, blustery night, we awoke Monday morning to find the wind continuing to blow the rain hard against the motorhome windows. It was January 29, our fifth day out and a chilly 42 degrees—quite different from Sunday morning's pleasant weather! Paul bundled up and walked in the rain to the Visitor's Center where he asked about floodwater warnings and directions for the best way to exit the park going south. As we left the campground, even Paul felt anxious about what weather or high waters lay ahead.

Gradually, the rain stopped and the highway dried. Calmer nerves prevailed. In addition, when we entered Louisiana on U.S. 59, the person at the Louisiana Information Center didn't say anything about flooding when I asked her the best way to go sightseeing in New Orleans. Yet as we drove on U.S. 59, which was elevated several feet above level land on either side, we saw swollen river water alongside so high that at one place only the top of a car showed. We assumed it had been parked on a frontage road beside the main highway when it was overtaken by the high waters. We were in the Pearl River and West Pearl River area. When we crossed a bridge over the Pearl River, the high, swift waters rushed violently beneath. Murky waters lay menacingly backed up into woodlands and onto side roads where I saw the driver of a car back up rather than go through brown, muddy water at a place where the road dipped.

By 1:30, we arrived at our destination for the day, a soggy Fontainebleau State Park at Mandeville, Louisiana, northwest of New Orleans. Paul paid the registration fee at the entrance gate, and we crept slowly around the park looking for a dry campsite. Many state parks allow campers to choose their own sites instead of assigning one to them. Water lay in pools and puddles on the low, level floor of the dripping-wet pine forest.

One of the few campers already there hospitably pointed out a site after seeing us drive around the circles of roads several times. Since the campsite was not a pull-through, we unhooked the tow car, backed the motorhome into a bowery sanctuary, and parked Patches in front of the motorhome.

We hadn't stopped for lunch on the road, and so that was our first order of business. As we did at home, each of us prepared our own sandwich. Paul usually ate sliced turkey breast while I chose baked ham. He cut his sandwich in half lengthwise whereas I sliced mine diagonally. We each decided what fruit, dessert, and beverage we wanted. Before I retired, because our schedules were so different, we began the practice of each getting our own breakfast and lunch. It made life simpler because we didn't always get up at the same time in the morning, we weren't always ready to eat lunch at the same time, and we each had our own food needs and wants. If we were eating alone, we had our own blessing; if together, Paul prayed it aloud. So even on the road, we followed that same habit. I always prepared the main meal—dinner—and Paul did the dishes afterward. In the motorhome, we often happily enjoyed high-quality, commercially frozen entrees and added more vegetables, fruit, and dessert we wanted.

As we ate at the dinette table, we marveled at the high waters and strong current we had seen that day and felt grateful that the bridges were high. Since we had come south to see the legendary city of New Orleans because neither Paul nor I had seen that antebellum metropolis, our thoughts turned to what we would do the remainder of the afternoon. Earlier that day, a helpful agent at the Louisiana Information Center gave me the telephone number for a Holiday Inn at Slidell that offered guided tours of the city. So shortly after we ate lunch, while Paul did the few dishes, I walked to a nearby public telephone and called the inn to be sure we could get tour tickets for the next day. And so we set out in Patches for Slidell, about 20 minutes east, to pick up the tickets.

Realizing how difficult it would have been to get around without Patches, it was time to give credit where credit was due. I said, "I think we did the right thing in bringing it along. You were right."

Paul agreed. "I do think it was worth all the hard, hard work I did in that freezing wind. I thought I'd freeze my fingers off. It's good to have it for short trips like this one and then for tomorrow morning when we want to catch the tour to New Orleans. We can let the motorhome stay parked, save gas, and have a change of vehicles all at the same time. Yes, I think we're going to be very glad we brought it."

(As I mentioned, Paul liked to fully cover his subject, sometimes with run-on sentences. I remember one especially long one that went on and on so long that I got up out of bed to write it down. Earlier that evening, I had attended a fancy bridal shower given for my predecessor at the college. As a newcomer to the college social scene, I was somewhat intimidated by mingling with administrative women staffers and faculty wives, including the wife of the college president. Later at home, I commented to Paul how far removed the evening had been from when I was a little barefooted girl on the farm "back in the sticks," as living in the country was referred to where I grew up. I had already gotten into bed; Paul was about to turn out the light and get into his bed when he began to reply slowly and thoughtfully, "You were in a better position to judge and evaluate the true contribution and significance of the social function to the cultural development of the country . . .," whereupon, the lights now out, I began to get out of bed, saying, "I've got to write all that down. That's too good to miss!" I grabbed an envelope and pen from the dining room. As I walked back to the bedroom writing, I had just turned the corner when Paul, now lying flat in bed, continued, ". . . by virtue of the fact that . . . ," and I just howled with laughter! Nonplussed, he continued, ". . . by virtue of the fact that your upbringing was one which was constituted with the simple life." It's truly fascinating what we appreciate and find attractive in our mates. That same trait might drive others buggy.)

We bought tickets for a combined tour of New Orleans and a cruise on the Mississippi and returned to the park. Following supper, I washed our few dishes and Paul dried them. Then I sat at the dinette table to sign a birthday card to my good friend Betty June in Maryland, whose birthday would be Saturday. I decided to leave the envelope unsealed so that I could include a postcard from New Orleans for her and her husband, Albert, after our tour.

Before leaving home, I had shopped for greeting cards—birthday, Valentine, sympathy—I thought I would need on the trip. When on superhighways in new territories trying to cover long distances, we tended to want to keep going rather than stop for something like cards. Sometimes diversions of the road caused me to lose track of time. Being prepared avoided, "Oh Paul, it's Ruth's birthday. We'll need to find a store that sells cards."

I paused in writing the address on the envelope when a television meteorologist warned that the Pearl River would crest that night.

How many miles was that from us, I quickly asked Paul. He assured me that the river was about 14 miles east at Slidell. If those waters got to where we were, he would be very surprised. When I visualized those 14 miles, I could not picture floodwaters moving over that much land and reaching our campsite.

As I completed writing the address on the envelope, I realized we were getting far away from Maryland. After New Orleans, we would go even farther from home as we headed west to the Texas border and Houston, and then south toward Corpus Christi en route to Brownsville. I was anxious to reach Brownsville where I hoped we would find a warm respite for a few days.

· 10 ·

Sightseeing and Moving On

ABRUPTLY, at 5:15 A.M. Tuesday, the electric alarm clock went off. We had to get up early so we could get back to Slidell to take a city and river tour that would focus on the famous city of New Orleans and a cruise down the even more famous Mississippi River. Although we did not get tickets for it, the night club tour sounded exciting with a visit to a jazz club in the French Quarter and a show in a famous cabaret on Bourbon Street. It would be fun to see what the city was like at night. Even Mother and Dad Beard had taken this type of tour years ago. We are all teetotalers, but we enjoy shows and music. Paul and I thought we would take the day tour and then decide afterward whether and when to do the night tour.

I wasn't sure what to expect that day in New Orleans except lovely old homes with ironwork balconies. Uncertainty, of course, was part of the adventure of traveling, with sightseeing and learning as its joyful benefits.

I poked my head outside the motorhome to decide what to wear. It was cold, misty, and dark; I hoped the sun would come out later. Not knowing for sure, I put on my long, hooded coat and flat-heeled, black leather boots in case of rainy, cold wind on the boat ride. Paul wore his blue, fleece-lined jacket and tan twill cap.

Somewhere on our tour today, I wanted to buy a postcard depicting New Orleans to enclose in Betty June's birthday card. I still had time to mail it; her birthday would be Saturday.

With Paul driving Patches, we arrived at the Slidell Holiday Inn ahead of the other people going on the tour. Happily, we climbed aboard the bus and claimed comfortable seats that offered a full front and side view just inside the front entry steps.

Of Cajun heritage, the delightfully witty driver and tour guide took us and the other 20 or so people who accompanied us into the city, drove us around, dropped us off for the sternwheeler cruise, and picked us up again, continuing the sightseeing narrative as he guided us out of New Orleans and returned to Slidell. In between travel commentary, he made up entertaining captions about people he saw walking or standing on the sidewalk. He noted streets in some parts of the city that seemed to change names for no apparent rhyme or reason.

He showed us the beautiful City Park, the Garden District with its elegant homes, various churches including St. Louis Cathedral, and the historic French Quarter. Along the way, I observed handsome ornamental ironwork balconies for which the city was famous. At St. Louis Cemetery, I walked in awe among the rows of unique aboveground vaults. Many of the old cemeteries were originally built above ground because water would fill the empty graves before caskets were placed in them. In the end, walking beside these tiers of vaults in the cemetery moved me more than anything else I saw in the city. I was literally one of the living walking among the dead!

Near noon, our sagacious guide took us to the Toulouse Street Wharf area where he suggested we browse through the Jackson Brewery, perhaps eat lunch there, and then walk across the railroad tracks to exchange our tour tickets for boarding passes on the sternwheeler *Natchez*. Everyone on the bus went their separate ways until it was time to board the *Natchez* at 2:00 P.M.

Following his suggestion, we wandered in the renovated brewery that was now a busy, multistory shopping mall with many restaurants. Paul knew that the Cajun food would be too spicy for his digestive system. To be on the safe side, I too ordered what turned out to be the largest hamburger I had ever seen—or consumed. This was only the second time our palettes had been treated to something other than Beard cooking on our journey.

After lunch, we found a shop where I bought postcards. Then we headed for the *Natchez* and got our boarding passes, but before going up the gangplank, we looked wide-eyed at the enormous red paddle wheel at the stern of the boat. It must have been 40 feet in diameter and reminded me of the musical *Showboat,* which I had seen years ago in New York. The *Natchez* itself was reminiscent of the old riverboats on the Mississippi.

About 2:00, we boarded the floating vessel and climbed to the second level where we sat on chairs facing the wharf. Under cloudy skies, a cool breeze made me put up my hood. From the top of the riverboat, a young woman played a calliope, giving a carnival air to the scene around us. I began to write a postcard to Mother Beard. She would identify with New Orleans because she and Dad had visited before. Suddenly, Paul nudged me with his elbow, "Look down there!"

On the concrete pier in front of us, a man in his early forties dressed in a plaid shirt, gray pants, and open-zippered gray jacket danced to the rhythm of the calliope, his shoes certainly taking a beating. He looked like a store clerk on his lunch hour—a tall, slim gentleman with his coattail flying—the epitome of spontaneity, a free spirit.

At the end of the number, he looked up toward the musician and requested "Dark Town Strutter's Ball." As she pumped into that song, he danced more soft-shoe improvisations below us. When the music ended, the dancer raised his hands and clapped for the calliope player, showing his own appreciation. People waiting on the pier and those on the boat applauded, too, including Paul and me.

I felt the boat move, taking us downstream. Shortly after the two-hour tour and live narration by the captain began, I stood at the rail and looked down at the water—I was actually floating for the first time on the bigger-than-life Mississippi River, the river of "Old Man River" and *The Adventures of Huckleberry Finn.* Along its banks, I gazed at piers, old plantation houses, and barracks of the Louisiana National Guard while listening to the captain reveal their history through the loudspeaker. He impressed upon us the importance of the levee along the sides of the river, saying that it made it possible to build homes and other structures on the land. Otherwise, the acreage, which was below the level of the river, would be under water.

I took several pictures; one was of Angler's Restaurant and Bar, a new building made of old lumber and junk to give it an antiquated look; it was one of the more unusual buildings in the city. From the *Natchez*, when the captain pointed it out, I could plainly see where Canal Street separated the newer high-rise buildings from the older, lower French Quarter structures and snapped a view of that skyline.

Had the weather been balmy, I would have truly enjoyed the cruise. It became too cool and breezy to sit or stand outside, however. I was glad I had worn my hooded, insulated coat; Paul wished for his heavier winter one. We explored the boat, a much warmer way to spend our time. Paul found the hot engine room and gave me a tour of its intricacies. Many people sat at tables in the handsomely appointed main lounge, where a buffet looked tempting, but we had already eaten that huge lunch.

At the end of the round-trip cruise, I bid an audible, fond good-bye to the Mississippi, which continued to flow mightily to the Gulf of Mexico. Paul and I again boarded our bus for the return to Slidell. After we left the city and the driver had less to say, Paul and I talked with other motorhomers staying at various parks in the area. The couple sitting behind us was from Oregon, and a single woman across the aisle kept praising her Vogue motorhome. The Oregon couple agreed that the tour was not as exciting as they expected. Perhaps it was the weather—you can always blame the weather. It certainly wasn't the tour guide. For me, perhaps it was that I had previously visited Charleston, South Carolina, had seen its lovely old homes with iron-work railings, and loved its charm. Perhaps that took the edge off the excitement of seeing similar architecture in New Orleans.

In spite of the damp, cool weather and our overall disappointment, our guide had given us a delightful introduction to Cajun culture and the largest city in Louisiana. I was glad I'd added it to my education, but I was not enamored enough just yet to spend a lot of time there. I was more inspired by the river than by the city. (Please forgive me, New Orleans aficionados!) Yes, the cemetery was unique, but the Mississippi was a living, awesome, moving body of water that, like ocean waves, seemed like it had always been flowing and would go on forever.

As we talked on the bus, Paul and I concluded that with the weather so damp and cold, we would forego the night tour of New Orleans, at least for this trip, and instead turn westward the next day.

Back at Fontainebleau State Park, I gladly entered the warm familiarity of our waiting home on wheels. I had not yet tried the laptop computer for journal writing. I thought perhaps I would get it out while on the road the following day and that I really should if it was going to be useful this trip.

Before leaving the Louisiana campground on Wednesday, our sixth day out, Paul carefully checked the oil in the engine of the motorhome, a routine he performed every 300 miles or so—approximately every other day. Inside the coach, I went around its perimeter making sure I stowed items, such as the detergent bottle that usually sat on the kitchen counter, where they would not spill during travel and put the electric clock on the floor beside its bedside table. Betty White had unknowingly taught me this system when she played the role of Sue Ann Nivens on the *Mary Tyler Moore Show*. In her role of "happy homemaker," she officiously told Mary how to clean up after parties—just go right around the room doing whatever needs doing and you'll be done in no time, she had said (or something similar). Then Sue Ann had sashayed out without offering to help Mary!

A little after 9:00, on this last day of January, we left a still-saturated Fontainebleau State Park. Riding west on I-12, heading away from the floodwaters of eastern Louisiana, sunny skies belied outside temperatures only in the mid-fifties. If we had had an automatic pilot, we would have set it first for Orange, just inside the border of Texas, then west to Houston followed by south to Corpus Christi and lastly to Brownsville. That southernmost tip of Texas was one of the places we wanted to explore as a future winter retreat. That day, we would go as far as Orange and spend the night.

Already on the road almost a week, we were only in Louisiana, proving that retirement and traveling in a motorhome allowed us the luxury of lazing along (not poking along on the road and holding up traffic, however). Paul had taken many vehicle safety courses at the telephone company and applied what he had learned to motorhome driving. His education included extending courtesy toward other drivers, not tailgating, pulling over to the side of the road to let backed-up traffic pass, going with the flow of traffic unless it was above the speed limit, and not letting the rudeness of other drivers make him retaliate in kind. He stayed even-tempered, often making a chuckling comment like, "That fellow didn't look very carefully, did he?" or "That fellow should look again," when another vehicle pulled out in front of us. I learned road courtesy and tolerance from Paul's example. That morning, we reminded ourselves that we wanted to spend a month in Arizona and then have time to visit relatives and friends in California and Arkansas, all within about two months, of which a week was almost gone.

As we traveled along, I told Paul of my day's goal. "I think I'll get out my laptop computer. I want to see how I like writing with it while we ride along." So far on the trip, I had written by longhand in a bound, lined journal. Paul replied that it sounded good to him and that he had wondered why I hadn't used it before.

"I put it off for a couple of reasons, I guess," and I paused. "It just seemed easier to write in my journal by hand, at least until we got more into the trip. Also, I didn't know if you'd feel left out if I sat here writing at the computer instead of talking with you." I also knew that, to really concentrate, I wanted to seclude my writing environment just as I liked being in a private place to pray. I wanted to be able to capture the thought when it first came rather than putting it off until after interruptions. If I knew that interruptions would come, I preferred to put off writing until I could be alone.

Yet I knew that I could write anytime, anywhere. I proved that when I followed a teacher's instruction to decide in the morning upon a time that day to write. It turned out one day that the time I chose found me in the laundry room at a campground. With women and children speaking French and English, I opened my journal, laid it on an unused dryer, turned my back on everyone else and stood there writing for 15 minutes. I found that although I can write in untoward circumstances, I much prefer peace, quiet, and privacy.

Immediately Paul assured me, "Don't let that stop you! I've got plenty to do with driving. Also, I can listen to the CB with the ear phones, you know."

"Well, if you need me to look up something or help look for road signs, you'll let me know?"

"Yes, I'll let you know," he said gently, smiling at me.

Leaving my seat, I went back to a closet and brought forward the laptop computer enclosed in its zippered, black fabric case and laid it on the sofa.

At home, I had a hard drive computer connected to a laser printer. I used it as my journal. As I sat in front of the computer there, I looked through large sliding glass doors at green lawns and woods, writing what came. At some point unknown to me, the creative mind took over, sending thoughts and words through my fingers. That keyboard made putting thoughts on paper as effortless as driving with an automatic transmission instead of a stick shift.

With retirement and extensive motorhome travel in our dreams, I had bought a Toshiba T1000 and an Okidata Microline 380, 24-pin printer, which rode along on the carpeted floor behind the passenger chair. I had used both of these at home just enough to know how they worked but not enough to feel comfortable with them.

I lifted the laptop computer from its case and took it with me into the passenger's seat. It rested precariously on my lap since it slanted toward the floor—I needed to raise my feet!

Like a hen trying to get settled in her nest, I swiveled in and out of the passenger seat going for diskettes, handwritten instructions, the WordPerfect key code strip, and the WordPerfect reference manual. Lastly, I brought up a footstool.

Finally, my fingers flew over the battery-powered keys as I looked around at the scenery and typed:

> Across a median strip with dead-looking winter grass, traffic flows toward us like railroad cars. No clouds show in the blue expanse above this level road, I-12, lined with long-needled pine trees.

> Time out while I look at Baton Rouge and the wide, muddy, murky, mighty Mississippi River from this high, steel-girded bridge.

"Hi, Old Man River!" I said out loud to my new friend, the Mississippi. Now that I had paused in writing, Paul asked, "How far is it to Orange, Texas?"

I transferred the computer, at last initiated, to a turkish towel on top of the dashboard area so it wouldn't slide around. After looking at the map and answering Paul's question, I resumed writing with the computer. I discovered that I could write more descriptively when using the computer because my keyboarding fingers could keep up better with what I was seeing and thinking at 55 miles per hour than if I were writing with a pen.

Later, to give Paul a rest, I got into the driver's seat for about one and a half hours, sometimes going through highway construction areas and over long, long causeways. Several trucks had the nerve to pass from behind on a high, narrow, two-lane bridge, but I kept my wits about me and held on to the steering wheel, focusing on the center of the lane ahead. In road construction zones, I slowed down to the 45-mile-per-hour speed limit as I joined a line of backed-up traffic. It struck me that it took a certain amount of nerve to drive a large RV. Subsequent experience sustained my nerve. The technicalities were similar to those of driving a car; it was the larger size to which one had to adjust in a motorhome. As for the tow car, I hardly knew Patches was back there except when I had to allow for it as I turned sharply or slowed down.

After 239 miles, we arrived midafternoon at Oak Leaf Park Campground in Orange, Texas. It doesn't take much time before the laundry basket overflows in a motorhome. After almost a week on the road, it was time to check out the campground's laundry facilities. Some motorhomers like to do laundry en route so that they will not have a lot to do when they get home—along with catching up on mail and getting back into the daily routine. Other motorhomers take along enough clothes so that they do not have to do laundry until they get home—they store soiled laundry in plastic garbage bags in their tow car or a compartment under the coach. But, of course, on a really long trip such as ours, some laundry would have to be done en route. I had planned to do our laundry about once a week, just as I did at home. Usually campground laundries were busiest during evening hours, so I planned to go there as soon as we leveled the motorhome, ever vigilant in my position as "bubblechecker."

While Paul hooked up to water and electricity, I lifted our bulging laundry bag from its rod in the closet. I tucked a box of detergent inside and took along as many quarters as I could find in case the laundry room didn't have a change machine. Soon the machines sloshed and hummed with our clothes.

During cycles, I read jokes and anecdotes in a tattered *Reader's Digest*. Eventually, Paul surprised me by coming in and helping to carry the clean laundry back to the motorhome. At home, I do all phases of the laundry, including putting it away.

Afterward, we sauntered over to the camp store, an interesting place to browse. Paul bought razor blades and a *USA Today*; I picked out a postcard for Mother Beard.

The next morning, Thursday, February 1, I woke up remembering that Betty June's birthday would be the day after tomorrow. Although I had prepared her card last Sunday, I wanted to write a message to her and Albert on the postcard I had selected in New Orleans and slip it into the envelope.

I needed to mail the card that morning. How could I be sure we would find a post office on the road? Post offices were like discount coupons—where were they when you needed them? Finding a post office on the road was another game Paul and I played. We had a running parody. I sometimes saw one as we were passing it. As I said, "There's a post office!" Paul kept on going, saying, "Oh, did you want to stop there?" He would chuckle. Eventually, we would get our act together and I would see a post office in time for him to slow down and see where we might park. Of course, we often saw post offices when we didn't need one.

While most campgounds offered mail boxes, this time I wanted to use the post office to be sure the envelope went out that day. Sometimes the mail at the campground didn't go out until late afternoon.

Since I had no idea where the nearest post office was, I decided to ask at the campground office. Fortunately, a member of the family that ran Oak Leaf, offered to take my letter to the post office. Bless them!

I walked briskly back to the motorhome, smiling about the mail solution. The chilly morning air made me draw my tan coat closer around me. I wondered if it was warm in Brownsville. The map showed it was almost as far south latitudinally as the tip of Florida. We were about 500 miles north of it and would have at least one more overnight, near Corpus Christi, before reaching it.

Brownsville

BEFORE LEAVING Oak Leaf Park Camp-
ground on Thursday morning, we pulled beside its large LP gas tank
and bought six gallons. We had used the furnace every night and
heated water for showers and dishes, and although we had not run
out of LP gas, Paul liked to replenish our supply whenever we had
the opportunity.

According to the tiny thermometer adhered to the driver's side
view mirror, the temperature was only 50 degrees. Specks of rain dab-
bled the windshield. High waters had alarmed us as we came through
Mississippi and Louisiana. That morning, the television weather forecaster had predicted possible thunderstorms, high winds, and tornadoes. Tornadoes—what next? Paul took the threatening weather in
stride; I watched for funnel-shaped clouds. Surely, surely, we would
find a warm, mild respite in Brownsville, Texas.

From Orange, we drove west on I-10 toward Houston. Once there,
we would take U.S. 59 south to the Lake Corpus Christi State Recreation Area at Mathis, our next overnight destination.

As we cruised into Houston on a three-lane, divided highway
under a myriad of overpasses, Paul exclaimed, "Boy, there's a mess of
roads here!" Huge green highway signs helped us find our way. When
we emerged from the downtown district, we were surprised to find
that Houston's outlying areas also contained skyscrapers that housed
banks, hotels, hospitals, and apartments.

Suddenly, the red light on my laptop computer signaled a low battery. Immediately, I saved my journal document, exited WordPerfect, turned off the computer, and got out the AC adaptor. Simultaneously, Paul pushed a switch on the dashboard near him that turned on the auxiliary generator, the ingenious machine that provided electricity to the motorhome's wall outlets when we could not hook up to campground electricity.

I plugged one end of the adaptor cord into the computer and then the other end into a wall outlet near the passenger's seat. Paul told me that if I plugged the cord into the wall outlet first that it would energize the plug end going into the computer. If I accidentally touched the electrified plug, I could get a shock or if the hot plug accidentally touched another piece of metal, it might ground out or short the circuit. (Our son, Jeff, who is a computer network analyst, later explained that it was always a good procedure to plug into the computer first because that would make the circuit that was to be energized complete. He told me to picture a large empty tub with an opening on one side near the top into which a hose would fit. I wanted to fill the tub with water. Then picture a faucet to which the other end of the hose would be attached. Then he asked me to visualize what would happen if I attached the hose to the faucet and turned on the water before I had put the other end of the hose into the opening on the tub. I got the picture and knew that I should make a practice of plugging the adaptor cord into the computer first and then the other end into the wall outlet that supplied the electricity.) I turned on the computer again and reopened my document. Now as we moved down the road and I typed into the computer, the marvelous auxiliary generator supplied the power.

Before long, Paul asked, "How far south of Houston does US 59 take us?"

Pausing in my typing, I reached for the Texas map already open on the dash in front of me.

"It looks like this double red line we're on turns into a double black line just north of Victoria, goes around Victoria, and hooks up with US 77 going south toward Corpus Christi."

"Good. Just what I needed," Paul said, then added, "I wonder if our gas mileage is as good today as it was yesterday on those level roads. Seven point seven miles to the gallon—I'm really pleased with that."

After lunch, when we stopped for gas at a Texaco station in Victoria, Texas, I called ahead to Lake Corpus Christi State Recreation Area to reserve a site for that night. Considering the large number of winter tourists vying for spaces in the excellent state parks in Texas, I didn't want to chance not getting a campsite.

"Sometime, somewhere this afternoon we need to stop for groceries," I told Paul.

Grocery shopping on the road was more appealing than at home, even exciting at times. We found an H-E-B grocery store in Victoria. I meandered through the aisles pushing a cart, enjoying being a stranger in town (not having to worry about how my hair looked!), searching for items on my list, all the time unaware of the new-fangled technology awaiting me at the checkout counter. To my surprise, when the woman moved my groceries across the scanner slot, a clear, computerized voice announced out loud each item and price. Fascinated, I listened, then laughed. What if somebody had bought something they wanted to keep private? What then!

I laughingly told Paul about the checkout voice as we put away the groceries, which included two gallons of drinking water. Sometimes instead of buying water, I filled plastic gallon containers at campgrounds or rest areas that offered good water. I liked to be sure we always had safe water with us in case the water in one area tasted funny or looked cloudy.

Next on my mental to-do list—I needed to find a hairdresser. Although my hair looked halfway decent, it was two days past its usual weekly shampoo and blow-dry, something I'd never let happen at home. When we got to Brownsville, I would make an appointment first thing.

Back on U.S. 59, we made our way to U.S. 77 South, where Paul asked from behind the steering wheel, "Are the water pump and water heater off?" I swirled the passenger seat to check them.

Two easy duties that we needed to do (but usually forgot) before driving away from a campsite or rest area were (1) turn off the water *pump* switch and (2) turn off the water *heater* switch, both of which were located handily above the entry door of our motorhome.

When using water as we traveled down the road or dry-camped (when water and electricity hookups were not available), we turned on a water pump switch that operated an on-demand pump, which in turn forced water into the plumbing system from the freshwater tank at the rear of the motorhome. When we hooked up to a campground water faucet, however, it had its own pressure and we did not use the motorhome's water pump at all.

We turned off the pump switch when on the road in case the automatic on/off pressure switch that is an integral part of the pump itself malfunctioned, causing the pump to operate without actually pumping water and thus possibly damaging the pump's bearings. Since this small pump was at the rear of the motorhome, we would not hear it running above the sounds of the engine and the road.

The water heater had a different story. Turning on its switch ignited the propane vapors to provide hot water for faucets in the kitchen and bath. Leaving the switch on when traveling, however, wasted propane gas since we did not normally use hot water as we cruised along. In any case, whenever we turned on the water heater switch, it took only a minute or so for the water to get hot. We tried to keep both the water pump and water heater switches turned off when driving the highways. That time, as usual, I had to turn them off.

So far on this dream journey from Maryland, the only mechanical problem that had concerned us was the locking up of the front wheels of the tow car. Happily, that was resolved. The motorhome itself had responded willingly to its long days of travel over some rough, bumpy roads. And then abruptly Paul asked, "Did you hear that noise?" cocking his head as though listening.

"I don't think so."

"I've been hearing a scraping kind of noise off and on today. I'll have to get down under there and take a look this evening when we get to the campground."

"Where do you think it might be?"

"I'm not sure, but somewhere underneath my feet. It's different from anything I've heard before in this vehicle," he said, keeping his eyes on the road.

"Something serious?"

"I don't know."

We continued on US 77, north of Corpus Christi. A four-lane divided highway took us through the Texas countryside. "I wonder what this would look like if it were June instead of February," I said to Paul. As it was, we saw bleak, gray, leafless, gnarled trees. The gray, cloudy sky darkened the already inky soil, newly plowed and harrowed, in miles and miles of level fields. Seeds and plants hid, waiting for spring. Only the median and side strips of the road showed green grass. Cattle grazed in what looked like an old orchard and somehow found some morsels near the highway. They and an occasional house or two and the moving traffic were the only signs of life. I wasn't sure I liked traveling through such desolation in winter, even to find a summer oasis.

About 5:00 P.M., after covering 334 miles, we pulled into site 9 at Lake Corpus Christi State Recreation Area. Unbelievably, 70-degree temperatures and a large flock of noisy grackles greeted us! I quickly shed my maroon, long-sleeved top, jeans, and black soft-soled shoes and put on a short-sleeved cotton top, cotton pants, and white tennis shoes. It had taken us eight days to find a warm place.

Before supper, Paul crawled under the left front side of the motorhome to look for the cause of the noise that he had heard earlier. Putting a rug on the ground, he worked it past the left front wheel and under the axle. Then lying on his back, he inched himself toward the suspected area, moving the beam from a large flashlight around slowly, searching the undercarriage of the motorhome. It didn't take long for him to see that the left front shock absorber bolt had come out of its hole in the chassis. As the bolt vibrated against the side of the chassis, it made the scraping noise that Paul had heard. The nut was missing from the bolt.

Paul knew that he had to find a nut and reattach the bolt soon; otherwise, the shock absorber would continue to hang. It might bounce into its original hole, damaging the threads of the bolt.

As evening tiptoed in at the park, it brought an eerie quiet. Although about ten RVs had parked in our circle of trees and thickets, I had seen only an occasional person moving about. "It's so quiet!" I said to Paul. The strange quiet made me wonder if some Pied Piper had lured away the children. I loved to hear children's squealing voices as they played and had fun, but Paul advised, "Let's just enjoy the peace while we can."

The next morning, Friday, warm, dense mist shrouded the camping circle. Since our entrance door opened away from view of other campers, I stepped outside in my soft, pink, quilted bathrobe and took a picture of bare trees, which looked like strange dancing figures in a steam bath. I heard a small flock of geese flying overhead. Warm air brushed my cheeks. Short sleeves that day!

"I stepped outside in my soft, pink, quilted bathrobe and took a picture of bare trees, which looked like strange dancing figures in a steam bath."

When the park service staff came by to collect garbage, Paul hurried outside to talk with them. They gave him directions to auto parts stores in the nearest town, Mathis.

By 9:15 A.M., we were weaving through Lake Corpus Christi State Recreation Area, Paul in the motorhome and I in Patches, leaving that warm, peaceful stopover. We hooked up the tow car to the motorhome just beyond the exit gate of the park on a level spot at the side of the road.

In Mathis, we searched for auto parts stores until we found one with easy parking along the curb. While I stayed in the motorhome, Paul walked into the store and soon returned carrying a small brown paper bag with nuts and bolts. Knowing that our Holiday Rambler had a Chevrolet chassis, Paul had learned in the auto parts store of a Chevrolet dealership in town. He wanted to find a higher-strength nut than the auto parts store carried. When Paul fixed something, he usually made it as good as or better than it was originally.

He decided to unhook Patches and drive it to the Chevy place because he would have to hunt for the showroom and did not know how much parking space would be available. He also would stop at a bank to replenish our cash supply.

While waiting for Paul to return, I thought about how competent and conscientious he had been in taking care of our vehicles. His beloved hobby had certainly come in handy. Yesterday, when I told him he was a natural for this motorhoming life, he smiled.

Paul soon drove past in Patches, tooting the horn, smiling and waving like a circus clown on a unicycle. I giggled and assumed he had more errands to do.

Eventually, he returned with high-strength nuts, corresponding washers, and cash, which he promptly divided with me. I didn't even ask!

We left Mathis towing the car, of course, and looked for the first rest area where we would eat lunch and Paul would try to install the nut. After eating, Paul scooted himself under the motorhome. His wrenches and socket set were lined up within easy reach. In minutes, he had successfully slipped the shock absorber bolt back into its hole in the chassis. He slid a washer and nut onto the bolt and fastened them securely in place. Job done. He wriggled out from under the vehicle, put away his tools, and was soon behind the wheel again, looking ahead.

After driving 193 miles that day, we reached one of our main goals for this trip, Brownsville. A warm, Gulf breeze welcomed us. I almost danced going into the office of the park to register. It appeared that our desire to go there had been validated. We paid for two nights, although we thought we might stay a few days longer since the weather seemed so nice.

"What are you folks interested in while you're here?" asked the manager of the Rio Mobile Home and RV Park.

His question surprised me. It was the first time that a campground staffer had asked it of us. We apparently were at a resort where the management catered to people who spent the winter with them. Most campgrounds near highways offer only recreation rooms, swimming, hiking, perhaps a lake, and sometimes planned weekend activities.

"The weather primarily," I said.

He gave us a calendar showing daily programs at the park—exercises, painting, music, and other activities. A full-time leader planned social events.

"Could you give me a suggestion for a hairdresser? I'd like to make an appointment," I said.

A young woman, who was in the adjoining office, soon made me an appointment for 11:30 the next morning.

After supper in the motorhome, we walked in the pleasant evening air to the activity building. Two older, itinerant couples gave a country western and gospel concert. Because he has an ear for harmony, Paul thought they needed more practice. But both the performers and the audience joined in the down-home conviviality of the evening.

Back at the motorhome, we ate frozen yogurt as we looked through colorful brochures from the Texas Welcome Centers at Orange and Harlingen. Unusual for Paul, he joined me in planning what to do and see in Brownsville. He normally didn't like to have a specific plan. (Could this be the beginning of a breakthrough for him?)

Before we left home, Paul had declared in no uncertain terms that he did not want to go to Mexico nor did he want to take the motorhome or even the tow car there. He'd heard too many stories of vandalism and legal troubles when one crossed the border.

Contrarily, I found Mexico fascinating—mostly because I had never been there. My inner eye saw romantic heroes from old western movies. I remembered cowboys like Gene Autry singing "Mexicali Rose" and "My Adobe Hacienda." I pictured colorful pageantry from brilliant photographs of Mexican fiestas in the *National Geographic* magazine. In elementary school I used all the colors in my box of crayons to color pictures of the Mexican boys and girls in their native costumes that were in my coloring book. I visualized Carmen Miranda and other beautiful Mexican women dancing in their cachucha costumes.

Brownsville offered the Art League, Historical, and Stillman House Museums; the modern Gladys Porter Zoo, without bars or cages; Fort Brown/Texas Southmost College; and the Palmito Hill and Palo Alto Battlefields. The city itself began in 1846 as Fort Brown, established by General Zachary Taylor as a national boundary between the United States and Mexico. The fort was later turned into a hospital, and later the original hospital became the administration building of Texas Southmost College. Brownsville offered access to Matamoros, Mexico, by the International Bridge. Matamoros catered to U.S. visitors with handicrafts, restaurants, nightclubs, and gift shops.

In spite of the many possibilities in Brownsville, we elected to visit Padre Island, a famous resort area off the mainland between Laguna Madre and the Gulf of Mexico. We would go there after my hair appointment. On our return from the island, we would eat dinner at the Fish House, a fine restaurant recommended by our park host.

Any thoughts I had about going to Mexico ended up on the cutting room floor. Still, I wanted to at least look across the border at our southern neighbor—something I didn't say to Paul, yet.

· 12 ·

A Difference of Opinion

BY SATURDAY MORNING, the warm Gulf breeze of the day before had blown itself away, leaving 50-degree temperatures and cloudy skies that threatened rain. On the trailer next door, a flag flapped noisily. We began to question how long to stay in Brownsville after our tour of Padre Island that day. Since we were so close, I hoped that somehow, sometime that day we might drive near enough to the Rio Grande to look across and see Mexico, but I still didn't say so to Paul.

As I thought about my upcoming appointment, I wondered briefly what the winds would do to my new hairdo when we went to the beach that afternoon, yet I wanted to see the Gulf waves rolling onto the shore of Padre Island and my shampoo was overdue. I'd adjust to it all somehow, I told myself.

In spite of the cold gusts, Paul washed the windows on Patches for our forthcoming trips that day to the hairdresser, the island, and a restaurant for dinner. After being towed behind the motorhome, the car's windshield and windows had collected dust and rain splatters. He rearranged tools and materials in the outside compartments of the motorhome. I heard him laughing and chatting with the next-door neighbor and then saw him standing out in the driveway guiding another camper as he edged his huge fifth wheel past his neighbor's motorhome heading onto the narrow resort road.

I wished my spirits were as high as Paul's. While he busied himself outside, I wrote in my bound journal by hand:

Journal, we've not been very close this trip. Not much really private time with you.

I had planned to use the laptop computer as my journal. So far, to my surprise, I have not found it as handy to use as I expected. I'm sure it's because it's new and I just need to use it more to be comfortable with it. I know I will be glad to have written in the laptop when I get home because I will be able to easily edit or print out my notes should I want to do that. With my handwritten journal, I will have to key them into the hard drive computer after I get home. I also feel uncertain about how to keep the battery of the laptop charged. The paradox is that I have both the computer and the bound journal with me but am not using either very much. When I want to write, I think that I should use the computer—that writing in the bound journal would be contrary to my plans to use the computer as I travel. What a dither!

Am I just tired, Journal? Am I keeping my thoughts and feelings in my safe deposit box instead of sharing them? Introvert that I am, I must force myself to say what I think. How cautious I am! I must risk sharing. Of what am I afraid? I assume too readily that others will react negatively.

I assume also that I know what Paul thinks, but I need to talk with him and listen to what he says so that I really know what he thinks, and I need to let him know what I think. Heavy stuff, as my former, sensitive professor of religious studies would have observed.

Well, Journal, it's time now to eat a snack before leaving for the hairdresser and our trip to the island. Maybe that's it; maybe I just need to get my hair done! Bye for now.

With my hair freshly shampooed and blown dry, Paul and I rode in Patches 27 miles from Brownsville to Padre Island, which is off the east coast of Texas. Varying in width from one-eighth mile to three miles, the island lay between Laguna Madre and the Gulf of Mexico. Our windshield wipers swished quickly as we crossed a causeway from the mainland and moved along a busy street in the resort town called South Padre Island that occupied the five southernmost miles of Padre Island. The town drew many tourists looking for fishing, boating, shelling, sailing, diving, and windsurfing, as well as golf, tennis, racquetball, and shuffleboard. It offered a wide range of accommodations from campgrounds to family motels to luxury hotels and condo rentals. We looked for a place to park close to the beach.

Suddenly, Paul swung into a parking area beside a tall building. "How's this?" he asked. "This is about as close as we're going to get from what I can tell." I saw the blue Gulf ahead.

"Are you coming?" I asked.

"No, I think I'll just look at the water from here. But you take your time."

In rushing wind and rain, I struggled to open the door of Patches and raise the red umbrella. As I walked down gray, wooden steps onto spongy sand toward the white caps, wind with rain rushed at the plastic rain bonnet inside my hooded long coat. Backing into the gusts, I moved sideways toward the moving edge of the water.

Still with my back to the wind, I looked down the beach. Two stout-hearted souls strode toward me. They soon passed and I reached into my pocket for the Canon AE-1. After moving the camera back and forth several times to find just the right lines and place of interest, I pushed the shutter button.

Turning the opposite way, I took another picture. With the wind now in my face and messing up my hair, I didn't spend time searching for the right angle or moment. After all, I hadn't gone there to take pictures. I wanted to *feel* the Gulf, to listen to its water rolling in, to smell the sea spray, and to sense the eternity of wave after wave unfolding on the shore. The water's vastness stretched my appreciation of nature and made me feel in awe of God.

At the water's edge hardly more than a minute, I leaned over at just the right moment between waves and touched the cool water with my fingers as it bore its way up the sand; then I turned reluctantly toward the car. Had it been a beautiful, sunny day, I would have looked for shells and just sat and sensed the vastness of the Gulf waters. With tennis shoes sinking into the sand, I walked back to the steps, my face turned away from the wind.

"Did you see what you wanted to?" Paul asked.

"I could have stayed longer, but the wind was so strong. I just love to watch the waves and hear the surf."

We drove on. Then Paul saw an opening to drive onto the beach itself. He stayed on tracks already in the sand. Several four-wheel-drive vehicles ventured beyond these tracks closer to the water. Two men in a car whizzed past us in the wet sand. When they tried to turn around, they couldn't move no matter how much they revved the motor. Their wheels sank deeper into the sand. Luckily for them, people came to help.

"That's why I didn't want to get any closer to the water and why I wanted to stay in these tracks," Paul said.

"Yeah. That's smart." (I could see that Paul's "better safe than sorry" cautiousness this time really paid off.)

We drove back to the main street and then toward the north end of the island, leaving the resort town of South Padre Island behind. Sand dunes lined the road. Looking back, I saw a landscape of high-rise condominiums and hotels—quite a contrast to the bleak stretches around us.

The map showed a channel dividing the 113-mile-long Padre Island. We were on the southern portion heading toward its northern end. After perhaps 20 miles, the paved road ended at a simple, three-stake barrier. We parked along the roadside and climbed the dunes where we stood on top looking all around—to the Gulf on one side and Laguna Madre on the other. He wouldn't want to have missed this, Paul shared with me. Wind whipped at my hair, even inside my plastic rain bonnet.

I looked down at the black paved road where our car waited in front of the barricade and then beyond the simple barricade at drifts of gritty sand. Not even a commercial sign disturbed the barren desolation that led to the end of the south island and into the water. I saw the end of the road, the end of the island, and the beginning of the water. Those endings and beginnings seemed so obvious as physical landmarks and yet so enigmatic—which were symbols of death and which of life?

After taking a few more pictures, we skied down the dunes like they were snow, our arms flailing in the wind to keep our balance, laughing, getting sand in our shoes, and then hurrying into the car.

"Boy, it's good to be out of that wind," I said, grateful to be back inside Patches.

Paul reached to turn on the ignition, looked over at me, and teased in his gentle way, "Did the wind get into your hair?"

"How could it not?" I retorted, looking at my disheveled hair in the mirror on the sun visor.

On the road back to the city of South Padre Island, we saw a large group of motorhomes and trailers dry-camping on packed sand beside Laguna Madre. We could not decide if we would ever want to permanently join them—although we loved *visiting* the beach, we didn't want to *live* there.

We left the island, making our way back toward Brownsville. "I'm ready to move on tomorrow and see what McAllen is like," Paul said. I agreed.

Back at the motorhome, we changed clothes. Soon we were on our way to dinner at the Fish House in Brownsville when we came to a sign that pointed to the International Bridge that crossed the Rio Grande and led into Mexico. A spark of hope ignited within me.

"Could we go down that way and just look across into Mexico?" I asked. I had given up going to Mexico since Paul was so wary of it. But since we were so close, I wanted very much to see Mexico, if only from across the river.

"I don't want to get on a road that takes us across the bridge—one where we can't get off and have to go on across," Paul warned as he steered the car in the direction of the International Bridge.

I strained to look for views of either the river or Mexico or a parking lot beside the bridge on our side, but traffic and buildings blocked the view. The closer we got to the bridge, the more concerned Paul became about being in a lane of traffic in which there was no turning off or turning back. The streets and signs puzzled us. Sitting upright, searching hard in all directions, I steadfastly pictured a parking area at the bridge like those at Niagara Falls where people stood at a fence or wall and looked across the river.

Suddenly, Paul turned off the street leading toward the bridge. He turned around and headed in the opposite direction.

I couldn't believe it. A huge sledge hammer had squashed my rising hope. As if from a great distance, I heard Paul explain patiently that he was afraid that if he kept on that other street he would have been caught in the traffic going across the bridge. I heard the words, but I didn't accept them. I kept looking behind us for a glimpse of Mexico. Too many buildings, cars, and trucks blocked the view.

As we traveled instead toward the Fish House, away from Mexico, Paul said, "Did you want to see Mexico?" as if he were kidding me about a post office that we had passed without stopping to mail a card I had written.

"It hurts enough without your teasing me," I blurted out.

"I'm sorry, honey. I just didn't want to get caught in the lane of traffic going across," he tried to explain.

My insides seared. Why was he so cautious? I didn't understand his reasoning. Couldn't he take a little risk?

At the Fish House, with its tablecloths and candles in a softly lit ambiance, we ordered dinner. I fought to gain control of my feelings. I knew I had to talk about them. I thought of what I had written in my journal earlier that day and made myself open up to Paul. "I really wanted to see Mexico. I didn't realize how much until we turned back. I felt like someone had played a cruel trick on me."

"I just didn't want to get caught on a road that went across the bridge," Paul said again.

"But why? What would have been so terrible about going across? Couldn't we simply have come back?"

"Maybe yes, maybe no. Maybe we would have had to go through a lot of red tape. I just didn't know and didn't want to take the chance."

"But what about just getting close enough on this side to look across the river? In my mind, I saw a parking area and lookout, a place to stand and look across the river, like at Niagara Falls."

"Neither one of us could see what really lay ahead. I thought there would be a road leading across the bridge, and once we got on it, we would have no choice but to go on across. Think how it is with the Harbor Tunnel at home," Paul stated earnestly.

I visualized the time I took a wrong road and was headed toward the Harbor Tunnel at Baltimore; there was absolutely no place to get off at that point, so I had to go through whether I wanted to or not. I remembered feeling frustrated and foolish.

"Oh, yeah," I mused, trying hard to hold onto the image of how I felt at the Harbor Tunnel.

Paul reiterated what he thought could happen in Mexico—vandalism, legal and insurance problems perhaps. As I listened to his repetition, I tried to figure out what really happened inside me to trigger my hurt. I knew that I had pinned my hopes on there being a parking lot on our side of the bridge. When would I learn not to assume things? Every now and then those assumptions tripped me up. And what an upset this one was! But could I admit that to Paul? Hard as it was to do so, I sighed and said, "I guess I was so caught up in getting a sight of the real Mexico that I depended too much on my assumption of a parking lot on this side."

He and I continued to talk and our food came. Other people were filling up tables nearby. "Well, I should concentrate on the main destinations for this trip, which are Arizona and California, not Mexico," I said, as much to console myself as to tell Paul.

The next day, Sunday, we planned to move on from Brownsville, Texas, and continue west. Who knew, maybe I would see Mexico during our travels west.

· 13 ·

A Fulfilling Moment

"YOU KNOW, DEAR, there's something different about today," Paul said lightly. We had just gotten up and were making the bed on Sunday morning in Brownsville, the day after my major disappointment of not seeing Mexico from across the Rio Grande. Paul leaned toward the head of his side of the queen bed to line up the broad hem of the top sheet with the head of the mattress.

After retiring from Western Maryland College, I had tried Paul's way of doing household tasks, even though it sometimes went "against the grain." When he made the bed, for example, he simply stretched the bedspread from the bottom of the bed to the top, letting it shape itself as it would over the pillows, whereas when I made it, I tucked the bedspread a little way under the pillows and then continued it over their top. But when we made the bed together, I did it his way, telling myself it really didn't matter—it's for "everyday" (not for company, just us). It was our relationship that mattered.

Although Paul made the bed one way and I made it totally different, I realized it was more important to keep the peace and to go along. In a confined space, especially, I had to think about the whole picture more than an individual decision or choice.

"What's that?" I asked, stretching and smoothing the sheet on my side toward its top corner.

"The sun is shining."

Yawning, I squinted at the yellow brightness coming through the window and its closed draperies. "Right! A welcome change!"

We continued making the bed. I consciously slowed down my usually quicker pace and let Paul lead. We pulled, stretched, and smoothed the thermal, knitted bedspread. Then to my surprise, for the first time in our bedmaking teamwork, Paul tucked the bedspread *under* the pillows and laid the remaining part over them. We ended with the *House Beautiful* look! That change in Paul's bedmaking style had come of his own free will.

As we ate cereal with sliced bananas and drank hot water (Paul added sugar and cream to his) at the dinette table on that day of rest and worship, we watched local religious services on television.

Later Paul went outside to unhook the motorhome while I drove Patches to the activity building's phone booth. There I called Bentsen-Rio Grande Valley State Park for reservations for that night. Located just west of McAllen, near Mission, Texas, it would be less than a two-hour trip from Brownsville.

About 9:30 A.M., Paul drove the motorhome while I followed in the tow car as we left Rio Mobile Home and RV Park. After a brief stop at a nearby car wash to jet spray the motorhome, we hooked up Patches and then pulled out toward McAllen.

On the way to McAllen, I forced myself to write so that using the computer would become as natural as using a pen and paper. When Paul asked questions like, "Is Mission (Texas) right on US 83?" I interrupted my writing and reached for the map on the dashboard.

By noon, we had covered the 74 miles to Bentsen-Rio Grande Valley State Park, where Paul registered us at the entry office. When he returned with the campsite map, I noticed that the park bordered on the Rio Grande. He also handed me a booklet he had picked up in the office: *The Rio Grande Hiking Trail of Bentsen-Rio Grande Valley State Park*. My heart beat faster, yet I didn't dare count on seeing Mexico because it would involve hiking. Paul didn't like to hike because he sometimes got a "catch" in his side from an old hernia operation and also because walking sometimes made his knees hurt. I knew that I shouldn't walk alone in unfamiliar territory.

We parked in site 48. Motorhomes and trailers kept rolling in and filling the campground. Weird, clutching, briery, gray trees clustered around us. Surely they would have sported green leaves if it had been June instead of February.

After hooking up, Paul went back to the park office and telephoned his first cousin, Jesse Yingling. Each year around the first of December, he and his wife, Emagene, drove their trailer from their home in Ohio to Lazy Palms Ranch, near Edinburg, which is about 20 miles northeast of McAllen. As members of the ranch, they stayed until April. Paul had to leave a message for Jesse with the ranch's campground manager.

"What message did you leave?"

"I told him that we were here. If it suited him and Emagene to come visit, we'd be glad to see them."

On Sunday afternoon, we drove into Mission to a Camping World supply center, one of a large chain that sells RV parts, equipment, and other products. Many RVs populated the parking lot. Inside, we joined other campers wandering around, looking, searching, and chatting with one another.

We continually discovered better ways of doing things or organizing the motorhome. At Camping World, we bought four quart-size, clear plastic bottles in which to store a gallon of milk. Milk costs less by the gallon, and the quart containers would be easier to handle and fit neatly in the refrigerator door; it would also increase our capacity to keep more milk on hand. We found a small, oak message center that held a memo pad and pencils. It had three hooks on the bottom, one of which was just right for the bottle brush that we would use to wash the new plastic milk bottles.

On the way back to the campground, I said, "This McAllen area seems inviting."

"Yeah, I agree," Paul responded.

"The wind doesn't blow as much as at Brownsville, and the air has enough moisture to be good for a person's skin. But I'm not ready to make a decision on where to spend our time next winter until we've seen Arizona."

"Good idea."

At twilight, someone knocked. Our first visitor! A quick look out the window revealed a pickup truck with a shell on the back.

Jesse entered—how good to see him! What fun to visit in an unexpected place! He told us that Emagene had a bad cold and was taking prescription medicine so she couldn't come. As we talked, Jesse sat in the swivel chair beside the entry door. Paul climbed into the passenger chair that had already been turned toward the living room, and I settled on the sofa. We sat comfortably in this arrangement with room to spare. We had a lively session of reminiscing and catching up on what had been happening in our lives. It was Jesse who told us that there was indeed no way of turning around once a car was headed for the International Bridge at Brownsville—absolving Paul again of being overly cautious. Before Jesse left, we promised to stop by his trailer, although it was off our course.

The next morning, Monday, unexpectedly and without any request from me, Paul said he wanted to hike the two-mile loop to the Rio Grande and back. (I had only commented after he handed me the booklet yesterday that the park bordered on the river.)

We drove Patches to a parking area at the trailhead. In winter boots, red sweatpants, and zippered red, white, and blue sweat jacket, I smiled for the camera beside a sign that said Rio Grande River Hiking Trail. I smiled inside, too, but guardedly, not counting on reaching the river. After all, I had already been disappointed once.

We stepped into the woods. Hikers came toward us; others passed us from behind. Paul liked nature; he just did not like walking, at least not just for exercise, which I enjoyed. We strolled along the sunshine-stenciled dirt path through the woodland, taking our time. Paul carried the booklet about the trail, which, along with small signs with numbers near trees and bushes, helped us identify the flora. Number seven identified the weird one I had been seeing—honey mesquite. I learned that in summer, its pods are eaten by wildlife and livestock. Its beans make good jelly, and its hard wood is used for fence posts, furniture, and charcoal.

The trail wound around and forked through trees so that a hiker could not be sure which path went to the river. Then as we walked through open brush, including cacti, I looked ahead and saw what appeared to be muddy blue water beyond winter-bare branches of the mesquite.

Hurrying, I looked for an open place in the frenzied, hedgelike growth of trees and brush along the bank. Finding one, I stood still and gaped.

The Rio Grande flowed by smoothly between banks about 650 feet apart. It looked narrow and shallow, as if one could wade across, but who knew what depth lurked beneath!

Across the river, a man got into a pickup truck and, with dust trailing, drove away. He left behind a two-story, boxlike, flat-roofed farm house with porches on both floors on one side; run-down out-buildings; and sounds of a cowbell and gobbling turkey. The ground looked barren with only a few scraggly trees and a fence, its wood posts leaning in seemingly random directions.

"Could that be Mexico?"

"If it isn't, I don't know what it is," Paul replied.

"Mexico!" I said it out loud. The solitary remoteness of that house seemed an interesting contrast to the fiesta-loving civilization that was surely farther south. I looked hard at the sight across the river and felt its presence. I would forever feel in touch with it.

I lingered to soak up the view and then reluctantly turned away from this fulfilling moment and place.

Something affirming leaped up inside me: Everything comes to she who waits—and perseveres! Right there, heading away from the river, I thanked God for the joy of seeing Mexico! I thought of the scripture where the angel told Mary that her relative Elizabeth was six months pregnant, although she was old, and then said, "For with God nothing will be impossible." God had such singular ways to bless his believers.

On the trail back, Paul clowned for the camera near a huge cactus plant and then moved ahead, chuckling. I soon caught up with him on the single-file path, and we played follow the leader back to the car.

There comes a time when traveling that one must say "whoa" to sightseeing and "giddyup" to catching up on paperwork and domestic duties. By Monday afternoon, following my momentous encounter with Mexico, I had decided to do just that—stay in the motorhome while Paul went into Mission for groceries.

Sitting at the dinette table, I taped campground diagrams and registration receipts into a three-ring notebook, bringing it up to date. This notebook served as a log and a reference for future trips. I wrote birthday cards and postcards to friends and family, including a postcard to Mother Beard.

Next, I cleaned the motorhome with the central vacuum cleaner, using the hose and attachments that were stored under the living room sofa. When plugged into the power unit situated under one of the dinette seats, the vacuum cleaner hose easily reached every part of the interior of the motorhome, from the rear, including the overhead cabinet doors at the farthest point, to the dashboard and the windshield. To me, the central vacuum cleaner was one of the most satisfying options that we had ordered for the motorhome.

I vacuumed the fabric ceiling, cabinet panels, venetian blinds, counters, dashboard instruments, and, of course, the carpeted floor using the round brush, floor nozzle, or carpet brush as needed. Although a normal vacuum pass takes ten minutes, all of this took several hours. After being on the road 12 days, a clean coach would refresh us.

Early Tuesday morning, we left Bentsen-Rio Grande Valley State Park. By 10:00 A.M., we turned into Lazy Palms Ranch to visit Jesse and Emogene. With its location well off a main artery, Lazy Palms Ranch offered peaceful, clean, level, ample, and well-organized sites—an inviting scene.

Jesse was outside, waiting to show us where to park. Emagene's cold was on the mend he told us.

Since retiring, Emogene and Jesse had found themselves involved in all sorts of exciting adventures. They had served as volunteers in Haiti at a children's hospital—she as nurse and he as plumber. Last summer, they had driven a large passenger van to take Amish Mennonites on a sightseeing trip through the West.

They showed us the huge activity building where ranch members taught one another crafts such as crocheting and whittling. Members also planned tours to Mexico and other places. The Pan American University in nearby McAllen offered classes that senior citizens could attend.

As we wandered among tables with craft activities, I thought I saw a cowboy in a small gathering at the other end of the enormous room. "Who's that?" I asked Jesse, pointing.

"Oh, he's a touring cowboy," Jesse said.

"Do you think I could meet him?" My interest in cowboys stemmed from my father, who must have read every Zane Grey western novel. When I thought of my youthful father, who died at age 34 of a streptococcus infection in the bloodstream before penicillin was available, I pictured him grinning and talking with other readers of Zane Grey about the West. I got a warm feeling that carried over to a liking for cowboys and the West in general. My interest in cowboys kept me in close touch with my father.

Circumventing tables, chairs, and people, Jesse and I reached the star.

"May I shake your hand? Are you a real cowboy?" I asked.

"Well, yes, but these aren't my regular working duds. These clothes are like ones worn in earlier days," and he went on to explain in some detail. His leather chaps looked just like those worn in old-time western movies. A real cowboy! Yet everybody around me, including the cowpoke himself, seemed nonchalant about it all.

From this encounter, I surmised that we were getting into cowboy country. Now that I'd seen Mexico, my next passion was seeing real western cowboys.

After a delicious, home-cooked meal of sizzling fried chicken, peas, stuffing, gravy, and sections of sweet Texas oranges and grapefruit in the trailer, we took pictures, got directions from Jesse on the best route to our campground for that night, and thanked him and Emagene for their warm, generous hospitality. From there, we headed south to Falcon State Recreation Area near Falcon Heights, Texas, for the night.

At 4:15 P.M., we drove through the gate at Falcon State Recreation Area, off US 83. A telephone booth beside the office building reminded me of phone calls to make. At our campsite, a bleak scene of sandy soil, dry grass, and gray mesquite trees greeted us—winter in Texas.

· 14 ·

The Joke's On Me

AFTER SUPPER on Tuesday evening, in the dark, Paul and I rode in Patches to the Falcon State Recreation Area office. Outside telephone booths, like sentinels, stood lighted and ready for callers. I hoped to make reservations for San Antonio, city of the famous Alamo. On the way, actually out of the way, we would visit Laredo, where I hoped to see a cowboy environment.

But first, I dialed the Family Motor Coach Association (FMCA) office to check for messages. We had joined this national group shortly after buying our motorhome. In addition to the message service, it offered a subscription to its official publication, *Family Motor Coaching*; technical information exchange; mail forwarding; national conventions; and a number of other member benefits.

"No messages, Mrs. Beard," the friendly young woman said.

I aimed to call FMCA each day, usually at night when we arrived at a campground, keeping in mind that its hours of operation in Cincinnati, Ohio, were 8 A.M. to 11 P.M., eastern time, Monday through Friday, except holidays.

If Jeff or Hazel needed to get in touch with us, they could dial the toll-free emergency message number and leave word for us to call them. When we, in turn, called that number, an operator would tell us if we had any messages. While it took extra effort to make the telephone call when traveling, it gave us peace of mind to know that no emergencies had come up at home.

I then called the Alamo KOA Kampground at San Antonio for reservations for the next night (Wednesday) through Friday night. During the call, I mentioned that Ralph and Dot John, good friends from Maryland, had reservations beginning Thursday and asked if we might be placed near them. The person helping me could not promise anything since the sites had not yet been assigned for Thursday.

During Ralph John's 12-year presidency at Western Maryland College, I had been his executive assistant. His wife, Dorothy, and I had become close friends. Together, we frequently had lunch, shopped, and went to meetings of the American Association of University Women. When Ralph retired, he and Dot were joyfully surprised with a 28-foot Taurus travel trailer given by the Board of Trustees. With the Johns' trailer and our motorhome, we enjoyed another common bond, the RV lifestyle, although we had never actually camped together.

The day before we left home on this trip, I had called Dot and Ralph at their home. Ralph said they planned to be at the Alamo KOA Kampground in San Antonio on Thursday, February 8, for a week and in Corpus Christi the following week. We talked about possibly getting together, although I had no idea where we would be in early February. I had kept the thought in the back of my mind.

We had already passed Corpus Christi and didn't plan to drive close to it again on this trip, which left only San Antonio as a possible meeting place with the Johns. We would be ahead of them in arriving in San Antonio, but we were ready to stay in one place for a few days before heading west to Arizona.

Driving back to the motorhome, we passed a sign: Falcon Dam.

"I'd like to see that in the morning before we leave," Paul said. Since I'd seen Mexico, I was more than willing to see something Paul wanted.

During the chilly, dark side of daybreak the following morning, Wednesday, my flashlight illuminated the keyhole on the passenger's door of Patches. The car's cold, black vinyl seat made me draw my jacket closer around me. With Paul driving, we searched for Falcon Dam.

While trying to read road signs in the darkness, we made a wrong turn that took us downhill to a sandy beach at the edge of the dam's back waters, where the radiant glow of the unrisen sun surprised and greeted us. With the dark horizon silhouetted, a great V-shaped sweep of sunlight searched its way through low-hanging clouds, their undersides almost white. The same sunlight served as a backdrop for clumps of higher, overhead gray cirrocumulus clouds. Near earth, a soft, golden glow looked hand painted in several lengths and widths of parallel strokes. This glorious painting changed in hue and composition as we watched. I breathed in deeply as I felt overwhelming respect for the Creator of this dawn panorama, newly designed every day, every minute.

Turning the car around, we drove until we came to the parking area at Falcon Dam. A lone fisherman seemed not to notice us as he worked behind his pickup truck, which he had backed down a long

"The rising sun reflected a long, narrow, golden bar in the water as the fisherman disappeared in the distance."

concrete ramp to the water's edge. He launched his boat, parked his truck and empty trailer among several deserted others, stepped precariously from the dock to the boat, and started the motor. The rising sun reflected a long, narrow, golden bar in the water as the fisherman backed his craft away from the ramp and disappeared in the distance.

Cool morning stillness surrounded us; the quiet beauty of the early dawn crept into our awareness. Are fishermen captivated by all of this wonder, too?

Several minutes later, we left the reservoir. Already the enchantment of early dawn ebbed. Daylight made us think about what we must do before breaking camp. We returned to the motorhome.

In the morning's freshness, Paul steered the motorhome out of our overnight refuge. I followed in Patches. With no sewer hookup at the campsite, we stopped at the disposal station near the exit of Falcon State Recreation Area.

Dumping took only a few minutes. It was simply the procedure of emptying the contents of the vehicle's holding tanks into a sewage

"Dumping took only a few minutes."

receptacle at either an individual campsite or at a common dumping station at a campground. (Paul always wears leather work gloves for this chore.) Motorhomes have two separate holding tanks: one for "gray" water drained from the kitchen and bathroom sinks and shower and the other for "black" water flushed down the toilet.

I watched from Patches as Paul placed the outlet end of the blue sewer hose into a concrete opening at the dump site; then he connected the inlet end of the sewer hose to the motorhome after removing a safety cap. Paul drained the black water tank first and then the gray water tank. When the tanks were drained, he disconnected the sewer hose from the motorhome and flushed it with water. Paul reattached the safety cap to the discharge pipe from the holding tanks. He returned the blue sewer hose to its storage place and washed down any waste spilled on the concrete apron at the dumping station opening before recapping it.

Either Paul or I would complete the operation later by pouring Aqua-Kem into the toilet and flushing it into the black water tank. This chemical deodorizes and helps disintegrate incoming waste and tissue and also helps keep the holding tank clean.

The first few times Paul went through this process, I wanted to look the other way and deny the fact of dumping, but after seeing how other campers took it in stride, I accepted this reality of life, too. Paul and others often chatted with anyone who waited to dump or who walked by. They were as nonchalant as if we were getting gasoline at a filling station.

By 8:15 A.M., under sunny skies with 60-degree temperatures, we left Falcon State Recreation Area bound for Laredo and San Antonio. I wore jeans, a light blue cotton knit top with short sleeves, and a long-sleeved navy blue sweat jacket, which I would take off when I got out of the passenger seat to retrieve the laptop computer.

The day before, I was either tired or else my left brain won out over my right brain because I procrastinated in getting out the computer and ended the day without using it. It seemed that my left brain, with its rational nature, often discouraged me from using my right brain, with its creative powers. I'd learned to recognize that when I worried about something I had to write; it was the left brain working, but when I got into the writing project, the right brain happily took over and the project got done. The worrying was useless. So I knew that all I had to do was start writing, not put it off.

We were going out of our way so that I might experience the mystique of Laredo. The Texas tourist guide booklet said it was "rich in south-of-the-border flavor." The publication showed a color picture of mariachis serenading visitors. I visualized Gene Autry and other movie cowboys talking and singing about Laredo.

I was not sure what to expect: perhaps a Mexican with a striped serape and huge tilted sombrero, or a sheriff's office with a jail behind it, or a singing cowboy rounding up doggies, or a bunkhouse near a corral where fellows in chaps pushed their hats back off their sweaty brows. Surely there would be something of this in Laredo; surely the cowboy at Lazy Palms Ranch was the prologue.

We moved along US 83 toward Zapata, a small town east of Laredo. "Look at that wide main street! It looks just like those in the old western movies," I told Paul as we entered Zapata.

"A grocery store, Radio Shack, Western Auto. If you see a hardware store, let me know," said Paul, his eyes searching both sides of the street as he slowed down.

"They even park heading into the curb! Texaco, Los Pasteles Bakery, Your Place Cafeteria, Alvarez Flowers & Gifts, Elizondo Auto Parts," I read off the names of stores while being enthralled that we were riding down an actual, wide, western main street. "Too bad you're not still looking for an auto parts store; right there was one."

We continued past a Spanish church of white stucco, Conoco, Chevron, Cortijo Restaurant, and law offices. Then Paul saw it. "Plumbing and Hardware," he read and steered immediately to the wide shoulder.

By now we were at the western end of Zapata, almost out in the country. Opening the driver's door, Paul climbed down the ladder-like steps and crossed the wide street to the store.

Just outside the motorhome on my right, several stands of flat-leaf cactus plants mingled with low mesquite trees and rooted tumbleweed, all trying to survive in what looked like sand. Old tires, bottles, paper, and cardboard littered the area.

On the opposite side of the street, the ground appeared windswept. Apparently, the low trees and brush on my side captured debris blown there from across the street by strong winds. The foliage served as a "snow fence" for trash.

Suddenly, a pickup truck pulling a fifth-wheel travel trailer swung to the shoulder and parked just ahead of us. A man and woman left the truck and went back to their trailer. "They needed a pit stop," Paul concluded when he returned from the store. The couple had to get out of their truck and go back to their fifth wheel in order to enjoy its rest break facilities, which is one of the trade-offs when purchasing a trailer rather than a motorhome. They may already have possessed the truck and their most economical option was to add a trailer, or they may have opted for more living space for the money. While rest room facilities and galley ride conveniently with you in a motorhome, the driving area reduces the amount of living space, and the total cost for the entire rig is appreciably higher.

"The plumbing and hardware store didn't have the pressure gauge that I wanted, but I got a light switch for your lamp. I got a brown one intentionally because then you can see it easily," Paul said.

The switch was for a white cord attached to a small lamp that I used for extra light when I wrote at night. I had mentioned to Paul how inconvenient it was to use the light. I had to plug the cord into a wall outlet to turn on the light and then unplug the cord to turn it off.

"I'll try someplace else for the pressure gauge," Paul commented. He said the gauge would measure the water pressure coming from a campground spigot. The regulator on the gauge would allow him to set the amount of pressure entering the plumbing system of the motorhome. Too much pressure can pop loose various connections and cause leaks.

"Once something starts leaking, it's kind of hard to get it stopped unless you take it all apart and put it together again," explained Paul. "Our motorhome's designed for about 40 pounds of pressure, but I usually keep it at 30 pounds." This gives plenty of pressure for the sinks, shower, and toilet. At home, our water pump comes on when the water pressure gets down to 20 and goes off at 40. Usually, the water pressure in the motorhome seems about the same as at home.

We continued toward Laredo, the highway like a long, narrow leather belt under the expansive Texas sky. A small flock of wild ducks seemed to float just above the distant horizon, and then another appeared, both in wing-shaped formations. The land and vegetation around us looked very dry, although green tidbits showed along the highway and just inside fences. We rode along with Paul driving and me using the computer and getting more used to it.

"It's easy to see how you could lose cattle out here. They get into the brush and you can't even see them," said Paul as he looked at rolling hills of scrub and low trees. A herd of beef cattle, red with white heads, stood and chewed or grazed next to a gray shed fringed with dormant brush. Run-down and deserted stores drew our sympathy as we passed. A slab of concrete against a slope emphasized the dry riverbed from which the abandoned boat ramp rose. "This is Gene Autry country," said Paul.

"You think so?" I wasn't so sure.

"Yeah," he replied. Paul yawned aloud, then said jokingly. "Did we get up before breakfast this morning?"

I laughed, feeling sleepy, too, "Yeah, I think so." And so we rode along looking at the landscape, making observations, and thinking our own thoughts.

I wondered what Laredo would be like. I wanted to get the flavor of it somehow. I had read the Laredo description in both the American Automobile Association (AAA) *Tour Book* for Texas and the *Texas State Travel Guide*.

About 26 miles east of Laredo, irrigation standpipes punctuated the far-reaching fields planted with crops. Somebody cared about cleanliness because highway shoulders were free of litter. We passed our first corral in Texas. Farther on, mesquite, cacti, and yuccas stretched for miles like a gray and wine plush carpet. What are those small trees with a wine-colored leaf or bud? I wondered.

"We've been on the road two weeks already. This is our 14th day," I observed.

"We're getting this traveling thing down pretty well," Paul said. We seemed to be coordinating tasks with good humor and in good spirit.

At first, we had been perfectionistic conversationalists—at least I was. We got into competitive, precision discussions that became a kind of "accuracynoia" (a combination of the word *accuracy* and the combining form *-noia*, meaning "thought"). One or both of us picked at the exact language of the other. We asked picayune questions to make the words of the speaker match what the listener thought they should be. It was often irritating. I remembered one example:

Bernice: "Over there's a satellite dish. First one I've seen today."

Paul: "Where? Oh, yeah. That's a ten-foot one. I've seen some others."

Bernice: "How can you tell it's a ten-footer? It's some distance away."

Paul: "Well, from looking at a lot of them."

Bernice: "Did you measure any?"

Paul: "Well, no, but I have a good idea."

Bernice: "I wouldn't be sure unless I measured it or saw it written on the dish."

Paul: "That's the difference between us. I can look at something and give an educated guess, whereas you want to measure."

So it went. After a few days into the trip, I tried to accept Paul's statements without running them into the ground and tried not to criticize or find fault. If our trip was to be enjoyable, it was up to us to make it so, and I was one-half of that "us."

As we rode toward Laredo, I kept looking for cowboys riding the range. Not seeing any, I consoled myself by visualizing the surprise of the glorious sunrise at Falcon Dam that morning.

At midmorning we entered Laredo and made our way to the north side of the city. We parked outside the glass-fronted tourist bureau. While Paul headed for an outdoor telephone booth, I entered the bureau with high hopes of getting specific information on cowboys.

A young woman behind a long counter waited as I approached, the only visitor in the large room.

"Is there anywhere in Laredo where one can catch the south-of-the-border flavor and see cowboys as they were shown in old movies?" I asked.

"Not around here," the young agent shook her head slowly with a flicker of amusement in her eyes.

"No?"

"No," she repeated. "You would have to go out into the hill country to see cowboys."

"Where is the hill country?" I asked.

"In the San Antonio area," she said, getting out the map of Texas and showing me a brown shaded area of elevated topography northwest of San Antonio.

I could not believe that we had come all the way to Laredo to catch its old-movie flavor and the tourist bureau agent denied its existence. Was she too new to know? Other agents behind the same counter surely had overheard us and would have offered correct information. We could have gone directly to San Antonio!

Leaving the bureau, I walked up an adjacent arched pedestrian bridge to view the city. Again, disappointment, as I saw only industrial buildings occupying the area. While on the bridge, I thought of another question for the agent.

"Could you tell me the names of the flora we passed as we drove here from Zapata? Do you have a leaflet or booklet showing them?" I asked.

The young woman looked blank. She could neither tell me the name of the wine-colored bushes nor provide any information on the local vegetation. Deflated, I wondered, Did I ask the right questions? How else could I have expressed it?

In a way, I was relieved. I felt more inclined to get to San Antonio than to sightsee in Laredo. My body wanted to stay in one place a while. Yet we had driven out of our way to come here. How would I tell Paul?

He returned to the motorhome and filled me in on his phone call to our bank. As requested before leaving home, monies had been transferred by our hometown bank to a debit account at another local bank because our bank did not offer such an option. We used a Visa debit card as we traveled. While some people use a debit card, other RVers have told us they use a credit card. If an RVer likes the idea of arriving at home without accumulated debt, then the debit card is one way to go. With the credit card, of course, one buys on credit and pays it back at a later time. With the debit card, the expenditures come out of monies already deposited in a checking account at the bank. There is no annual service charge and depending on the type of active checking account you have, you may or may not receive interest. Using either the debit card or the credit card with your PIN (personal identification number) at an automatic teller machine costs a service charge of about $2.00 per use. If you use a debit card as you travel, when you get home your checking account is lower than when you started but all your bills are paid from the trip. If you use a credit card, your credit account debt is higher than when you started on the trip and until it is paid, finance charges will accumulate.

He was pleased that the bank had carried out our prior arrangements. "What did *you* find out?" he asked.

I turned my body sideways in the passenger seat so that I faced him and took a deep breath.

"Guess what?" I said a bit sheepishly, not knowing what Paul's reaction would be when I told him the news.

"What?"

"You know how we drove here to Laredo to see the south-of-the-border environment and cowboys like we used to see in the movies?"

"Yes."

"Well, they're not here. That young woman in the tourist bureau said we would have to go to San Antonio to see cowboys!" I said.

Paul threw his head back and guffawed. "You mean we traveled 1,200 miles out of our way for nothing?"

"Yeah," I grinned.

"Well, then, I guess we head for San Antonio."

"I'd say so, unless there's something you want to see here."

Still laughing, he started the motor and we headed north. Every now and then, he chuckled about going out of our way to see Laredo and it being a bust. "Something good will come of it, if only your good laugh," I said. It added actually only 61 miles to our travels, but it had required spending an extra night, which was at Falcon State Recreation Area. Yet we had seen such an awesome Texas sunrise at Falcon Dam; we could hardly write off the detour as a total loss.

North of Laredo, we came to a checkpoint. A uniformed officer walked to the driver's side of the motorhome.

"Are you United States' citizens?" He spoke fast with a Spanish accent. "Yes," Paul answered.

The officer waved us on and Paul said to him, "Have a nice day!"

We counted five uniformed officers. A large billboard showed a drug-sniffing police dog. One officer escorted two young men into the checkpoint building while a third young man stood beside a black Trans Am parked on the right side of the road.

As we headed toward San Antonio, I continued typing into the laptop computer. Paul asked if the computer battery was low. I had typed all morning after having plugged the adaptor cord into the wall outlet.

"I'm plugged into electricity," I replied confidently.

"No generator, no juice," he announced. The generator was not turned on!

I looked quickly at the warning light; it was red, indicating a low battery.

"Could you turn on the generator?" I asked urgently, unplugging the electrical cord from the wall outlet to protect the computer from any surges the generator might create until its voltage had stabilized. Activating and stabilizing the generator took no more than a minute from the time the switch was turned on.

Paul immediately pushed the generator switch on the dashboard. The "ready" relay of the generator switch clicked a few seconds later, showing it was supplying electric current to the wall outlets. I plugged the computer's AC adaptor cord into the wall outlet again, and the red warning light turned green, indicating that the computer was receiving current.

My mind raced with thoughts of what I would do if my morning's work was lost. With relief, I watched as every word reappeared. Another lesson learned: the auxiliary generator *must* be turned on to activate the electrical outlets when we were on the road. Where had my mind been?

In the passenger seat, I continued to write. On this winter day, we rode through dry countryside with leafless gray trees and low cactus clumps that looked like huge cabbages. Long, low hills broke the flatness to the north. Many clouds lingered, but in this wide sky country, blue prevailed. Sunshine warmed my right arm.

I felt glad for our KOA reservations in San Antonio for the next three days. It would be pleasant to stay in one place. We hoped to have a fun visit with Ralph and Dot, perhaps taking a tour with them of San Antonio and the Alamo. Then westward again to the hill country and cowboys, I hoped!

We had stopped four times since leaving Falcon State Recreation Area: the plumbing and hardware store in Zapata, a Conoco station for gasoline, the Laredo tourist bureau, and the border checkpoint. The next stop would surely be lunch; it was almost noon.

The early morning ride in the dark to Falcon Dam seemed long ago. Our final stop that day would be San Antonio later that afternoon.

You never know what to expect when you enter a campground. After driving from Falcon State Recreation Area and Laredo, we were ready to register quickly and relax. It was 3:01 P.M. when Paul turned left into the Alamo KOA Kampground in San Antonio. To our surprise, *two* lines of RVs waited ahead. People walked to the office and others from the office back to their vehicles. Many volunteers in bright red T-shirts congenially directed traffic and answered questions from incoming campers.

Paul drove slowly toward the last RV in one line and stopped.

"With all this traffic, I think I'd better stay with the coach. Would you mind going to the office?" he asked.

Dust floated up around my tennis shoes as I crossed the unpaved common area to the office in hot sunshine. I could hardly squeeze inside the office. People stood waiting or milled around. After spotting the registration counter, I waited patiently behind another camper. Looking around and between people, I saw that the large room also housed the camp store.

My turn came, and the registrar handed me a registration form, which is customary in camp offices. It asked for my name, address, make and model of vehicle, license number, number of persons in our party, and number of nights staying. After looking at my KOA membership card, the registrar deducted 10 percent from the cost of the campsite. This reduced the fee to about $15 per night, which included water, electricity, and sewer hookups.

"Are you always this busy?" I asked.

"It's rodeo week," she explained.

"Rodeo week?"

"This is the week we have our annual rodeo and stock show over at the fairgrounds."

Sounded interesting.

"Some of the rodeo people are camping at the far end with their horses and trailers," the registrar added. Looking around again, I picked out live cowboys with hats, spurs, and fringed shirts. I could hardly wait to tell Paul.

"Cowboys?" he teased, pretending he didn't know what they were.

We soon inhabited site W-47 in a grove of barren trees.

· 15 ·

San Antonio

WHEN WE WOKE UP the next morning in San Antonio, countless birds sang in a clamorous chorus of chirps and coos throughout the campground. It was Thursday, the eighth of February, due day for Dot and Ralph, but how would we find them in the 400-site campground that resembled a small village? After breakfast, I walked on dusty paths to the office to see if I could learn anything. To my astonishment, the office had assigned them site W-46, right next to ours. First the rodeo and now this. My cup runneth over! San Antonio was getting more exciting by the minute. Would such hospitality be the hallmark of our stay?

That morning, Paul and I did errands. We dropped off clothes at a nearby dry cleaners. We had seen publicity notices at the campground office and at a full-service H-E-B grocery store where we bought tickets for the Sunday night performance of the Oak Ridge Boys at the rodeo arena. I remembered them as guitar-strumming country singers, a group playing old-time western favorites and perhaps a hymn or two. Later I would learn how innocently behind the times I was!

In the adjacent mall, we made appointments in the same salon for a haircut for Paul and a shampoo and blow-dry for me. In the interim, we ate lunch at the Wyatt Cafeteria.

By early afternoon, all spruced up, we drove back through the campground entrance. Bright sunshine highlighted a familiar-looking Taurus 28-foot trailer that waited in a registration line. Paul guided Patches to the side of the registration parking area and shouted out his window toward a tall figure making a beeline toward the office, "They're all out of campsites!"

Frowning at first at this news, Ralph looked our way. Quickly recognizing Paul, he broke into a chuckle and strode over, extending his hand.

Meanwhile, I jumped out of Patches and headed toward Dot, who sat in their Suburban laughing at Ralph's reaction to Paul's shout.

"We were just coming back from some errands, and here you are! How great to see you! You'll never believe this, but our campsites are side by side!" I said to Dot.

After hugs all around, Paul and I returned excitedly to our campsite and put away groceries, marveling that we and the Johns were actually camping together for the first time—and in Texas no less, not a state nearer home.

The Johns arrived shortly. Ralph backed their cream-colored trailer, with tan, rust, and brown stripes banding it about three-fourths of the distance from the top, into their site, unhooked the Suburban, and parked it behind the trailer almost before you could say "tiddlywinks." A large-framed, dynamic man, with high intelligence and an all-encompassing mind, he always got a lot done in a brief time. While diminutive, Dot, too, was quick of mind and body. Her sense of humor and good heart brought much joy into the lives of those around her.

Always gracious, they soon invited us to come over. We stepped into their living/dining/kitchen area and it immediately had a feeling of greater spaciousness than our motorhome did. Their sofa lined the front wall of the trailer to our right with a window at each end and above its back, giving a wider open area to stretch out our legs when sitting there. Across the room from the entry door was a large dinette table with bench seats ample for two persons on each side. It sat perpendicular to a large set of windows, with six jalousied panes, which matched the one at the end of the sofa. To our left, along the wall was a kitchen counter with a double sink and work space and window above it, a stove, and a refrigerator. Wall cabinets hung in the kitchen area as well as in the dinette. The color scheme was deep rust and tan with the carpet a solid brown. The sofa and dinette cushions sported matching tan, rust, and brown striped material. The windows had venetian blinds with a valance that matched the upholstery material of the furniture. A beige tile floor in the kitchen area led down a hallway toward the rear bedroom. There, a night table cabinet stood between twin beds with cabinets overhead and short clothes cabinets at the foot of each bed. Off the hallway were a three-quarter-length, deep clothes closet on one side and opposite it, the bathroom with a tub and shower, toilet, and wash basin with a medicine cabinet above. All together it was a very livable space, and its cheerful hosts added to its relaxing aura.

As we chatted merrily in their living area, we learned that they had been visiting relatives en route and would spend a week in San Antonio before going to Corpus Christi for another week. We told them that we would head west toward Arizona and California after our stay in San Antonio. We began to make a few plans for our time together.

When we camped with others, a church group for instance, we tried not to infringe on anyone's autonomy. Freedom was basic to camping—freedom to relax, or to shop, or to cook, or to read, or to eat in your own vehicle, or to stay inside when others sit at a group campfire, or to sleep late, or to sightsee. Camping was vacation.

So it was with Dot and Ralph. We didn't want to infringe on their freedom, nor they on ours. We planned loosely. On Friday evening, we would visit the River Walk together in downtown San Antonio and have dinner there. On Saturday, the Johns would visit the Lyndon B. Johnson National Historical Park, particularly the LBJ Ranch, which was northeast of the campground, while Paul and I took a city tour. And on late Sunday afternoon, we would all go to the rodeo and concert. We planned to leave on Monday morning, and the Johns would stay on a few days more before going to Corpus Christi.

After they decided to go to the rodeo, we all got into Johns' Suburban (our Patches would have been too cramped for Ralph's lofty frame) and returned to the same H-E-B store where we had bought our tickets. Happily, they got tickets for seats in the row just behind us.

Back at the campground, I registered at the office for two more nights, Saturday and Sunday. While browsing in the camp store, I spied digital wrist watches for only $4.99. Something to ponder.

Meanwhile, Paul had noticed a man washing RVs right where they were parked at the campground. When he asked at the office about getting our coach washed, an employee suggested he catch up with Arthur Campos, a professional RV washer and waxer. So Paul drove around the campground until he found Arthur, who agreed to wash and wax our rig the next morning.

Friday arrived cloudy but in the 70s. By midmorning, I wrote in my journal:

I am "alone" among 400 campsites with trailers, motor-homes, and horse trailers (at the far end of the campground where their country aroma would not offend horseless campers). Paul has driven Patches to pick up the dry cleaning and scout around the area. Dot and Ralph left a while ago to see the Alamo in downtown San Antonio. The laptop computer sits in front of me on the table across from the sofa; I need to sit on top of three sofa cushions in the upholstered swivel chair to reach the keyboard comfortably.

I have these beautiful moments alone to focus on whatever I want to write. Exciting, special, coveted moments. Now that I have them, what shall I say? Perhaps their value is in just *being*.

A little gray bird with a perky white tail lands and walks on the dusty paved road. Seconds later it lifts aloft and away. It never stopped—must be on a search for its daily bread.

As I look around inside our motorhome, I recognize that we keep our cupboards and living area organized, although we don't follow a set pattern of behavior. In a small area like this, we both work at keeping things picked up and put away. A place for everything and everything in its place, the saying goes, and we try to follow it. Also, we have no hard and fast procedure for entering and leaving campgrounds. Each time differs. Sometimes Paul registers, sometimes I do. We decide when the time comes.

Outside, Arthur and Vivian, his wife and assistant, came to wash and wax the motorhome. I closed the windows and the door. I was hardly back at writing when I saw Paul return. A wide smile crossed his face when he saw the wash and wax operation in progress. He greeted them and stood back as he watched them working, he on the roof and she at the tires. I resumed writing:

> Have you ever been in a camper when it is being washed? It reminds me of being in the car when it's slowly going through the car wash. You feel a bit unsure about whether the water will come in. Right now, the motorhome shakes as the man on the roof walks and sprays water. You hear brush strokes and water dripping off the sides like snow melting from a roof in spring. You feel as though you are getting a bath, too.

I stopped writing when Paul came into the coach ready for lunch. As we ate, the team continued washing.

After lunch, Paul and I both went outside and watched with fascination as Arthur and Vivian moved from back to front on the driver's side of the motorhome. Arthur used a step ladder as necessary. Vivian wielded a large, thick, rectangular sponge overflowing with suds. She scrubbed the bottom half as high as she could reach; Arthur did the top half. He used a long-handled brush to wash the rounded sides of the roof. When he came to a window, Arthur took a blue plastic, short-handled rubber squeegee from his right hip pocket and scraped the glass dry.

Vivian protected her dark hair with a black-and-white bandanna. As we watched, it caught a large glob of soapsuds from above where Arthur worked. When she progressed far enough ahead of him, she looked at the part Arthur was finishing, pointing out places that needed more attention. They worked well as a team.

I went back inside the coach and continued writing:

> Arthur and Vivian have worked their way around the front of the motorhome and are now right outside the window where I am writing this. She is wearing a yellow knit top covered by a blue hooded sweatshirt. Printed in pale gold letters lengthwise

down one leg of her thin gray stretch pants is the slogan "Don't Worry, Be Happy."

Arthur is wearing blue jeans and a dark blue knit top. His curly black hair frames Latin features, a dark mustache, and a growing beard.

In talking with him, Paul learned that Arthur wants to develop and expand his washing business. This husband and wife team clean our coach exceptionally well.

I'm going up to the office now to arrange for our tour of San Antonio tomorrow.

At the campground office, after making reservations for the tour, I lingered in front of the $4.99 wrist watches. I asked a young man arranging merchandise nearby if the watch really worked.

"Well, if it doesn't, bring it back and we'll give you another one," he responded.

"Has anyone brought one back?"

"Yes, a woman brought one back last week and we gave her another one," he reassured me.

What if I were in Arizona and the watch stopped? Yet at $4.99 what could I expect? I realized I did indeed need to know the time, especially when I entered notes in the motorhome log. The watch was digital, which I liked because it showed the exact time in numbers. My previous watch had been digital. I paid the $4.99 plus 8 percent tax and wore the silvery timepiece with fake leather band out of the store. Later I could (and did) replace the band with a stretchy, silver-toned one.

The last few days had been full. On Wednesday, we arrived at the Alamo KOA Kampground in San Antonio. Thursday, we did errands and welcomed Dot and Ralph next door. Friday morning, Arthur and Vivian washed and waxed the motorhome. And in a few hours, we would join the Johns for Paul's and my first excursion to downtown San Antonio.

Late Friday afternoon, we rode downtown with Dot and Ralph in their Suburban. We talked excitedly about our upcoming plans.

Arriving in the busy business section, Ralph easily found a parking lot. Soon the four of us made our way to the celebrated River

Walk, where we lightheartedly strolled the lush, peaceful, cobble-stone walkway below street level that followed an offshoot of the Rio Grande as it wound through San Antonio. We walked past a variety of gift shops, sidewalk cafes, and restaurants in a warm afternoon breeze.

Laughing, we scrambled into an open-air cruise boat for a short ride on the river. As we disembarked, rain rushed us into the Bayous Restaurant nearby for dinner. From a table by a window in the second-floor dining room, we looked down on the river and the River Walk that we had just enjoyed.

Being with Dot and Ralph was always fun. We joked about our-selves as senior citizens—already?—and the accompanying custom of paying one's own way when camping and socializing with others in that stratum. After a convivial meal, during which darkness had crept in and the rain had stopped, we walked downstairs, crossed to the other side of the River Walk, and slowly left its charm and glit-tering night lights behind. Yet the magic of the River Walk contin-ued as we gazed ahead at the famed cream-colored Alamo enshrined in the glow of a full moon.

On Saturday morning, Ralph and Dot set off northeast to see the LBJ Ranch. Paul and I boarded a bus that came to the campground for a day-long tour of the city—seven and three-fourths hours, according to the brochure.

Our veteran tour guide and bus driver ably answered our ques-tions and provided historical commentary. He told us about the great variety of things to see and do in that Texas metropolis. He showed us the four early missions founded by the Franciscans, including the famous Alamo. He took us to the Arneson River Theater, the Japan-ese Tea Garden, Fort Sam Houston, the McNay Art Museum, the Insti-tute of Texan Cultures, the Buckhorn Hall of Horns Museum, and the Lone Star Brewery. My heart skipped a beat as I stepped into the nearby O. Henry House, a small white stuccoed building rented for two years by the famous author (William Sydney Porter) of short sto-ries while he published his humorous newspaper, *The Rolling Stone*.

We even saw a Mexican street singer at Market Square wearing a tall straw sombrero and sitting on a low concrete table. A gray, black, and white serape draped from his shoulders to his black boots. He strummed a brown guitar. Beside him sat a basket for donations and a red-tipped maraca, a gourd-shaped rattle used to keep rhythm with the music.

In late afternoon, the tour bus dropped us off at the campground. "Great tour! A real winner!" we told our guide.

I walked back to the motorhome while Paul stopped at an outdoor telephone to call his sister Hazel. He kept in touch with her to learn how Mother Beard was doing. It turned out this time that Hazel herself had gone into the hospital the day before for a biopsy of a lump in her breast. Paul asked how she was doing. She told him she was optimistic and would learn the test results the following Monday when she would see the surgeon. Hazel also told Paul that Mother's health remained about the same, with perhaps a little deterioration. I tried to think positively about the news.

Earlier, Dot and Ralph had invited us to come over for a social hour when we returned from our bus tour. As we sat comfortably at their dinette table, they worked at the kitchen counter preparing and serving freshly squeezed orange juice and generous hors d'oeuvres. Chatting as they moved back and forth between the counter and table, we asked about their visit to the LBJ Ranch and they wanted to know about our tour. After much congenial conversation, we invited them to our motorhome after the rodeo and concert on Sunday evening and went all the way home to our campsite next door.

On Sunday morning, the 11th of February, Paul and I attended chapel services in the activities room at the campground. A retired army chaplain led about 75 campers in familiar hymns of praise and gave a meaningful sermon. It meant a lot to me to get back to a worship service, even if it was in the casual atmosphere of the campground.

Ralph and Dot went downtown to a mariachi mass at the oldest cathedral in the United States, the San Fernando Cathedral. Before his career in higher education, Ralph was an active United Methodist minister. He had never attended a mariachi mass and wanted to learn about that style of worship. During the mass, Spanish musicians in costumes played guitar music.

After lunch, Paul and I called Jeff and Nancy to get caught up on our mail and the news. We tried to do that every Sunday. We told them about our camping neighbors and the great time we were having. In contrast to our 70-degree temperatures in San Antonio, they said their weather was cold and snowy. They had gone to church, but attendance was down because of the snow. Jeff said we had gotten a gas and electric bill and told Paul the amount so that we could send a check en route. They both sounded happy, and so were we.

Later that Sunday afternoon, we again rode with the Johns just a few blocks to the Forty-First Annual San Antonio Stock Show and Rodeo. I wore a short-sleeved top, blue denims, and black winter boots. In my fantasy, the part that showed below my denim pant legs became cowgirl boots.

I soon found the event was like a huge county fair. There were so many buildings we hardly knew where to go first. The equestrian building looked interesting. Inside, we witnessed handsomely clad horseback riders being judged as they put their steeds through their paces, or at least tried to. Some horses shied when their riders tried to guide them over a wood platform; others could not back around a barrel without knocking it over.

We roamed into a huge building that stabled American Gray Brahmans. With a hump between their shoulders, droopy ears, and slanted eyes softened with a fringe of white hair, they looked unconcernedly at us from their stalls, as if they wouldn't hurt a flea. In the same building, we joined other fair goers sitting on a small grandstand to watch the judging of the grand champion and reserve grand champion Red Brangus breeding cattle. A breeder sitting in front of us heard our questions and told us that most of the cattle in the show came from the plains ranches, meaning the Rio Grande Valley.

In another large building, we joined the cafeteria line for a plate of ham or beef ribs and sat at one of the long tables, eating and chatting.

After dinner, we moseyed on down to the main grandstand for our first authentic rodeo. We bought a colorful program and perused it while waiting for the main event to begin. I read a write-up about the Oak Ridge Boys, but it did not say specifically what kind of music they played. It did say they sang country and gospel in the '50s. I was puzzled about what to expect but hung onto my hopes.

The spirited opening ceremony began. Riders on horseback rushed out of the main gate, their steeds galloping like race horses around the inside circumference of the arena, their brilliant flags flowing behind them.

Soon competitions began with *real cowboys and real cowgirls*: bareback bronco riding, calf roping, calf scrambling, steer wrestling, team roping, saddle bronc riding, barrel racing, and bull riding.

During the calf scramble, young boys and girls chased frisky calves, trying to pin them to the ground with their bare hands and then slip a halter on them. Successful scramblers could keep the calf to raise and show at next year's stock show.

For the rodeo finale, bull riding, a cowboy clad in tightly strapped spurs, a riding glove, and chaps waited on top of a chute gate, poised to ride a crossbred Brahma girded in a flat-braided manila rope. Suddenly, the gate opened and there they were, the rider holding on for dear life as the bull kicked and bucked. With his gloved hand holding the rope, the cowboy had to stay mounted for eight seconds without letting his free arm touch either the bull or himself. Rodeo clowns ran around, sometimes retreating inside barrels for protection against the kicking and butting bulls.

What I had seen previously only on television was now real, right in front of me. I held my breath as cowboy after cowboy tried to hang on. I felt excited, frightened, and sorry for both the riders and the bulls, all at the same time. I worried that someone might get trampled. It turned out that no one got seriously hurt as far as I could tell. I knew seeing one rodeo would be enough for my lifetime. I would always, however, admire the cowboys for their courage and the bulls for their performance.

When the rodeo concluded, workers cleared and cleaned the sawdust arena. A round, spotlighted stage dropped into its center. The Oak Ridge Boys rode in standing on the back of a shiny pickup truck. As the lights dimmed and all became dark except for the glaring white lights focused on the stage, I hoped to hear country and gospel singing. I leaned forward toward the spotlighted platform.

The first number forced me to the back of my seat. It was deafening country rock. My hands moved up and discreetly covered my ears. I feared for my eardrums. Wanting to give the rock music a chance, I tried to listen to the words but was unable to make out anything, even when I removed my hands. Perhaps the next number would be more country or gospel. I wanted to give them a chance to slip in at least one familiar number or for me to get a handle on their music genre.

I could hardly believe that they were singing only rock music. (I learned from the program that this group had gold and platinum albums and received a Grammy Award and several Country Music Association awards, which certainly indicated that many people liked their music.) After three or four more numbers, I asked Paul if he wanted to leave.

"Any time."

Then I leaned back and said to Ralph, "We're ready to leave whenever you and Dot are. I had no idea the music would be like this!"

"I wondered, when you said you wanted to come, if this was the kind of music you expected," Ralph said. "We're ready to go, too."

As we left the stands and the grounds, we heard the banging and thumping music behind us all the way to the Suburban parked a block or two away.

The four of us returned to our RVs at the campground. The Johns would come over to ours for dessert later.

Even with the rock music still echoing in my head, I continued to feel affection for the city of San Antonio. The people we had met on our tour and everywhere were friendly and gracious. It seemed unusual for a large city to radiate a welcoming feel. We *liked* San

Antonio! With its western, Mexican milieu, it was everything I had hoped to see and experience in Laredo!

I had a lot to be thankful for—being with good friends, having a nice motorhome in which to travel and stay, and having good health, which is a blessing especially when traveling.

· 16 ·

On the Road
Heading West

SAN ANTONIO WAS TURNING out to be a wonderful, unexpected segment of our dream journey, one we might have missed had it not been for the Johns. I was glad that we were in good health (in our so-called senior years) and able to enjoy the city's activities and the congenial company of our friends and next-door camping neighbors, Dot and Ralph. The most serious health problem that we had encountered in any of our motorhome travels had been when Paul developed painful bursitis just before our Oregon trip two years earlier and couldn't drive the motorhome for a while. But so far on the dream journey, he had no complaints. At that moment, in fact, he was sweeping the welcome mat at the entry steps of the coach, preparing for our guests' arrival.

Entertaining in a motorhome comes without the stress and anxiety that one suffers at home where the house must be perfect, clothes right for the occasion, and food extraordinary. No wonder we put off inviting guests over. On the road in an RV, however, everybody makes do with living quarters, traveling clothes, and available food. Informality and understanding come naturally with the territory.

Inside the coach, I moved about getting ready for the Johns' visit. Since Ralph's birthday would be in a week or so, I had baked a ready-mix, microwaveable yellow cake and frosted it with white icing with carnival-colored sprinkles that came in a squeezable package in the same box. With the frosted cake still in its microwaveable plastic dish, I crowned it with three candles, one each for past, present, and future, and hid the pièce de résistance on the bed at the rear of the coach. I laid matches beside it.

On the dinette table, I laid out forks and spoons, birthday napkins, small plates for the cake and ice cream, and clear acrylic tumblers for sodas (the tumblers were from a handsome set that Ralph and Dot had given us earlier for the motorhome). The utensils were part of four beautiful place settings of Oneida stainless silverware that I had bought for almost a song when a local jeweler went out of business. I could hardly believe my good fortune in coming upon them just as I was outfitting our new motorhome. The pretty beige plates with light blue and white trim that matched the motorhome's decor were from a Corelle tableware pattern by Corningware. I had purchased them at an outlet store, another good buy of a high-quality product. I turned out ice cubes from their trays into a handy plastic container and returned them to the freezer so they would be easy to put into the tumblers after our guests arrived.

My dear mother, who died of cancer six years earlier at age 79, had taught me some great things about entertaining. She had been a caterer and owner of Sunset View Inn, which was our home, where she served group meals by reservation. She also often cooked meals and had picnics for various reunions that she enjoyed hosting at our house. I had observed that she did as much as possible ahead of time. For example, she would fry chicken the day before an event and put it in a granite roaster. The next day, she would take the roaster out of the refrigerator, add a little water, cover it with the roaster lid, and put it in a 350-degree oven for about an hour. Succulent chicken! When her guests arrived, she would be relaxing in a rocking chair either on the front porch or in the living room, reading or talking with the waitresses she hired to help set up, serve, and do the dishes. Somehow she always managed to be ready at least five or ten minutes ahead of the appointed hour, even when serving 30 people one of her locally famous fried chicken or Swiss steak dinners with homemade sticky buns.

She enjoyed people. Not at all a perfectionist, as I turned out to be in my earlier years, she laughed at her own imperfections, including her large nose and wing-footed walk.

I'd often helped her as a waitress. Keeping in mind her model of an unpretentious hostess, I wasn't afraid to entertain. And with motorhoming, I had gotten over my mania for perfection!

"Come in! Come in!" Paul said, opening the motorhome door to Dot and Ralph.

Laughing and chatting, we settled into the living room area with Ralph on the sofa, Dot in the swivel chair, and Paul in the passenger chair turned toward the sofa. I sat on the edge of the dinette seat, a part of the conversational group but in the area where I could fix and serve the dessert. Soon I went to the bedroom, lit the candles, and slowly walked forward bearing the glowing birthday cake. Paul and Dot joined me in singing the traditional "happy birthday" ditty. A surprised and laughing Ralph easily blew out the tapers. Considering the small size of the one-layer cake, he could easily have blown the whole thing out of my hands, for that matter! But I figured it was the thought that counted. Paul helped serve ice cream and sodas with the cake.

It seemed incredible that the four of us were together in Texas. We talked about philosophy and religion—at least Ralph did as the rest of us marveled at the depth and scope of his thinking and vocabulary.

I asked if they had any suggestions on how to plan vacations with adult friends who didn't have RVs. We agreed that hosting or sightseeing with adult friends during the day or evening in an RV is fun, but it's more comfortable all around when grown-up guests have their own separate sleeping arrangements in a cabin or motel nearby. Vacations in an RV with one's grown-up and small children and grandchildren would be excepted, of course. Many families in our church camping group regularly enjoyed and exchanged tales about the adventures of camping with their children and grandchildren.

We moved on to travel stories and plans, sharing good humor and laughing heartily, feeling like old shoes together. We reminisced about the good time we had had those last few days. It was hard to believe that our reunion time with Dot and Ralph would run out the next day already. We had almost forgotten that we were headed west.

Monday morning, February 12th, seemed like the first day of school—we had to get back on our schedule! It was time to leave behind good times with cherished friends, our Alamo KOA Kampground home, and the hospitable environment of San Antonio, and head back to the road with its unknown people, places, and adventures, all of which could add to our education if we so chose.

Paul was leaning over the front of the motorhome as he checked the oil level when Dot emerged from their trailer next door, carrying a towel and shampoo. He looked up. "The maid's doing the laundry. I'm going over to wash my hair," she giggled to Paul as she walked toward a nearby building that housed campground showers. The maid she referred to, of course, was Ralph who was already at the campground laundry facility. In the RV lifestyle, domestic duties often knew no gender.

"What fun this has been! Did you ever think we'd camp together?" I heard myself saying. The four of us stood in front of Ralph and Dot's trailer in the sunny grove of the campground.

We hugged goodbye, wishing one another safe travel. Then Paul and I walked the few feet to our motorhome where he got behind the steering wheel and I perched on the passenger's seat, travel log on my lap ready to write down our leaving time, and turned toward our camping neighbors.

Paul slowly steered away. I waved goodbye to Ralph and Dot until we turned a corner and they were out of view. As we drove past the campground store, I looked at my $4.99 watch—it still worked after three days on my arm—and logged the time: 9:30 A.M. Deep inside, I felt sad about having to say goodbye, but I knew we needed to continue our quest, and I was sure they looked forward to some time to themselves. Paul and I gave an A+ to the campground, the city of San Antonio, and our serendipitous time together with Dot and Ralph.

We headed toward Tucson, 981 miles west, which was probably three travel days away. Eighteen days since we had left home, yet we were still in Texas! This would be a travel day, not a stop-and-sight-see day.

Since I had seen real rodeo cowboys in San Antonio, we went through the hill country without stopping to visit any of the guest ranches advertised along Interstate Highway 10. When we stopped for lunch at a picnic area, I took a picture of the hill country northwest of Boerne, where the cowboys were supposed to be. From where I stood, I could see no ranch buildings; rather, I looked out over the highway below to a thick grove of trees, acres of trees. Beyond them was an upland plateau, perhaps a field for cattle grazing, and at the distant horizon rose rounded hills slashed with wide white lines that looked like accumulations of snow in crevasses. Above, in the blue sky, a solitary white cloud drifted. I didn't see any cattle or modern-day cowboys, but I could imagine ones from the Old West roaming those distant fields and hear them yodeling and singing "Whoopi Ti Yi Yo," "Yellow Rose of Texas," and "Home on the Range."

At 3:30 P.M., we turned off I-10 at Exit 372 near Ozona, Texas. Soon we found Circle Bar RV Park, which made me think of T. S. Eliot's poem "The Waste Land." It was as level as a concrete runway, tree-less as a piece of cardboard, and monochromatic as a beige carpet; its barren sandy soil and blowing wind in this wide open country were images of desolation. I wondered why this RV park merited a high rating and half-page advertisement in the *Trailer Life Directory*. As we drove around looking for the office, I began to see why. It had everything a traveler could want—a truck stop, convenience store, gift shop, swimming pool, hot tub, and restaurant. I exclaimed, "I've never seen such a well laid out campground! And so neat, in spite of the sand and the wind!" It had convenient hookups at each campsite.

We took advantage of the park's restaurant for dinner. I'm always willing to eat out, even at home. As we ate, Paul mentioned that his right shoulder was giving him a fit. When I asked him what he meant, he said that it pained every time he moved it—he thought it might be bursitis.

The next morning, Tuesday, the sunrise across the wide horizon was so beautiful that I braved the 35-degree howling wind, rested my camera on a fence post at the edge of the campground, and snapped a picture. I wore my long coat and had put up the hood. By the time I got back to our coach, Paul knew for sure that he had bursitis again and that driving would be extremely painful. So we left Circle Bar RV Park at 7:19 A.M. with me behind the wheel. When we reached the wide, smooth highway and were cruising along, I picked up a small, portable tape recorder in my right hand, talking into it instead of keying into the laptop computer. At 9:36 A.M., when we stopped for gasoline at Fort Stockton, Texas, Paul operated the gasoline pump and paid the bill in spite of his pain.

Back on I-10, I thought of Dot and Ralph, still back in San Antonio, and their plans to go south to Corpus Christi and South Padre Island before heading east. Today we would go to El Paso on the southwestern boundary of Texas and tomorrow reach Tucson, Arizona.

Some days we didn't begin to look for a campsite listing until the middle of the afternoon when we had some notion of where we'd be by four or five o'clock. Today we knew we wanted to reach El Paso, so we did our research in the morning as we rode. Across from me, Paul reached for the *Trailer Life Directory* and opened it to Texas and then to El Paso.

"Boy, there are a million campgrounds in El Paso!"

He continued to search El Paso, rubbing his chin as he read silently and then putting his hand on his forehead as if thinking.

The long, level road stretched ahead, almost hypnotic in its straightness. Tall hills to the left only slightly relieved the plane. Low shrubs somehow existed on the sandy soil on both sides of this four-lane highway. Frontage roads ran along each side of the highway. Sunbeams tried to break through clouds. I guessed it was about 60 degrees outside. As the coach moved forward into moderate headwinds, a sign indicated that we were 225 miles east of El Paso.

"The Mission RV Park is 15 miles east of El Paso on I-10; the Roadrunner is 10½ miles east on I-10. According to the map in here, the Roadrunner is close to a mall," said Paul. I needed to buy some tapes for my recorder and restock the groceries.

"So you're leaning toward the Roadrunner?"

"Yeah, but you can look at what the book says before we make a decision."

"Okay. Thanks."

Near Van Horn, Texas, we stopped for lunch at a rest area. While I washed my hands, Paul one-handedly got from the refrigerator sliced ham, sliced cheese, and rolls. According to our custom at home, he fixed his own lunch and I fixed mine. We added applesauce and Pudding Pops purchased at Fort Stockton earlier that morning.

As we ate lunch sitting at the dinette table, we noticed a young couple in their 20s, with a small baby, parked across the road from us. They had three vehicles, all of them old, dented, and dilapidated-looking; they were apparently moving their belongings. The young man drove a passenger car with a tow car attached, and both vehicles were stuffed to the roof with personal possessions. Behind was an old-model white van with the hood and front bumper dented like an accordion. The young woman drove it. The young man, in greasy overalls, got back into the car with the baby and waited for the young woman to return from changing her pink sweatpants into blue jeans. Their license plates were from South Dakota, so they were headed in the same direction as we, but we pulled out ahead of them. My heart went out to the young couple and also my respect; I knew that their struggle was once our struggle and prayed for their safety and success.

Paul seemed determined to do as much for himself as possible in spite of his bursitis. After lunch, he wanted to drive for an hour so that I wouldn't overdo it. His arm felt better, he said. I napped on the sofa while he drove.

At 1:10 P.M., I again stepped over the hump into the driver's area. The steering wheel felt amenable, the engine powerful, and the sheer bulk of the motorhome impregnable. A secret little flicker of delight surprised me. I *liked* driving this vehicle, even with the tow car! Paul's continuing encouragement gave me confidence.

Except when passing, parking, and turning sharply, I wasn't aware that Patches followed. As I passed a slow-moving pickup truck,

I made sure that both the motorhome and tow car were completely past before going back into the right-hand lane. When I pulled into a rest area parking lot, I allowed for the added length of the tow car.

I too believed in and practiced driver courtesy. As I drove, a tractor trailer came alongside and then passed. Following Paul's example, I switched on our headlights to signal the truck driver that he or she was far enough ahead of me to pull back into the right-hand lane. I turned off my headlights when the driver turned on the right blinker as the truck began to change lanes. Had it been at night, I would have momentarily put the headlights on high then quickly back on low. When the driver completed the passing maneuver, he or she usually thanked me by giving a double wink with clearance lights.

That morning when I started out driving, I knew I'd be driving a long time so I tried to be relaxed and at the same time make each movement of my arms and wrists count. I let my arms rest on the steering wheel, steering only when necessary. As the wind shifted and became a cross wind, I steered more actively. I changed the position of my hands on the wheel according to the kind of grip I needed to steer against the wind, or to relax them, or just to change.

I paced my psyche as well. Instead of thinking about how many miles I had to go, I drove along looking at the scenery, talking with Paul, sometimes talking into the recorder, and occasionally looking at the odometer to see how far we had come, surprising myself at the miles already behind us. At work, I would have pushed myself, thinking of all that had to be done by a deadline, but on the road, I just drove, and the miles decreased without emotional trauma. After all, no deadline faced us that day—when we got there, we got there.

The great things about driving on the Texas Mission Trail, I-10, were sparse traffic, large vistas of fields, and the wide, all-encircling horizon. As the motorhome climbed into mountains, the smooth, modern highway was well lined and well maintained, and thereby a joy to use.

Just a few miles east of El Paso, I felt dust in my throat and Paul complained of it in his nose. We saw the dust blowing all around outside the coach, so we closed the dash air vent and turned on the dash air conditioning.

At 3:08 P.M., Paul took the wheel to steer us into campsite no. 60, a pull-through, at Roadrunner RV Park, El Paso, Texas. He usually did the parking, leveling, and hooking-up duties. If necessary, I could do it, but Paul seemed to enjoy the processes and did them quicker than I could. The map showed that the time zones changed from central standard time to mountain standard time just west of Van Horn, Texas, so we set our clock back an hour to 2:08 P.M. We had previously set our clock back an hour when we left the eastern standard time zone somewhere in Alabama.

I had seen outside public telephone booths as we pulled into the campground and knew I should call several Tucson resorts for a reservation for the next night. But first we decided to find the mall.

· 17 ·

El Paso

WARM BREEZES GREETED US in El Paso—Paul and I didn't even wear sweaters as we shifted from the motorhome into Patches to find the shopping mall. We shopped leisurely at Kmart, Safeway, and Best Products, glad to have our feet on the ground for a change of venue but noticing that as the afternoon advanced, the air turned chilly. By the time we returned to the campground, a cold wind made us shiver and hustle into the warm coach.

Following dinner in the motorhome, Paul and I walked across the dusty campground to a trio of telephone booths standing outside the office. Other campers leaned inside two of them, holding the earpiece, smiling, and looking out but not actually focusing on anything.

Inside the third booth, I called two resorts in Tucson to make a reservation for the next several days and learned that both offices had closed for the day. A security officer at one resort suggested calling tomorrow morning when the office opened at 8:00 A.M. For the first time, I wondered if we'd find a place we liked on short notice.

I turned the phone booth over to Paul who wanted to call Hazel. He expected to learn the results of her recent biopsy. Optimistic when Paul talked with her Saturday, she was to learn the test results from her surgeon on Monday.

As Paul punched in Hazel's telephone number, I talked with a woman standing in front of the next booth. She was from Calgary,

Canada. Shortly, her husband, who had been on the telephone, called her to it and then he and I spoke briefly until Paul motioned to me, "You're to get on this phone."

I hesitated, trying to assess his urgent tone, unusual for him.

"You're to get on this phone," he repeated.

After telling him hurriedly that the man I was talking with was from Calgary and that he knew some Beards, I stepped into the booth.

"Hi! How *are* you?" I asked.

Hazel's voice sounded amazingly clear and steady as she told me that her test results showed that the mass was cancer, using the word "cancer" without hesitation.

"Oh, no!"

She said she wanted so much to talk with me because of my experience with mastectomies. She asked me to describe what I went through. Usually, I didn't say much about my double mastectomies with silicone implants and the following five and a half months of chemotherapy. This was different—she really wanted to know, so I went into the details.

I told Hazel about the numerous biopsies I had gone through for fibrocystitis, or "lumpy breast." I explained that although the condition wasn't considered life-threatening, each lump had to be checked out for cancer, and there was no knowing how many more biopsies would be required. When a sixth biopsy was ordered, I consulted with a plastic surgeon and decided to have a bilateral (both breasts), subcutaneous (under the skin) mastectomy (removal of breast tissue) with silicone implants beneath the pectoral muscles.

"Well, it turned out to be a lifesaving operation because they discovered cancer the size of a pea in the tissue they removed from the right breast. Because they had found cancer, however, they needed to examine some of my adjacent lymph nodes.

"Two days after the first operation, they took me back into the operating room and removed some of the lymph nodes from my right arm closest to the breast where they found the cancer. They found only two or three cancer cells in the nodes closest to the right breast, so they felt that the disease had not spread further into my body. Are you still there?" I asked.

She asked for details of the therapy as well.

"The oncologist said that it was marginal as to whether or not I really needed chemotherapy, but he did recommend it. And so I had chemotherapy for about five and a half months, which was a shorter time than originally planned.

"I took the treatments by injection every ten days. Each injection made me nauseous for several days, but I never missed a day of work. The oncologist gave me antinausea pills, which helped somewhat but not entirely. As you know, I didn't lose my hair. I'd say it took me about a year to get my energy back and feel like myself again after the chemo was over, but I did have a feeling of assurance that the treatments were continuing to protect me for some time after they had been stopped."

As I talked, Hazel's disciplined voice covered the long distance. She asked more questions. Then she told me that the love and support from family and friends amazed her. She felt lifted up; I sensed her peace. Visualizing my own hospital stay, I identified with her. I, too, had felt close to God, that all would be well, and had been grateful for the prayers and good wishes going out to me.

At the end of our conversation, Hazel told me that she was going to discuss the surgeon's options with her family physician, but she leaned toward a modified radical mastectomy with no further treatment.

She thanked me for the telephone time. I hoped that I hadn't forgotten something important or given her a wrong slant. It seemed unbelievable that this was happening to her; she took such good care of her health, always eating nutritiously and searching out answers to her allergies or other health questions.

Shaken, I handed the telephone back to Paul, who talked with Hazel again. Then I realized I had something else to ask her so Paul stepped aside.

"How's Mother doing?" I asked Hazel.

Hazel said that her condition appeared to be deteriorating. Her physician said that she had poor circulation, which occasionally caused memory lapses and obstinacy. Ordinarily, she had a superior memory and was kind, loving, sensitive, and thoughtful.

I wondered if we should return to help care for Mother during Hazel's coming operation and recuperation, but Hazel said that Harold, her and Paul's brother, was willing to help and that Al, her husband, had volunteered to do Mother's laundry. She stated that they'd be able to manage things; her voice sounded confident and reassuring. When she and Al went west the previous November on their "big trip" in their motorhome after retiring, Paul and I looked after Mother, so apparently Hazel wanted to handle things while we were away.

On our dusty walk back to the motorhome, I felt uneasy about staying too long once we reached Arizona, which would be the following day.

It was pitch dark and raining lightly at 6:30 A.M. on Valentine's Day in El Paso. The city of over 400,000 people stretched for miles and miles along the Rio Grande to the south and ran into the border of New Mexico on the northwest.

"It looks like they're rolling already," Paul said as he pulled away from our campsite at Roadrunner RV Park and looked toward I-10. He referred to trucks and other traffic that moved along the interstate highway, their bright lights blazing in the early morning darkness. We momentarily traveled east on a frontage road, then up a ramp, and then turned westward onto I-10. Our goal for that day: Tucson, Arizona.

At breakfast earlier, we had talked briefly about our family concerns, which led to recognizing our own blessings. Now Paul referred to that chat.

"Aren't we—like you said—aren't we fortunate?" Paul commented. "I really feel blessed." His bursitis had eased enough for him to at least start out driving.

"Yes. I do, too!" I thought of our good health. I wondered how Hazel was feeling that morning.

"There's the Safeway where we got our groceries last night," Paul pointed out as we drove past.

Street lights glowed. In the dark span ahead and on both sides, the lights of El Paso made the city seem as spread out as the great night sky above it. Riding up high in the motorhome with massive windows in front, beside, and behind us, I could see so much better than if I had been riding in a car. Cradled in a valley, the metropolis looked like a huge sparkling Christmas garden outlined against inky, curving, jagged forms of mountains to its west. Under the heavily overcast sky, traffic moved along, lights luminous.

"My, my, my, my, my! Look-a-there!" Paul referred to El Paso.

"Isn't it beautiful?"

"Looks like Christmas."

"Yeah, it's just beautiful! El Paso just before dawn!"

"See. It's not dusty out there this morning," Paul kidded as the rain continued. He referred to the dust that blew like a whirlwind on a dirt schoolyard when we arrived at the RV park the evening before.

We rode past a large, illuminated heart silhouetted by red electric lights on the slanted roof of an El Paso restaurant. Happy Valentine's Day, it beamed.

"Gosh, it's still beautiful! I didn't realize El Paso was this big. It just goes all around the wide sweep of the horizon from one side to the other and up ahead." I swiveled in the passenger seat from north to south and back.

"Boy, I tell you—a lot of El Paso's strung out along the border, isn't it?"

As we continued through the city, Paul asked about an upcoming sign, "Does that say 10 West over there to the right?"

We both leaned forward to read several signs ahead. We were still finding our way through and out of El Paso. Paul remembered that the map showed I-10 taking a dip down into the middle of El Paso and then up through the mountains. Together we decided that we should stay in the present lane; it turned out to be the right decision.

An electric sign beside a bank blinked "Happy Valentine's Day" across a rectangular screen with white lights announcing the words and red lights providing the background. The city had a heart!

We left El Paso, Texas, continuing north on I-10 to Las Cruces, New Mexico, where the interstate highway turned westward again. The rain had eased up.

"That reminds me," I said as I saw a huge billboard along the interstate beyond Las Cruces advertising Rincon Country RV Resort in Tucson. There were two resorts with this name, one east and the other west. At home, I had called toll-free telephone numbers for information on cost, discounts, activities offered, description of sites, and the view from the campsites at these two resorts. I also had called Voyager RV Resort and Mission View RV Resort, both in Tucson. They each reported that they were full at the time but suggested I call when we reached New Mexico.

"When we see a telephone, I should try to call a resort again," I said. By that time, we were near Deming, New Mexico, where we thought we might need gasoline. "I think the sooner we stop the better our chances will be of getting in."

"I don't have any problem with that," Paul replied.

As we rode along, I prayed that all would go well for Hazel, whatever her decision. I was concerned, too, for Mother Beard and how she was feeling. As he drove, Paul didn't seem disturbed and had not suggested cutting our trip short in order to go back and look after his mother. We were having a wonderful tour, but I had uncertainty about having a good time. Was it the Puritan ethic or was it Mother Beard's health?

I took a turn at driving, using my right hand to hold the micro-cassette tape recorder.

At 8:37 A.M., we stopped at the Chevron station in Deming, New Mexico, where gasoline cost $1.20 per gallon. In my excitement to call the resorts, I forgot to take along a quarter for the pay telephone and my VISA card in case I needed to make a deposit to hold the reservation. In the cold wind, I hurried back to the motorhome and then returned to the outside telephone.

The first two resorts I called were full and did not expect any vacancies. The third, Mission View RV Resort, gave me a reservation—with temporary limitations. Campground office people are usually pleasant, as was the man at Mission View. He said we might not have electricity at our site because they were expanding their park and planned to put the new area on line that day unless it rained, in which case they might have to postpone it. When I asked if we could use our generator in the expanded area, he said yes. Water and sewer connections had already been installed. Obviously, campgrounds in Tucson filled early with "snowbirds" (people going south for the winter).

Cheered to have a reservation of sorts at a place we chose, our next goal was to travel the 211 miles from Deming to Tucson and find Mission View RV Resort.

Gasoline stops were also bathroom breaks, as was that one at Deming. How grateful many times over we were for our coach's bath facilities. While not as large as those at home, the motorhome bathroom's rectangular shape measures 64.5 by 40 inches, including the

"Paul replaced the separate hot and cold water spigots with a brass mixer spigot so it would be easier to maintain the water temperature we wanted."

shower/tub area, and is ample for use by one person at a time. The entry door can be locked and unlocked from the inside. Across from it is the sink with a mirror above it. To the left is the toilet and to the right is the shower/tub enclosure. A neat package.

The wash basin originally had separate plastic, burnished brass-colored spigots for hot and cold water, which Paul replaced with a brass mixer spigot so it would be easier to maintain the water temperature we wanted. A large, framed wall mirror, topped by clear light bulbs, hangs above the wash basin. A tan chemical- and heat-proof countertop surrounds the basin and extends to the left side, fitting snugly at the intersection of the street side wall and the interior wall next to the rear bedroom. Oak-paneled cabinets in which we keep medicines, bath linens, cosmetics, and shaving equipment hang above the counter and toilet fixture. Towel racks, some of which we added, abound on the door and walls. Beneath the counter, more storage space holds baking soda, other toilet chemicals, and supplies such as toilet paper. The toilet paper holder itself hangs on the inside of the sink cabinet door. A fluorescent ceiling light fixture adds more light to the room, and wallpaper with tiny blue flowers on an ivory background bedecks the area.

The toilet itself, in my mind, is a marvel of design and mechanics because it not only functions well but also does so in the least embarrassing way. It is a Thetford Aqua-Magic Starlite Low unit. It allows one to press a foot pedal at its base in front on the right that lets the amount of clean water one wishes to swirl down inside the bowl and its outlet neck. As long as one presses this pedal, water flows into the bowl. To the left of this water pedal and attached to it is another pedal that, when pressed downward with one's foot, connects with the water-release pedal for the purpose of flushing down waste through the neck valve of the toilet into a holding tank for "black water" beneath the floor of the motorhome. These versatile mechanics mean that one can adjust the amount of water in the toilet bowl so that it neither splashes back up on one's body nor broadcasts sounds. To further alleviate embarrassment, just above the shower/tub is a roof vent with an electric exhaust fan. Although most motorhome bathrooms are small, they can be just as comfortable as at home, even when you are traveling down the road at 60 miles an hour.

The shower includes a tub with a seat at the showerhead end. It also had hot and cold water spigots that had to be adjusted in order to achieve one's ideal water temperature. It took me some time to remember which way to turn those spigots to get hotter or colder water through the showerhead until Paul replaced those spigots with a single-control mixer faucet. (The kitchen sink came with a single-control unit.)

The showerhead itself offers options. One can turn a valve to have a lot or a little water pressure, depending on the campground's water pressure or what Paul has allowed to come into the coach, and one can turn the water on or off by pushing a rounded pin to one side or the other of the head. In addition, one can let the shower arm stay in its wall holder or slide it out of the holder and turn the flexible metal hose on one's body. I don't have this latter luxury at home.

I am less enthused about the amount of water and length of time I have in the shower. Any water that comes out of the showerhead eventually flows down the drain into a holding tank for "gray water" beneath the coach. When the holding tank becomes full, the water can back up into the tub and one can be standing in such water in the shower/tub. Not that the water looks dirtier than it would if one were taking a bath, but it's the idea that repulses me. I remind myself that the gray water is only either dishwater or bath water; it is not sewerage (the waste from the toilet goes into the black water holding tank). Actually, we haven't had the gray water back up very often. When we stay at a campground for several days running, we can stay hooked up to the sewer site and let the gray water run into it as it drains from our sinks.

At any rate, I never feel as free to use water when I shower in the motorhome as I do at home, and that detracts from my enjoyment. But then, I much prefer using the shower in the motorhome to those at campgrounds, although many campers regularly enjoy using campground bathhouses. For me, I find that everything is handy in the motorhome and there's no carrying toiletries and clothes outside to a bathhouse. Campgrounds have high standards of cleanliness, but I *know* my shower stall is clean.

Having a tiled shower/tub requires that it be wiped down after each use. We keep a towel hanging on the retractable clothesline above the tub for this duty.

Having bed, board, and bathroom with us when we travel relaxes me even when I have no idea where we will stay on any given night.

· 18 ·

Arizona
Reached

WITH THE PROMISE of a site waiting for us at Mission View RV Resort in Tucson, we took to the road again. I settled into the high-backed passenger seat with a plastic container in my lap holding two oranges and an apple. I just felt hungry for fresh fruit, and Paul said he'd enjoy some, too. As we drove on, with fields moving past, I peeled and sectioned the fruit, the orange aroma and juicy squirts teasing my taste buds. I felt like my grandmother, who used to sit in a low armless rocker, her aproned lap holding a tin pan of potatoes that she was peeling for supper. My domestic task seemed homey and intimate as we rode along. For Paul, I piled fruit pieces into a cup that fit into one of the plastic holders hanging on the door window frames. Paul could tip the cup to his mouth and eat the fruit without getting his fingers sticky. When I handed him his fruit, he pecked me lovingly on the cheek. And we didn't run off the road in the maneuver! We pleasantly anticipated the journey to Mission View on I-10.

We drove over the Continental Divide—4,585 feet in elevation—on I-10 in New Mexico. I had learned about the Continental Divide in school. (Didn't we all?) Although Paul and I had crossed it at various places in our travels, I always expected it to be something I could visually see. But the only indication was a sign simply stating it—kind of a letdown. Its importance, fascination even, comes from the fact that water flows toward the Gulf of California and the Pacific on one side of the Rocky Mountains, and it flows toward the Gulf of Mexico, Hudson Bay, and the Arctic Ocean on the other side.

Following an early lunch at a rest area, I took the wheel again. A beautiful scene lay ahead—my eyes swept over the level countryside and distant mountains. The sky remained heavily overcast with a few islands of blue. Rain spattered the windshield, which it had done intermittently since we left El Paso that morning. I stopped tape recording while driving to figure out how to turn on the windshield wipers. With Paul coaching me, the blades began swishing back and forth.

"Turn your headlights on," Paul said.

"How come?"

"When it rains, in most of these states out here, you're supposed to have your headlights on."

The sun shone to our right; the rain already had let up. It was a brief shower, as if we had run through someone's lawn sprinkler. I turned off the wipers and the headlights.

Looking ahead, Paul said, "Looks like snow on the mountains out there." He reached for the binoculars on the floor in front of his feet. "Yep, I'd say that's what it is—snow." (My husband's curiosity is constant. He loves to make observations and feels rewarded when he is right.)

I loved western scenes like the one ahead. Cloud shadows moved across the earth, saturating the whole landscape in an elegant blue-gray haze.

As usual, Paul wore the earphones that plugged into the CB while I drove.

"Any activity on the CB?"

"No, pretty quiet," he responded, arms folded, looking ahead.

We changed drivers again at the Welcome Center for Arizona, which is located in New Mexico. As we approached the Arizona Agriculture Inspection Station nearer the border, signs directed drivers of RVs and campers to enter the left lane. Paul steered over to the left and greeted the inspector. "Mornin'."

"Got any fruit?" asked the official.

"We've got some oranges and bananas that we bought in Texas. That all you need?"

"That's okay. Go ahead." Paul drove on into Arizona.

Still on I-10, a dust flurry suddenly enveloped our coach. Wind kicked up fine, dry particles of earth from bare fields to our left. The gritty gust blew against the motorhome. Tumbleweeds crossed the road in front of us. Paul turned on the headlights and made sure the dashboard vent was closed. Just as suddenly, the dust disappeared.

Up ahead on the other side of the median strip, several tractor trailers were lined up on the shoulder because of an accident ahead of them involving a semitractor trailer.

I grabbed my camera, which I kept beside the passenger seat. In spite of Paul's previous admonitions to keep it cocked and ready, I hadn't done so. We passed the moment of truth without a picture. I only had time to see that the trailer had gone off the road, remaining upright, while the cab remained on the highway but had swiveled at the linkage so that it faced the rear of its long trailer. "Complete jack-knife," Paul summed up.

Barely past the accident, we again ran into thick dust even denser than before. We could see only eight or nine feet ahead.

"Slow down!" I gasped.

Paul slowed the coach and leaned forward, straining to see even a few feet ahead. If he stopped, he said, someone might plow into us from the rear. We crept along. Also leaning forward to see the road, I prepared mentally for the impact of someone hitting the back of our vehicles. One part of my mind focused ahead, another part opened wide for possible accident scenarios, and yet another searched for God's protection.

"Back there," Paul surmised, "that truck must suddenly have run into a thick cloud of dust like we're in and lost its way."

As if someone raised the veil of dust in front of us, we abruptly came out of it. "It's gone," I said. "At least for now," Paul conceded. "These things can happen in this area." I sat back, jubilant to see ahead again and thankful no one had banged into us. Strangely, light raindrops immediately splattered the windshield. Paul didn't use the wipers, however, because the grit might scratch the glass. We could see okay through the drops on the windshield.

"I see snow on the mountains way over there." I still felt a bit shaky and wanted to focus on something stable. We had already left behind the snowy mountain that Paul had seen earlier.

Turning his head, Paul said. "Snow on the mountains and sand in the valley." Good contrast, I thought, but I hoped we wouldn't run into blowing sand again.

Just beyond Bowie, Arizona, a sign read: Tucson, 101 miles; Junction 666N, 5 miles. The dark sky looked threatening. "I think we're in for some hard rain," Paul cautioned. Large raindrops again fell against the windshield and Paul slowed down to 50 from his usual 55.

Another motorhome towing a car traveled east on the other side of the median strip. A close observer, Paul commented, "When I see how some other people have attached their tow cars and the angles at which they ride, I can tell that they don't pay attention to the rules for towing. They probably just hook up the best way they can and go."

Paul had made sure our towing arrangement was safe. Well before this trip had begun, Paul hooked up the tow car to the motorhome and drove to a level parking place. There he made careful measurements to ensure that the center of the ball on the motorhome hitch was about an inch and a half higher than the pivotal point on the tow bar attached to the car. This was to keep the car from pole vaulting into the motorhome during a sudden stop.

Paul learned about such subjects from other campers, dealers, truck drivers, observation, and reading articles and books on regulations. Like many RVers, he easily talked shop. And like a three-ply paper towel, he absorbed information, adding to his own understanding, and then generously passed it on to me and others.

There on I-10 en route to Tucson, we didn't run into the heavy rain or dust that we had anticipated a few miles back. Whatever the cloud contained, it moved off to our left where it shrouded the mountains. Zany weather! Clear with long vistas ahead, rain and gray mist, and road-level dust clouds—all in the same day!

"I definitely want to change the oil and the oil filter after going through all that dust," Paul said. Many campgrounds don't allow guests to change oil at the campsite because of possible oil spillage on the ground. Paul said he'd try to find an RV supplier with space for changing oil or go to a large shopping center parking lot if necessary.

"When does this motorhome normally need to have the oil and filter changed?" I asked. Earlier on the trip, he had told me that he checked the oil in the engine every 300 miles or so or about every other day. That was to see if it was low and more should be added. Now we were talking about removing all of the old oil and the dirty filter and replacing it with a fresh filter and oil.

"I like to change it every 2,000 miles, but we're already at 3,000. The maintenance record book also shows when I changed the oil the last time."

"Do you write it down in the book every time you change the oil? What else do you keep in there?"

"All the changes—oil filter, oil, air filter, transmission fluid, and transmission filter."

"The book that came with the motorhome recommends how often all of that needs to be done?" I asked Paul, who nodded in the affirmative.

"Goodness! The rain's really coming down again." I exclaimed, glad that Paul was driving. He turned on the wipers.

"It's coming in sheets! The wind must be blowing really hard." I saw Paul grip the wheel and lean onto it to keep the vehicle on the road against the wind and rain. When the rain subsided, Paul asked how far it was between Willcox and Benson, Arizona.

I looked at the map. "Thirty-seven miles."

Towering gasoline station signs were silhouetted against the big sky as we approached Willcox. Paul estimated that we had enough gasoline to get to Benson with a quarter of a tank remaining, so we drove past the town. Our gas tank held 60 gallons, and the gas gauge needle was slightly below the halfway mark. Calculating that the motorhome used about a gallon of gasoline for every six miles, driving 37 miles would take about six gallons. Since we still had about 25 gallons, that gave us ten gallons to go on before the quarter tank mark.

"Want anything to drink?"

"I don't believe right now, thank you," Paul replied in his usual courteous way.

"I think I'm going to get something. My throat seems dry."

"How's that?" Paul asked, so I repeated it. "Oh, if you're going to get up, why, yeah, then I'll drink. I think I have part of a Sprite in there," referring to the refrigerator.

I turned and moved out of the passenger seat. One of the enjoyable benefits of a motorhome was being able to go to the refrigerator or pantry for sodas and snacks as we sailed along. I kept screw-top bottles of Diet Sprite in the refrigerator door. The same bottles fit easily into the hanging cup holders in the cab area. Across the aisle from the refrigerator, our pantry had two large slide-out drawers, about 19 by 18½ inches. We opted for this storage area instead of a normal oven and had never regretted it. The space was large enough for tall boxes of cereal on the bottom shelf and canned goods and packages of cookies or pretzels on the top shelf. The great thing was that both shelves slid out for easy viewing and access. I retrieved Paul's Sprite from the refrigerator door and a bag of thin pretzels, from which Paul helped himself to three.

When we stopped for gasoline at Benson, a few snow flurries circled. It was 1:01 P.M. After the fill-up, we continued toward Tucson. Strong winds buffeted the coach. "Boy, I wouldn't want to be dragging a trailer behind a car out here today, I'll tell you!" Paul said. He knew from experience that towing a trailer could be like holding a tiger by the tail. Yet motorhome drivers can't relax in strong winds either; they must reduce speed and keep a steady hand on the wheel.

"I just heard on the CB it's snowing in Tucson," said Paul. Simultaneously, we passed a road sign telling us that our next stop was now only 41 miles away.

"Tucson, here we come!" I quipped. I felt excited as we got closer to our long-planned and long-awaited destination—our sojourn in Arizona.

Precipitation hit the windshield again. "Looks like snow or rain—I don't know what the outside temperature is," Paul said, sipping his Sprite.

"Well, maybe the few snow flurries that we had back there at Benson were an indication of things to come," I half-kidded.

Then identifiable snow came at our windshield and blew across the road in front of us. It was a fine-textured snow, the kind that at home meant it may accumulate and drift.

"Do we have chains along?" I asked, shocked that I was asking it on this dream journey to escape winter.

"Yeah. Remember we got them before we went to Florida last February? But chains on the dual driving wheels won't necessarily help in deep snow. They might keep us going in light snow or just a little bit of ice."

"I'm glad you brought them along anyway."

Snow collected in spaces on the windshield where the wipers, set on Delay, did not reach. Paul turned on the CB again to see if he could hear anything about snow on I-10 and in Tucson.

From my passenger seat, I looked down at the side of the road rushing past. Snow clung to branches of shrubs and small trees. It lay in hollow places. Mixed with long, straw-like strands of grass, it looked like coconut icing on a cake. Snow was both artist and balm as it created wintry scenes of peaceful beauty.

"It's hard to believe we drove all this way to get out of snow and are running right into it!" I exclaimed in spite of its beauty.

"Somebody on the CB is talking about coming south to get warm and having only a couple of days that were warmer than where they came from," Paul chuckled.

As we reached the outskirts of Tucson on I-10, the snow stopped. No snow lay on the ground; the sky remained cloudy.

We got off I-10 at Valencia Road, found Sixth Avenue, drove through the arched entrance of Mission View RV Resort, and pulled up beside the office.

Both Paul and I went inside to register so that we could decide if we wanted to stay longer than one night. We learned that the expanded area *did* get electricity that day and that the weekly rate was a better deal than the daily rate ($12.00), so we registered for a week from February 14 to 21. The weekly fee of $72.00 was about $10.25 a day, an excellent rate.

At 2:50 P.M., in sleet that began while we registered, we drove a short distance to site 407 in the expanded area and then unhooked Patches. Paul backed the motorhome into our freshly graveled parking space, and I backed Patches in beside it. Quickly, I ducked into the coach while Paul hooked up to electricity and water. The sleet stopped. I looked forward to a cozy evening without the thought of being on the road the next day.

After supper, I climbed into the passenger seat to look at the evening scene. When we had arrived, clouds shrouded what I had hoped would be a majestic, snow-covered peak. The mountain turned out to be a sawed-off, plateau-type butte. Even so, I thought,

"We got off I-10 at Valencia Road, found Sixth Street, and drove to Mission View RV Resort."

"But you got us here safely, Lord, and I'm glad for that. Thank you very, very much!" I remembered the times when we could have had accidents en route, particularly when we ran into the dust storms.

When I left the cab area, I released the draperies from their side cloth tiebacks and pulled each one across the side window and around the curve to the center of the windshield. They served as privacy curtains at night. When closed, the draperies fell in back of the steering wheel and television set and in front of the glove compartment. They made a pleasant, beige fabric backdrop for the front of the coach.

The weather forecaster on television called for light rain or snow and cold temperatures that night. It was about 38 degrees; the forecast for the next day was a *high* of only 48. When we left El Paso that morning, it was rainy but at least 60 degrees. The afternoon before in El Paso, it must have been in the mid-70s. So in Tucson we were back into winter temperatures like we had in Maryland. Were we snowbirds or snowhounds? I felt rather defeated when I thought that we had driven 3,294 miles to "enjoy" the kind of weather we would have had at home. Were we foolish to scout around on our own like this? Should we have contacted some "expert"? What would I say and how embarrassed would I feel when our friends asked if we found a sunny paradise?

Paul put on his felt-lined boots, goose-down cap, and dark blue insulated winter coat. He took the garbage across the road to a hefty dumpster. At our site, he dumped the contents of the black and gray water tanks into the sewer connection.

To my surprise, when he came back inside, he got out the U.S. and Arizona maps, spreading them on the dinette table. We talked about where we wanted to go and who we wanted to visit on this trip. Could Paul actually be *planning* again?

As he looked at the map and the calendar, he said, "Two weeks for the trip home—I think we should reserve two weeks. I definitely want to stop and see Alice and Ray in Arkansas." Alice is Paul's first cousin. We hadn't visited her and her husband since they sold their motel and moved into their present home, which was probably 15 years ago.

We decided to stay in Tucson two weeks; visit Sedona, Arizona, a beautiful area according to many people; and visit friends and relatives in Escondido and Modesto, California.

Good navigator that he was, Paul suggested that we go from Tucson by I-10 to Escondido, up to Modesto, back to Arizona and Sedona, on to Arkansas, and then home by April 1. This route would include visits with friends and relatives as well as sights we wanted to see. While we camped in Tucson, we would take a day trip north to Phoenix in Patches. In Phoenix, we would scout out resorts and campgrounds and generally see if we preferred that area to Tucson. The next day, we hoped to go to the visitor's bureau of Tucson for maps and information on sights, tours, and activities in the metropolitan area.

Meanwhile, the weather puzzled us. How often at home during our cold winters had I heard the television meteorologist report temperatures in the 60s, 70s, and 80s for Arizona? I'd say to Paul, "See how warm it is in Arizona? I think that'd be a good place to spend the winter."

Alas, to our list of clear vistas, rain, and dust, we added snow and sleet, all in one day's drive from El Paso to Tucson, our goal for this Valentine's Day and one of the main destinations of our dream journey. Good weather or not, something inside made me willing to reach out for what else Tucson offered.

Getting Settled

IT WAS 8:40 Thursday morning, February 15, our first full day in Arizona. We had finally arrived at that long-awaited destination. Now it was up to us to enjoy and explore it.

I thought back to when I had sat at my desk in Maryland, before this dream journey began, making telephone calls to RV resorts in Arizona. As I had made the calls, I visualized spending a month or two with our motorhome parked on an idyllic site in a mountain sanctuary with shade trees and a beautiful view of a lake in the valley. I imagined that I set up my easel and immediately brushed on canvas my view of the lake with snow-capped mountains in the distance. I could get help in oil painting from an instructor at the activities center of the resort if I wished.

I should have picked up on a clue about the desert environment at resorts in southwest Arizona when I asked each resort that I called, "Do you have shaded sites?" One after another said, "No shade," although one had a palm tree at each site. When we camped at home in the mid-Atlantic region, we expected sites with shade trees. I could not visualize enjoying camping in the desert, but I told myself that all would fall into place once we got to Arizona. I felt excited about exploring new territory and especially about soaking up the warm sunshine.

Once we were in Arizona, doubts pelted me about my unrealistic expectations, but optimist that I was, I knew we'd cope. I asked myself what other RVers (or smart people, whether RVers or not) would do in this situation. On that Thursday morning, I thought of my mother, how she laughed when something didn't go perfectly. I suppose it was her way of coping. The weather in Tucson was anything but perfect! I, too, tried to see the funny side of our weather dilemma. In fact, I almost laughed out loud at the difference between what I expected and what I saw through the motorhome windows at that moment.

Snow melted off the sloping back window of Patches. Earlier that morning, the outside thermometer read 28 degrees! Cold winds blew south from an Alaskan front that had swept down the Pacific Coast and turned inland toward Chicago. Weather reports on television predicted cold temperatures for the next few days. That day's estimated high was only 48 degrees.

Overnight, water froze in both the campground spigot and in the hose leading into our coach. That morning, we had to use water from the freshwater tank under the bed. Paul detached the frozen hose and placed it in the shower tub to thaw.

"Well, you look like Maryland," I told Paul as he put on his brown suede, fleece-lined winter gloves, preparing to drive Patches to the campground office. He already wore a goose-down cap; heavy, long winter jacket; and felt-lined boots. He wanted to ask the office staff if we could buy LP gas at the resort. He had checked the gauge inside the motorhome as well as the gauge on the LP gas tank itself, which was located outside and attached underneath the motorhome just behind the right front wheel. The tank was half full. If the cold spell continued, he thought we'd need more LP gas to run the furnace and water heater.

From the office, Paul would go into Tucson to look for a new carburetor air filter for the motorhome engine, which was located inside the coach under the hump between the driver and passenger seats. Earlier he had removed the beige-carpeted engine cover, a huge form that looked like a giant turtle shell, that measured 33 by 41 inches and had a three-inch rise around its perimeter and a ten-inch hump toward the middle of the front. He laid it upside down on the sofa.

He wanted to take the old filter along with him to be sure he got the right kind. The cover had to be removed to change the carburetor air filter and carburetor gasoline filter, check the level of transmission fluid, and replace engine belts when needed. Fortunately, we didn't have to remove the cover very often.

Paul loved keeping the motorhome in excellent running condition and appearance. He liked to search out an exact part and, before installing it, make sure the surrounding parts were clean and in good working order. He cared about both the quality of his work and that the coach ran well.

Alone now, I realized that my computer, printer, lamp, and accessories monopolized the dinette table and that Paul should have a convenient workspace available for his projects. So I lifted a table extension from its storage area behind the console table and slid it between its runners onto the console table top, a feature that came with the motorhome. I moved my writing equipment onto it and claimed it as my desk, leaving the dinette table for Paul, who seemed to naturally put his keys and whatever he took from his pants pockets on that table. Once settled, I began touching the keys of the laptop.

Dear Tucson Journal,

In frosty air, people come and go in cars and pickup trucks. Walkers hurry, but take time to greet one another as they toss small bags of trash into the dumpster at the same time. A man in a cap and plaid jacket walks past, hands in pockets. Another, without a cap, in only shirt sleeves and gray sweatpants, hurries toward the office.

No wind stirs. All radiates harmony and life. Airplanes soar in the distance. A door slams; people say "Mornin'" as they walk their dogs. A long dump truck releases its load of quarry stones onto a dirt road in this expansion area, sending loud reverberations outward. This resort is an unfinished piece of business. Nevertheless, I'm grateful for its "welcome mat." Next year, this area may be paved and spruced up for visitors. For now, we have the essentials—water, electricity, and sewer.

Our motorhome rests on a newly prepared corner site that must be 30 feet wide. It has breathing space. From inside the coach, my eye sweeps around at level, mostly dirt, light brown land that leads to foliaged hills, a plateau-like butte, and snow-capped mountains in the distance. I see how one can be in the desert yet see mountains all around. I am beginning to feel peace and joy for this time to be settled in one place. In spite of my Arizona dream's illusion, my spirits are beginning to lift.

Paul returned from town and I finished my journal entry, leaving the laptop on the console table since we didn't plan to move the coach for a week. After lunch, Paul installed the new air filter. He asked if I were in a hurry to go to the hairdresser's. If not, while he had the engine cover off, he'd start the motor and let it warm up so that he could check the level of the transmission fluid. Since a man at the office had suggested a beauty college where appointments weren't necessary, I waited willingly.

After the motorhome engine ran about 15 minutes, Paul checked the level of transmission oil with its dipstick. Satisfied, he turned off the ignition and replaced the engine cover. He returned the television set to its oak pedestal on top of the engine cover.

I learned a lesson at the beauty school that I was able to use in future travels—if I want my hair to look right, insist on an experienced stylist. The timid student who shampooed and blew dry my hair confided at the end that she really wanted to be a manicurist! Meanwhile, my hair, although clean, was limp, frizzy, and styleless. I wanted to hide, even from Paul. Dear soul, she hadn't yet learned to use a brush to curl the hair as she blew it dry. She simply pulled the hair straight out as she dried it. As she worked, I couldn't help wondering why an instructor didn't come by to check on the operation. After that experience, I went to shopping malls for appointments at well-known beauty salon chains or got recommendations for hairdressers in beauty shops.

Friday, February 16th, arrived freezing cold! At 6:15 A.M., Paul slept under the goose-down comforter in the queen-sized bed behind the oak-paneled bedroom door that I had closed quietly when I came through a few minutes earlier. I wore flannel pajamas, a quilted robe, goose-down bootees, and a sweat jacket thrown around my shoulders. The coach's furnace, as well as a small, portable disc furnace, blew warm air while cycling on and off. With all this, my fingers and knees still felt chilly! Bundled as I was, I sat down to write in the computer journal.

Here in the coach, we have a queen-sized bed, which we like because it has lots of room and is easier to make than twin beds built in against the walls. The bed platform has a new, shorter queen-sized mattress with mitered corners at the foot, giving more room to walk around the corners. That new mattress was part of a major motorhome renovation that Paul undertook so professionally last year.

I went on to write that the first few times we had slept in our new motorhome, we discovered that drafts floated down onto our heads from the large rear window. This bothered us. Also, while the bed had a lot of storage space beneath it, the only accesses were small rectangular doors in the oak framework supporting the mattress. Those small doors had protruding handles that often hit my ankles as I

"When we discovered that drafts floated down onto our heads from the large rear window, Paul added oak paneling across the rear wall, cut a hole in the paneling for later access to the rear window, and fastened a large, custom-made beveled mirror on top of the oak paneling."

walked around the bed. In addition, we needed more toe room around the three sides of the bed. Subsequently, Paul undertook a major bedroom renovation. He removed everything from the bedroom except the side window draperies and venetian blinds, the filigreed oak railing above them that held baseball-type caps on Paul's side and more ball caps, dominoes, and card games on mine, and rear overhead cabinets in which I stored our bed linens and covers. He closed in the rear window with black glass and sheet foam to eliminate its drafts. He added oak paneling (shipped from Holiday Rambler at Wakarusa in a new motorhome coming our way, thus saving us shipping costs) across the rear wall, cut a hole in that paneling for later access to the rear window if needed, and fastened a large, custom-made beveled mirror on top of the oak paneling. He reconstructed the bed (using genuine oak lumber to match what was already in place) so that it would lift up for easy access to the storage area beneath and added four inches of toe room on the sides of the bed and ten inches at the foot. If I were looking for a new motorhome, I would surely want adequate toe room at the base of the bed. We ordered a new queen-sized mattress with mitered corners at the foot from Holiday Rambler, which gave more space for walking past them. We were pleased with how the room looked and functioned when the renovation was done. Paul's careful, patient work paid off.

A light sleeper, Paul minded being too warm or too cool. He liked to use covers that he could throw back easily or pull up, ones that weren't bulky. I found a queen-size thermal blanket and a thermal bedspread, both in colors to match the blues and beiges in the draperies and wallpaper. The bedspread generously covered the backs of the pillows. Each day after making the bed, we placed Mary and her Little Lamb, whom we talked to as if they were alive, pertly against the pillows.

As I looked up from the computer, I saw slivers of sunlight coming through the venetian blinds above the sofa. The coach was quiet as Paul continued to sleep. I closed my journal entry and moved about getting breakfast.

Near lunchtime on Friday, I walked to the resort's laundry area about two blocks away and did a load of clothes. Later, Paul came by. When we decided to tour the clubhouse, of which the laundry room was a tiny part, Paul took our clean clothes back to the motorhome and rejoined me.

Located just inside two tall, white stucco entrance arches, the clubhouse at Mission View was a sprawling example of Spanish architecture. It housed a beautiful indoor swimming pool, a hot tub, lounge areas, and an auditorium. We climbed an interior stairway leading us up three stories to a tower where we stepped cautiously onto an outside balcony, gasping at the view and taking pictures. To the west, north, east, and south, the Tucson, Santa Catalina, Rincon, and Santa Rita Mountains surrounded the city, as if protecting this elevated basin of sand.

After lunch, we found a grocery store and I stocked up on milk and bananas. I felt more at home in a place when I knew where the grocery store was located. Later, the LP gas truck came by and replenished our supply. Normally, we would have driven to the location of the LP gas supply tank, but in that resort environment, with many of the dwellers living in units that stayed parked, a truck with a LP gas tank on it came conveniently to the sites. Paul had earlier informed the office staff that we would like our supply replenished and he paid $9.44 to the driver of the truck at the time of delivery.

That night, Paul was already in bed as I sat on the edge writing in my bound journal.

Felt weak in knees, trembly inside, listless, and sad today. Thought about myself a lot and how I was feeling; where was my pep, enthusiasm, motivation?

Then I realized I needed to think about others, needed to pull myself out of these doldrums, needed to take charge of my life. I shouldn't expect my life to work out the way I wanted on its own. For example, if I want to go to a different part of the coach and Paul unknowingly blocks the 23-inch passage between the dinette table and the part of the kitchen counter that contains the double sink, I should not put off letting him know that I would like to go past. I think I felt trapped by the narrow passing zone but didn't work at finding a solution.

"I think the motorhome is working out well," Paul commented earlier today. I was glad for his comment, but I still struggled with my own concerns.

I see clearly that I shouldn't put off doing things in the motorhome, like discarding old food from the refrigerator and vacuuming the carpet. It's too frustrating to keep putting something off; I should just *do* it! And another thing—I shouldn't assume that I know what Paul will or won't want to do; instead, I should *ask* him or do it myself and find out. "Don't keep questions on hold inside," I lecture myself, regaining peace.

With Paul's upbeat spirit and my own determination to focus on others and take charge of my situations, this day is ending on a positive note.

Putting aside the journal, I turned out the light above the bedside table and scooted down under the covers. The Arizona images that I had had in Maryland floated into my mind. Warm sunshine, idyllic views, and shade trees had eluded us. Yet this was only our second full day in Arizona; we had 12 more days to spend here. And the next day we hoped to begin sightseeing in Tucson. Perhaps it would even be warm.

· 20 ·

A Grand Balloon Ascension

PAUL AND I HAD NEVER visited Tucson. According to what I read in travel books, the name came from the Native American word *stjukshon*, which was pronounced like "Tucson." The city, at an elevation of 2,389 feet, had a population in its metropolitan area of approximately 675,000. It was noted for its sunshine, low humidity, mountains, and abundant desert vegetation and therefore attracted visitors for both vacation and health reasons. In addition, like most cities, it offered cultural activities— art, music, dance, opera, and the theater. When I had heard or read about the city of Tucson back East, I felt uncommonly drawn to it, so once in the actual place, I was ready to see what it was all about, as was Paul.

What better way to feel the ambiance of Tucson than to walk its downtown cultural and historic district? On Saturday morning, February 17, wearing winter coats, Paul and I joined eight others at the John Fremont House. The restored Mexican-American adobe home was occupied by John Fremont in the 1880s during part of his term as territorial governor. In the small, darkened dining room, a history student from the University of Arizona gave a slide lecture. Then he led us out into bright sunshine, occasionally pausing and at times walking backwards, as he shared the story of Tucson.

We strolled among a mixture of adobe and high-rise buildings, seeing mansions and simple houses as he described architecture and gave anecdotes. Serendipitously, we saw a few skydivers with colorful parachutes descend out of the bright blue sky. We wove through the El Presidio Historic District at a gentle pace.

Between monologues by the tour leader, the rest of us chatted among ourselves, finding common interests. After the walking tour, one tour member invited Paul and me to follow her and her husband back to Rincon Country East RV Resort, a place we had planned to visit on our own.

With these new friends as guides, Rincon Country East seemed like an ideal resort. Palm trees provided shade and the Rincon Mountains posed nearby. We passed an outdoor swimming pool and went into a recreation hall. Outside again, we walked along a row of craft rooms; one was for oil painting, which is a definite interest of mine. People smiled and said hello. We ended by visiting with our gracious hosts in the enclosed patio attached to their lengthy fifth wheel. They told us they had searched many places, including Escondido and Phoenix, but felt Tucson was ideal. They planned to sell their fifth wheel and settle permanently in a town house in Tucson.

Leaving Rincon Country East, we noticed a vacant campsite in a small section set aside for RVers staying overnight or for only a few days. When our week was up at Mission View, we might try for a week at Rincon to get the flavor of another facility. We would have to take our chances in getting a site, however, because they made reservations only for people staying for long periods.

Paul and I drove Patches back to our own campsite for a late lunch in the motorhome. I took a two-hour nap and woke up feeling like my old self again and realized something had happened to me while motorhoming. Fatigue crept in unannounced, making me feel weak, trembly, and down. That good nap had met my body's needs and had restored my spirit.

After my nap, we drove Patches to Mission San Xavier del Bac, the "White Dove of the Desert," just a few miles from our park. I had seen this white structure in the distance when I sat in the front seat of the motorhome surveying the scenery, but I didn't know what it was. Later, I realized that our resort must have gotten its name from its view of the huge, historic mission church.

Built between 1783 and 1797 by the Franciscans on the Papago Indian Reservation, Mission San Xavier exemplified Spanish mission architecture. Looking well used but distinguished, the mission remained active.

Following our visit, at 5:56 on Saturday evening, I began to cook dinner. "One thing for sure, you can't have a lot of activities going on at the same time in a motorhome," I said.

"This is supposed to be the simple life, you know," Paul commented from the nearby sofa where he read the newspaper. In his usual low-key wisdom, he hit another nail on the head: one can live the simple life even in a busy world, providing one does not complicate it by trying to do a lot of different things simultaneously.

As a result, before fixing dinner, I cleared the counter and washed the few dishes left in one section of the stainless steel double sink. I wanted to have as much clear counter space as possible. Actually, the counter next to the sinks was only 15 inches wide. Beside that small space, however, were two additional feet provided by the stainless steel cover that folded flat over the four-burner gas range. So I had a total of 39 inches. I could add 13 more inches if I laid the custom-made butcher block over one section of the sink. In addition, just across the aisle, the dinette table offered a 40-by-28-inch area. At home, I had much more counter space but tended to use just a small portion of it. So I discovered that although the actual space in the motorhome was small, I could manage quite well if I made sure it was cleared off to start with.

I retrieved from the refrigerator/freezer, across the aisle from the pantry, the food I planned to use and placed it on the adjacent dinette table. Although the motorhome refrigerator/freezer is only about one-half the size of my side-by-side one at home, I was always amazed at how much I could store in it. On the road, we only had to restock about once a week just as I would do at home, except for milk. We used a lot of that.

First, I prepared the food that would take the longest time to cook in the microwave/convection oven. That evening it was meat loaf. After putting it in the oven, I decided to check something in the microwave/convection cookbook and stopped the baking cycle. Sure enough, I had overlooked an instruction that allowed the oven to bake meat loaf and roast potatoes together. I had to read and reread the new procedures because they differed from range-top cooking and regular oven baking.

With the meat and potatoes rotating in the oven, I considered how to cook fresh broccoli. When we first got the motorhome, the stovetop burners looked so clean that I couldn't bring myself to use them, knowing how easily and soon they could look messy. I pictured the struggle I had at home trying to keep the burners clean. So after turning the burners on to be sure they worked, I hadn't used them again. Was now the time to break down and give them a go? Should I *assume* Paul's reaction? No, I'd take charge and ask him.

"I'm about to make a momentous decision," I said.

"What's that?"

"I'm about to use a gas burner for the first time to cook the broccoli."

"Why?"

"Well, I thought you might be tired of food cooked in the microwave."

"Heavens, no! If that's the only reason you're using it, you can forget it."

Relieved, I closed the overhead cupboard door from which I was about to remove a pan and glanced over at the metal cover on the range top that would continue to protect the pristine gas burners. Above it was the waiting microwave oven, which I really preferred to use—no hard-to-wash pans and no hard-to-reach mess that seem to be part of using stove burners. In addition, microwave cooking was supposed to retain more vitamins when cooking vegetables.

I went on to cut the broccoli and place it into a glass microwave-able dish with a lid. That was the first fresh broccoli we'd had on the trip.

After dinner, Paul went outside and changed the oil in the motor-home. He was very careful not to spill any on the ground, even going so far as to place a piece of carpeting under the container catching the oil. (It may seem extreme, but Paul has always been conscientious and meticulous.)

Before going to bed, I set our electric alarm clock for 4:30 A.M. The next day, Sunday, we planned to see the Grand Balloon Ascension, near Tucson, which was supposedly one of the ten best hot-air balloon events in the nation. We learned about it from articles and ads in the local newspaper.

Very early Sunday, awaking before the alarm went off, I brought the clock under the covers so that when its shrill whine sounded, it would not shock-start our day. Usually we do not need to set the alarm, but when we have a special event going on like catching a bus for a tour of New Orleans or getting to a balloon site before the scheduled liftoffs, we take no chances on being late.

We both got up when the muffled note sounded and I thought we must be crazy to do this of our own accord. By 5:30, in darkness, dressed for winter, we stepped down from the motorhome and climbed into Patches, noting stars and the moon. Except for people in one trailer with a light on, everyone else seemed sensibly asleep. We wound through the resort's labyrinth, trying to find the exit. At last we saw the clubhouse, drove through the nearby arched exit, headed down Sixth Avenue to I-19, then I-10, and then Cortaro Farm Road. By this time, many other cars filed along, directed by sheriff's department officers swinging flashlights. As we moved along, signs reminded us, "Admission $5 for Muscular Dystrophy." It was pitch dark.

We parked Patches on a dark, grassy field. "Wait a minute," Paul said as we headed away. "We'd better get our bearings here. Let's start counting rows so we can find Patches after this is all over."

"Good idea." I looked for shadowy landmarks as we counted and walked across dirt roads and between parked cars, straining our eyes.

Ahead, floodlights illuminated a scaffold superstructure with radio call letters. Stepping between a tent and a van, we came into an enormous, level, pasture-like circular arena. Its fringes were lit up with carnival-type booths featuring Indian fry bread, donuts, souvenirs, a pancake breakfast, and a Pace Arrow motorhome. Many people milled around already.

"Where are the balloons?" I asked Paul, slapping my gloved hands together in the cold Arizona air. I saw none of the festival's touted 80 hot-air balloons. As we meandered through the crowd, we saw three people laying a tarpaulin on the ground. In the back of their pickup truck, a huge basket waited, the kind used to carry passengers skyward.

We walked among a growing crowd in the early morning darkness. At last, we came upon some enthusiasts preparing their balloons for takeoff, spreading out the large, colorful bags of material on ground covers. More people than we knew worked simultaneously at pre-liftoff tasks in this huge area during the chilly dawn hours of that day.

About 7:20 A.M., in the light of early dawn, the first balloon left the ground with three passengers in its gondola; it was silent, except

"Balloon after balloon lifted and floated toward a narrow valley between two mountains. Like bubbles in a boiling kettle, they rose all around us."

for the whoosh of the burners that warmed the air inside the balloon. That final moment between basket on earth and basket in air fascinated me. Unceremoniously, the balloon pilot lifted off. Where was the drum roll? The liftoff seemed historic, important, acclamatory. I wanted to reach up and touch the basket as it lifted, but surprisingly, its ascent was too swift.

Balloon after balloon lifted and floated toward a narrow valley between two mountains. Like bubbles in a boiling kettle, they rose all around us. They featured brilliant fabrics and fanciful, huge shapes—an elephant, a peanut, and fabulous onions. Seeing them floating in the air took my breath away. As they drifted serenely in the early morning light, I envied the peace and beauty of their passengers' experiences. Balloonists say that when they're floating in a balloon, time loses meaning.

"Well, I think this was worth getting up for at four-thirty in the morning," Paul said as he watched the colorful balloons float away.

On the way back, I asked, "Would *you* take a balloon ride?"

"I don't think so. I'm just not up for that at this stage of my life."

I would have gone if offered the chance. Although I was afraid of heights, I thought I would feel safe within the walls of the gondola.

Back at the motorhome, I wrote to Mother Beard on an Arizona postcard, one that showed Joshua trees at sunset. I asked how her new glasses were, told her we were fine, and reported that the Grand Balloon Ascension was breathtaking at daybreak, as was the sunset that same evening as I watched from inside the motorhome at our resort site.

Unlike its travel book description, the weather in Tucson remained cold. Where were the 3,800 average hours of sunshine a year of which the city boasted?

· 21 ·

Record-Setting Snows

ON MONDAY, FEBRUARY 19TH, rain splattered gently on the roof as Paul and I fixed our breakfasts. (We each prepared our own because we seldom ate the same foods in the morning and we often got up at different times, an arrangement that worked well for us.) When I realized that the sound of the rain had stopped, I glanced out the dinette window. *Snow* had taken its place!

With the weather uncertain that day, we discussed our plans. We had intended to stay another week in Tucson, perhaps at Rincon Country East if we could get in there, to try out another resort. The adverse, cold weather made us decide differently, however. When our prepaid week ended at Mission View on Wednesday, we would head for Mesa. Although Mesa was 106 miles north of Tucson, its elevation was about 1,100 feet lower, giving it warmer temperatures for more hours each day.

We wanted to visit Rincon today, however, to meet some of the staff and learn about activities available and making reservations. After calling the Rincon office, we learned that the social director was off duty because of the President's Day holiday. So we drove instead to the large Vanity Fair outlet and adjoining mall where Paul bought a shoe polish kit, a wallet, and two pairs of Lee cotton jeans. Not to be outdone, I selected a black handbag big enough to carry my camera and pocketbook contents, a 12-inch round glass plate to use for microwaving, and a pair of pretty, lace-trimmed pajamas.

After a late lunch in the motorhome, Paul went to the Pima Air Museum and then to the Beaudry RV Service and Parts Center to buy air and oil filters for our auxiliary generator.

"Don't hurry. I'll be writing into the computer," I told him. Soon I lost myself in my journal.

> It frustrates me when I try to write with someone else close by or when I am apt to be interrupted. I've written in a camp-ground laundry room with people coming and going, but it makes me feel unsociable if someone I've met is near and I'm not available to talk.
>
> I notice also that when I've not been able to write, I turn inward, become reticent, and feel like a balloon about to burst. Things that I want to write about pile up in my mind; I know I'll never remember them when the moment comes to write them down. Discouraging. I must work through this dilemma.

Paul returned with the supplies for the generator. As an airplane enthusiast, he was glad he'd gone to the Pima Air Museum. It had over 185 airplanes of all ages, including one used by Presidents John F. Kennedy and Lyndon B. Johnson.

The next morning, Tuesday, February 20, I ate breakfast early. While finishing with a cup of plain, hot water, I wrote in my bound journal.

> At last I've conquered my feeling of guilt in retirement! For most of my adult life, I've worked at a full-time job. I felt right about working; its related sense of accomplishment gave me self-respect. When I first retired, I erroneously thought that one shouldn't work when retired. Therein lay the guilt. To my surprise, I felt guilty because I wasn't working; I hadn't expected that. Not working just wasn't morally respectable in my mind. What I'm seeing now is that I *do* work in retirement—I'm just not paid for it. I cook, clean, get groceries, and volunteer—all contributing to someone or some worthwhile organization.
>
> Most of the work I do in retirement seems like play because it doesn't usually have the stresses that go along with a paying

job. Last week, I talked with a retired woman in the laundry room at Mission View who said she also felt guilty about not "working." I wish I could talk with her now to let her know what I've learned—that we work in retirement and that we simply need to identify our work. Guilt disappears when we do that—at least it does for me.

In this motorhome, cooking and cleaning *seem* like child's play because of the small size of the "house." When I *really* play, I sightsee, go to movies, watch comedies on television, take leisurely walks, watch sunsets, joke, and travel.

Paul opened the folding door, emerging from the bedroom. We were off to another day of work and play! After he ate breakfast, we went to the rear of the motorhome to make the bed. I began pulling up the covers on my side of the bed. He was about to do the same on his side when he remembered that I had said earlier I wanted to wash the sheets in Tucson. I like to do that at least once every two weeks on the road. He asked, "Are we stripping the bed or making it?"

"We're making the bed. I decided not to do any more laundry until we get to the next place." The laundry room was a bit too far of a hike from our site to carry our bags of soiled laundry and then return with clean clothes on hangers.

As we continued pulling up the covers and making the bed, Paul said tentatively, "You mean you're finally *camping*—"

"Instead of living at the Ritz?" I finished, and we both laughed.

As we prepared to visit the Arizona-Sonora Desert Museum that morning, Paul lifted our plastic bag of garbage from a wooden square box he had made and that fit in the right-angled corner where the refrigerator met the extended back panel of the dinette seat. He took it across the park road to the dumpster. By the time he returned, I was coming down the motorhome steps.

"Heater's off. Pump's off. Furnace's off. And we're off," I laughed.

It was 9:36 A.M. as we headed for the pay telephone before going to the Desert Museum.

At the laundry room, which housed the public telephone, I dialed FMCA and gave them our membership number and name. We had no messages. Then I inserted a quarter and dialed Rincon Country East.

The social director told me that the prettiest and best time to come to Tucson was during March and April when the cacti were in bloom. I asked him about Phoenix and Mesa. He said they were about five degrees warmer and that their temperatures didn't get as low at night as those of Tucson. He said, however, they had smog and heavy traffic.

I explained that we were from Maryland and were trying to get away from cold winters, asking him to suggest a place to do this. He responded that this spell of cold weather was unusual for Tucson. He sounded helpful and friendly. I asked him to switch me over to the registration desk. There I asked for information on making reservations for next year. The desk clerk took my name and address and promised to send a brochure.

Before leaving the laundry area, I bought a newspaper from the vending machine. "Fifth Snowfall during One Winter Sets a Record for Tucson," shouted the headline for the lead article in *The Arizona Daily Star*. The article told of the unusually cold winter season. A cold front from the Arctic was blamed for the latest snowfall, which broke a 1949 record for the number of times it had snowed during a single season in Tucson. So the cold weather we had experienced was indeed unusual for the area. I felt validated in our decision to visit Tucson—we just happened to hit a season of bizarre temperatures and unexpected snowfall.

From the laundry area, we headed for the Arizona-Sonora Desert Museum, 14 miles west of Tucson. When we arrived near noon, the parking lot swarmed with vehicles and drivers looking for spaces. We squeezed Patches into a spot beside the road leading to the museum. We were glad we didn't try to bring the motorhome, although we saw five or six shorter ones parked in the filled lot. They must have come early.

We bought tickets at $6 each. While waiting for the next tour, we ate lunch in the crowded restaurant that was part of the complex of museum buildings. At one o'clock, a volunteer naturalist began a fascinating tour as she walked us along the arid hillside. She identified and described animals and plants that lived in the desert, from a colony of prairie dogs to an aviary of indigenous birds to many varieties of cacti. Following her tour, we walked indoors to a cavelike museum with windows that, like an aquarium, showed *living* species in their underground habitat—snakes included. In the crowded gift shop, I bought postcards with beautiful photographs of desert flowers and plants to send to family and friends.

I had no idea so many species of plants (1,200) lived in the Sonoran Desert region and that over 200 animal species existed there, too. The naturalist and the museum gave me an eye-opening education in desert life. We came to appreciate the hardy desert dwellers.

On the way back to Mission View RV Resort, we passed Old Tucson. Columbia Pictures built this town in 1939. The film company used it to shoot *Arizona*, starring William Holden and Jean Arthur, and other movies. Even with my interest in cowboys and old westerns, I was too tired to take in another sight that day. As we drove past, I strained to see all I could from the car. "You know, I think I'm realizing something from writing in my journal that I hadn't noticed before."

"Yes?"

"I think it's helping me feel freer to talk about what I think or feel."

"How's that?"

"When I read what I've written, my frustrations or hopes don't seem nearly as enormous or foolish or unusual as they did cooped up in my mind. I think the same kind of metamorphosis must take place when I say those things out loud. Saying them deflates the balloon effect my mind had given them. What do you think?"

"Well! Congratulations! I call that a major breakthrough," Paul said. "So, do you have any frustrations you want to talk about now?"

"No, but I'd like a rain check." And we both laughed.

A few seconds later, I thought of something and giggled as I asked if I might cash in my rain check. By this time, Paul was turning Patches into the entrance to our motorhome park.

I told him of the frustration that I wrote about the day before in my journal. It dealt with my feelings about writing when someone else was in the same area and how I couldn't concentrate or focus because I kept thinking I might be interrupted at a crucial time or that I might be considered antisocial.

"Well, I guess now you know how I feel when I'm at my desk at home working on the finances or in the motorhome reading the paper, and I seem to get interrupted," Paul replied.

"You mean it bothers you when I interrupt?"

"I'm afraid so, dear," Paul said gently.

I told him I was glad to know that and would try to do better.

"Back to your writing—when you want to write, just go ahead. I'll see that you're trying to concentrate. Don't let my being near interfere. I wouldn't want you to feel that way, not at all," Paul assured me.

What a relief! What a great person my husband was!

Soon we parked Patches beside the motorhome. This would be our last evening in Tucson. Our paid week was up the next day and the weather was atypically cold. On to Mesa and, hopefully, sunshine.

· 22 ·

Relocating
to Mesa

AS I AWOKE about three o'clock Wednes-
day morning, my nose felt cold and I shivered. Moving closer to Paul,
I mumbled, "I wonder if the furnace is on."

Too groggy to investigate, we tried instead to sleep, depending
on each other's warmth. About five o'clock, Paul got up and looked
at the thermometer hanging above the dinette table and then at the
thermostat on the bedroom wall. He discovered that the furnace was
not working and came back to bed muttering, "I'll look into that in
a while."

A few minutes later, too cold to sleep, I wiggled hurriedly into
my quilted robe. I had planned to get up early anyway because of our
leaving Mission View that day. The thermometer above the dinette
table showed 52 degrees. Hastily opening the motorhome entry door,
I read 32 degrees on the thermometer just outside. I put my long insulated coat over my robe and pulled on my socks and goose-down slippers. When we had loaded the goose-down comforter, slippers, and
Paul's cap into the motorhome back in Maryland, we had no idea we'd
be using them in Arizona!

Paul got up also and plugged in the disc furnace to warm the
living/dining area. Wearing long pants, a long-sleeved flannel shirt,
his heavy blue winter coat, and goose-down cap, he went outside and
retrieved an electric bulb heater (150 watts). He set it on the small

table across from the sofa and pointed it toward the dinette table. It radiated delightful heat. Even so, we ate breakfast dressed for the Arctic Circle instead of Arizona.

After breakfast, Paul began to diagnose the furnace problem. First, he checked the electrical fuses in the compartment under the wardrobe area in the hallway across the aisle from the bathroom—all okay. Second, he removed the thermostat itself from the bedroom wall and as he did so, he disconnected two wires, one red and one white, that led to the furnace. When he twisted those same red and white wires together—minus the thermostat—the furnace came on. The problem was in the thermostat.

Third, sitting at the cleared dinette table, he took apart the thermostat. Inside it, he saw a whitish ash color on both a tiny wire and the thermostat lever. By carefully moving the lever back and forth, he removed that oxidation from both the fine wire and the lever of the thermostat.

Last, he untwisted and reconnected the red and white wires to their proper terminals on the thermostat. He reattached the thermostat to the wall and then made sure its switch was in the On position. The furnace came on—a welcome swoosh as warm air began coming through the heat duct and floor registers.

I asked Paul what others would have done if they didn't know what to look for when the furnace failed to come on. He told me that they would have had to take the motorhome to an RV service shop. How glad I was that he knew and continued to learn about electricity and mechanics.

As our inside environment became livable again, Paul went outside to unplug our electric cord from the resort's outlet, a normal routine as we prepared to leave a campsite. As he did so, our neighbor strode past, digging his heels into the gravel like a marathon walker. He'd often walked past our corner site in a gray jersey sweat suit and briefly greeted Paul. That day, he wore the same outfit. Paul said to him, "Kind of chilly this morning."

He responded in his French accent, "I cannot believe it. I leave now!" Soon he pulled out of his campsite with both his 30-foot, Class

A motorhome and tow car frosted over. I wondered where he thought he'd find warm weather.

In a cosmetic way, Patches too had fallen victim to freezing temperatures. Paul had to scrape thick frost from its windows. Meanwhile, I worked inside the motorhome doing my usual routine of going around the perimeter and stowing loose objects.

At 7:15 A.M., we left our site at Mission View RV Resort in Tucson. Our week there had been a time of adjusting to the disappointment of not finding our dream situation. Paul drove the motorhome through the now familiar resort roads while I followed in Patches, wondering if we would return another winter, deep down sensing an ironic sadness because it wasn't likely—we'd not take the chance of another unique winter season.

Once outside the Spanish archways of the resort, we pulled into an enormous gravel parking area across the road and hooked Patches to the motorhome.

"The campground wasn't so bad," Paul said as he steered toward I-10 West and Mesa. "I could have lived with the campground. But the weather—20s at night, 50s during the day. The weather wasn't exactly ideal, was it?"

I agreed and felt let down from my high expectations of warm weather in Tucson. I could still picture the meteorologist on television last winter standing in front of the U.S. weather map and pointing to 70- and 80-degree temperatures in Arizona. I knew I hadn't dreamed it.

About 8:30 A.M., we turned into the Desert Inn Truck Stop off I-10. I wanted to call Valle del Oro RV Resort in Mesa to reserve a site for that night. When I called them from Maryland in January, the office assistant told me that they were filling, but they did have a few spaces left. She advised me to call when in the area to see if any were available. Valle del Oro was one of the resorts I called that had no shaded campsites. It was in the desert, the assistant explained. She said you could see Superstition Mountain from it, however, as if that were special. She described it as a park for people 55 and over. The average site width was 35 feet, which was a generous size. We'd been in some places barely wider than the motorhome, but most were between 20 and 25 feet.

Using a pay telephone outside the truck stop restaurant, I reached a security guard at Valle del Oro with a kind voice who told me to call back in 15 minutes when the office opened. I walked back to the motorhome to let Paul know the status of the call. Then, returning to the restaurant, I entered and chose a table with a telephone, a great convenience at some truck stops. I ordered something quick to pre-pare—two biscuits with jelly and decaffeinated coffee—in order to justify taking up a table. The food came just before I called the RV resort at nine o'clock.

"We have a few spaces," said a woman at the resort office. "They're on a first-come, first-served basis."

When I tried to pin down a reservation, saying we were near Eloy, she repeated that it was first-come, first-served.

Concluding our conversation, I placed the biscuits and jelly in my napkin and went to the counter, where I asked the server for my check. To say the least, it appeared to be in Paul's and my best inter-est to get to Valle del Oro as soon as possible. A man stood ahead of me at the cashier's register. I felt like everyone else was in slow motion. I had to tell myself to stay calm and prayed that the Lord would help us find a place to camp tonight.

Paul waited beside our rig in the enormous parking lot. After I told him the state of affairs, we hurried into the motorhome and headed for Mesa.

As we rode, Paul said he was going faster than normal for him—60 miles an hour. Our minds raced about what we'd do if the resort were full. Paul said maybe we could dry camp in an overflow area at Valle del Oro if they had one. We had ample fuel, fresh water, and space in the gray and black water holding tanks if we needed to dry camp a day or two.

"I don't know what we'll find at Valle del Oro or whether we'll like it, but *The Trailer Life Directory* gives it an excellent rating," I told Paul.

"Sounds good, and the weather should be warmer since it's at a lower elevation than Tucson," Paul said.

"This whole trip was meant to be exploratory. So I guess exploring is what we're doing," I said, trying to justify our circumstances.

On we went. Paul continued driving at 60 miles per hour, but the circumstances seemed to call for it.

In my haste to get back on the road near Eloy, I hadn't gotten specific directions to Valle del Oro. Once we arrived in Mesa, we stopped at a gas station to ask. The resort was located on desert flatland in the suburbs of Mesa, according to the directory. After having to turn around once and then going to the wrong entrance, we at last saw ahead the main entrance to Valle del Oro.

Three colorful flags flying on tall white poles beckoned from our left. At their base, on a six-foot-high, tan stuccoed wall, white block capital letters spelled out "Valle del Oro" as they directed us toward the two-lane entrance. A concrete block wall, about seven rows high, enclosed the huge compound. Young shade trees in a bed of gravel outside the wall somehow survived, adding charm. From our high motorhome seats, we saw tops of countless recreational vehicles inside the resort. Pausing at the entrance guard station, we asked directions to the office. Driving ahead, we saw avenues upon avenues of campsites that looked like a planned suburban community, each with a street name. We then arrived at a beautifully landscaped complex of buildings—an oasis in that desert environment.

Easily maneuvering into a vacant parking space for motorhomes and tow cars, we gazed at the vast, flat-roofed, sprawling, connected set of buildings that waited nearby, searching with our eyes for the office. Somewhere within that complex, someone would announce to us the result of our race for a place to stay. A friendly volunteer about to get into a golf cart used for resort errands pointed out the office.

Trying to be calm, we walked steadily toward the office, looking around. I liked the lush palm and deciduous trees, the tiled porch roofs above columned verandas, and the feel of activity. It was like a beehive with people over 55 making honey of their retirement. They brought movement, hubbub, laughter, smiles, and life to this artificial but welcoming edifice in the desert.

The office was bustling, and we had to wait in line to register—all the while hoping a site would be available. It was already eleven o'clock. As our turn came, we stepped to the window. Gratefully, we learned a site was available. Since we hoped to stay there at least two weeks, we paid for a week in advance. The total came to $122.48, which included $115.00 per week, $6.33 sales tax, and $1.15 space tax. The registrar told us to pick up our identification badges and a calendar of events the next day in a nearby room. I was excited yet uncertain about what activities were listed and what we would decide to participate in.

By noon, Paul had backed the motorhome into site 219 alongside a concrete patio, over which we would extend our awning. The tow car sat parallel to the other side of the patio, its front facing the long asphalt road. Like shoeboxes loosely set on a shelf, motorhomes and fifth wheels were parked with their noses toward the street, complying with resort policy. Our vehicle seemed like every other in this resort village of about 1,800 RVs.

With no trees or shrubbery in our immediate area, I thought of eggs frying on hot sidewalks in this gravel, concrete, and asphalt

" . . . motorhomes and fifth wheels were parked with their noses toward the street, complying with resort policy."

enclosure. Were we going from one extreme to the other—freezing cold in Tucson to boiling hot in Mesa? Compared to Maryland with its foliage and trees, this campsite in the desert seemed penitentiary-like and I wondered if this was where we really wanted to spend time.

I stopped myself. I wanted to be open to this new experience; this was part of learning what life was like in Arizona's winter. I thanked God for safe travel and for this place to settle for a week or two. Being thankful, even for small everyday things, like water coming from the spigot, helped me cope with life's accumulative stresses.

As Paul hooked up to water and electricity, I tried not to feel too disappointed by the gravel site. We seemed like just one more vehicle in this resort village, yet I did notice that the coaches and fifth wheels were in fine condition and there was no litter on the ground. It was a very civilized place.

Hot, hot sun penetrated me. Sweaters were certainly not needed here! I shed long cotton pants for walking shorts. We had come 3,433 miles for this!

After lunch at our new "home" site, I walked over to the office, a distance the length of a football field. An assistant there helped me find the name of a hairdresser, and I made an appointment for the next day by telephone. If I liked the way the stylist did my hair, I would get a permanent the following week.

Back at the motorhome, I gathered soiled articles and laundry supplies and walked in a different direction up the long, straight street to the laundry area. The stuccoed, flat-roofed building suggested Spanish architecture with its red-tiled roof covering a veranda with columns. On its spacious porch, I walked past pay telephones, newspaper stands, and a couple of folding chairs. Landscaped with trees and shrubbery, the building offered refreshing beauty as well as utility.

The laundry facility itself was in a large room with lots of washers and dryers and all the accompanying accessories, such as wire carts to carry wet loads from the washers to the dryers, that made doing the wash pleasurable. All laundry areas are different, depending on the size of the campground. Some have just a single washer and dryer; most have more than one of each. Laundry areas must be kept clean by the campground owners because they're included in the ratings given by campground directories. The area at Valle del Oro was exceptional in adequacy and cleanliness. But I'd been in smaller laundry facilities where I could also make that same assessment.

Later in the evening, Paul and I strolled back to the laundry building and called Jeff to let him know where we were and check in with FMCA for any messages from Hazel. There were none, and so we assumed Hazel was improving and that Mother Beard was at least holding her own.

At last, warm weather. But would we like the resort itself? Deep down, I hoped this would be "it" for us, our Shangri-la.

Replacing a Flat Tire

IN THE MORNING on Thursday, our first full day at Valle del Oro Resort, we drove the tow car to the office complex, wondering what the place really offered. So far, I felt as if I were in a set-apart, sophisticated world all its own rather than a down-to-earth campground—and I wasn't sure I would find it relaxing and enjoyable.

At the office complex, we picked up our identification badges and the weekly calendar of activities and events (no waiting in line like the day before because the materials were in a different room). We then returned to Patches for the trip to Mesa and the hairdresser's.

On the way, I scanned the calendar and then wondered what the resort did *not* offer! Six pages of 8½-by-11-inch sheets printed on both sides were jammed with schedules and plans for dance exercise, coed exercise, golf, T-shirt painting, ceramics, water exercise, wood-carving, lapidary, china painting, and other classes or workshops. The calendar also described specific classes (more than 40), announced the resort's chapel services and other events, listed lost articles as well as items for sale, and generally promised a potpourri of interesting happenings. In addition, the resort brochure that I picked up along with the badges listed 38 activities such as clogging, tennis, barbecues, billiards, big band dances, tournaments, and potluck meals.

The oil painting class met all day on Monday. A creative writing class would meet Friday from 9:00 to 11:00 in the Acapulco Room, wherever that was. I definitely wanted to pursue that class.

At the hairdresser's salon in Mesa, the stylist did a nice job and I set up an appointment for a permanent the following Tuesday.

Meanwhile, Paul shopped for and found a notebook in which to record motorhome maintenance activities such as the date and odometer reading when he changed the engine oil. Paul had found that there was not enough space in the instruction manual that came with the motorhome for all that he wanted to record. So he decided to set up his own record book with a separate page for oil changes, oil filter changes, and other maintenance duties.

When we returned from town, we walked over to the country store and craft fair being held in the ballroom. Every Thursday, those events filled the 9,600-square-foot space and flowed onto the spacious concrete patio by the swimming pools. Although unbelievable that we at last wanted to shield ourselves from the hot sun, each of us bought a straw hat with a broad brim.

After a quick lunch in the motorhome, we found a Vanity Fair outlet in Mesa. Since we planned to try the outdoor spa at the resort, we both bought swimwear. I hadn't been in a swimming pool for years—in fact, I never learned to swim—but I wanted to try the spa. And I didn't have to worry about my friends at home seeing my unseemly knobby knees and cellulite! I could hardly believe the temperature would stay warm enough for an *outdoor* dip. We also purchased clothing gifts for Nancy and Jeff.

Early Friday morning, I walked toward the office complex, looking for the theater, where the dance exercise class was scheduled for 8:00 A.M. A small, detached building, the theater soon filled with people wearing shorts, including me, ready for aerobics. (At home, I go regularly to an aerobics dance class.) Soon, we were exercising to a video tape shown on a huge screen. Some of the exercisers themselves added encouragement and tutoring as we followed the video instructor.

From the theater, I walked along a concrete path, looking for the Acapulco Room, where the creative writing class was scheduled at 9:00. The room was in an extension of the office oasis complex, but the exterior sliding glass door was locked. No one else waited nearby. I questioned if I were at the right place. Soon another woman joined me. As we waited together, she told me about the sessions. Others came, one unlocked the door, and we settled into chairs around a long table in the rectangular room. Some students had been in the class all winter; others were attending for the first time, as I was.

The teacher, Wanda Lund, was retired from the *Deseret News,* where she had reported on general assignments including hard news and features. She also took photographs to illustrate her articles. She helped us fit easily into the lesson. I was especially excited because her method was based on writing from the right side of the brain.

The previous fall, I had taken a drawing class in a continuing education program from an excellent instructor and artist, Shirley Lippy. She had based her instruction on the philosophy and techniques described by Betty Edwards in her book *Drawing on the Right Side of the Brain.* So I was familiar with the left/right brain idea. Even last fall, Shirley and I had discussed how creative writing comes from the brain's right hemisphere. Eagerly, I jotted down the name of the textbook, *Writing the Natural Way: Using Right-Brain Techniques to Release Your Expressive Powers*, by Gabriele Lusser Rico, published by J. P. Tarcher, Inc., Los Angeles.

Far from Maryland that day, I learned to take a dominant feeling from a night's dream and "cluster" it into a poem or essay. When using the technique, I wrote the name of the feeling, such as anxiety, in the center of a piece of paper. Then I drew a circle around that name and surrounded it with other encircled words or phrases that came to my mind as being associated with the dream's main feeling, such as "deadline," "errors," "dust storms," and "thankfulness." The author of the text called this process "clustering." It extracted creative expression from the right side of the brain that the more analytical left side would censor or reject.

Toward the end of the clustering process, the brain would focus on an idea that would be the basis or theme for the essay or poem, such as "how I conquered anxiety." The cluster of words would be a resource for the brain to use in composing the essay. It was a way of letting one's mind flow free with ideas and details before putting anything into sentences.

I later used the process to write thank you notes and letters. It made me think through what I wanted to include by having to jot down the items. I found that writing comes easier when I've got the meat of what I want to say already clustered.

Our assignment that Friday called for an essay on whatever came to mind from viewing a picture of Greg Hill's sculpture *Homochronos*. I walked on air back to the motorhome. The eternal student (having gotten my bachelor's and master's degrees as an older adult and forever taking classes in continuing education), I could hardly wait to work on the assignment using the clustering technique.

When I stepped onto patio 219, however, my attention took a different path. Paul said nonchalantly, "We must have picked up a nail or something in a motorhome tire. It seems to be lacking some air."

"Is it flat?"

"I think you could say that."

"What'll we do?"

"Well, I was waiting for you to come back. I think that after lunch, I'll go up to the office and see if I can find a Goodyear tire dealer around here," Paul said slowly.

"Don't we have road service coverage for the motorhome?"

"Yes." He paused, wiping his hands on a red handkerchief. "We do have road service with Good Sam. But if I let them come and take care of it, then I won't learn anything. If someone else examines the tire, I won't learn much." I'd learned to go along with his decisions on maintenance of the motorhome. I knew he really was curious and wanted to understand everything possible about our vehicle, although I would have called road service as many other motorhomers would do.

When we finished eating, Paul went outside to examine the tire more closely, then he drove to the office to find a tire dealer.

I began writing postcards while sitting at the dinette table. It was a pleasant, sunny afternoon. The entry door was open, and a breeze drifted between the screen door and the screened window at my left. Later I might have to close up the motorhome and turn on the air conditioner. The postcard to Mother Beard showed a picture of Valle del Oro. She would be interested in seeing where we were staying. I was about to sharpen a pencil with a tiny, old-fashioned wooden box sharpener from our utility drawer under the kitchen counter when Paul came to the screen door of the motorhome.

"I need you to go along to take the tire to a Goodyear place." With an urgent manner and tone, he added that he wanted to get there before they closed.

It was early in the afternoon and most places didn't close until 5:00 or later, so I didn't understand his hurry. Since he seldom did things in a pressing way, however, I made no comment; I just laid down the sharpener and pencil.

"Get your pocketbook and whatever else you want," instructed Paul.

"You found a Goodyear dealer?"

"Yeah. In the phone book. I called from the office. He can put another tire on the rim today. Don't we have some old rags somewhere to use for dirty jobs?"

"We have an old sheet and old counterpane."

"That's fine. Just the bedspread," Paul said. Knowing that as often as not he eventually needed the second item, I got out the sheet, too, from a cupboard above the bed at the rear of the coach.

Outside, Paul tilted the back of the front passenger seat of Patches as far back as it would go, where it rested on the back seat cushion. Then he made a bed on the passenger seat with the counterpane and sheet. We inched the big motorhome tire into it, using the bed clothes to protect the upholstery.

Paul said he needed me to go along and read the map and that I could also tell him if traffic was coming from his right. With that tire in the front passenger seat, he couldn't see very well, he added. "Can you get in the back seat? You can be 'Miss Daisy,'" he laughed.

I squeezed past the big tire into the back seat. Paul slid into the driver's bucket seat in front. We repositioned the tire so it leaned against the window on the passenger side and not against the center hand-brake lever.

Before long, we found Western States, the Goodyear tire dealer, at 1507 Country Club Drive. A man took the tire from the front passenger seat and rolled it adeptly into a service bay.

Alone, I sat hunched up in the back seat of Patches with the hot sun hitting me. I opened all the windows, then fashioned a paper tent using a Phoenix city map to shield myself from the burning rays.

Soon Paul and the man returned, the man having quickly and efficiently placed a new tire on the old rim. He lifted the new tire into the front seat where it leaned against the open window. They then retreated to the office to pay the bill and get the appropriate paperwork.

I repositioned my map tent and looked around at the service center. An ample, modern, clay-brick facility, it had three bays for service work and a large showroom.

Paul got back into the driver's seat and examined the new tire that now rested beside him. "One thing I want to be sure to do is look for the load range. That's it—'D.' Now I'm satisfied." (Later, at home, we bought all new tires and went to the "F" load range, which meant the sidewalls were stiffer and would take harsher treatment. The new tires were also low profile for a better ride and more stability.)

We pulled away as Paul continued, "Well, there were two things wrong with it. Not only was the sidewall cracked, but it had a broken piece of an Allen wrench in it. They allowed me $96 for the old tire. I had to pay $112.40 all told. I'm amazed that I could get this done so fast."

We headed back to Valle del Oro. "I learned one thing," Paul announced.

"What's that?"

"I'm only going to put 60 pounds in these tires instead of 65 since these are a summer tread. It'll help them wear better."

On we went with the hot, desert wind blowing my hair as I sat in the back seat writing furiously in my bound journal; I wanted to record Paul's conversation before it slipped away. The new tire leaned against the open front window. Dear Patches had no air conditioning, and I vowed that our next tow car would come equipped with it. (We later replaced dear Patches with a used four-door Ford Escort that had air conditioning, an absolute requirement in my mind.) Back at our site, Paul satisfyingly took his time and placed the new tire on the motorhome.

Later that day, Paul called Hazel to see how she was getting along following her modified radical mastectomy four days earlier. Happily, she was doing very well and reported that Mother Beard was about the same.

Things seemed to be looking up for us, too. We had at last found warm weather and a resort with activities that interested us. Since this was our first time at such a place, I wondered (too much, I know) how we would adjust to it.

"Back at our site, Paul satisfyingly took his time and placed the new tire on the motorhome."

The next day, Saturday, I awoke thinking objectively about our trip. Being together day and night demanded patience, a determination to understand and accept each other, and sometimes real effort to be funny and compatible. We kept learning about one another's likes and dislikes (yes, even after 41 years of marriage) and talking about problems, no matter how little. We were adjusting not only to the intimacies of motorhome travel but also to being together in retirement.

"May I see your list of things you want to do today?" I asked Paul. A fledgling in the practice of list making, Paul sat in the dinette seat, holding a small piece of note paper.

"Sure."

I began reading aloud, "Water pressure gauge—"

"Oh, I have to add some more," he interrupted.

When he finished writing and explaining the other items on his list, I asked if I should read to him what was on my list. An inveterate list maker, I usually had tried to accomplish my tasks as a second priority to Paul's—not fair to either of us. Now, with both of us making lists and planning, we could equalize priorities.

"Sure."

So I read my list. "Work on creative writing assignment; do journal writing; visit Phoenix, Silveridge, Carriage Manor, Gold Canyon Resorts; get groceries; attend orientation on Monday; get permanent on Tuesday; clean motorhome; hem Paul's pants; and write cards. The only ones I want to do today are the creative writing lesson, my journal writing, and getting groceries," I added. Then, realizing we each had a lot planned, I needed to know his schedule, if he had one. "When do you think you'll be away for the largest block of time today?"

"Trying to get rid of me?" he teased.

I assured him it had nothing to do with him personally, but the point was to find a way for each of us to do our list items. I was thinking specifically of my creative writing assignment, which I wanted to tackle when I had some time to myself.

"Well, I'll be looking over the resort this morning—I haven't really done that yet—and this afternoon, go over to Main Street."

Paul set out in Patches to scout Valle del Oro. Adhering to my list, I read the printed assignment from yesterday's creative writing class and tried the clustering technique, which worked like magic. By the time Paul returned, the essay needed only finishing touches. I'd complete it when he went to town after lunch.

About 2:00, Paul went over to Main Street. He was still looking for a water pressure gauge for the motorhome. He also wanted to wash the desert sand from Patches.

While he was away, I keyed into the laptop computer the essay that I'd hand-written earlier. After editing, I printed it on the Okidata Microline 380 that we'd brought along. I wouldn't be here for the next class because we'd decided to go on to California instead of staying another week in Mesa. We wanted to allow more time for visits and sightseeing in California and Sedona, Arizona, and on the way back east. I planned to drop off my essay at Wanda's campsite when I went to dance exercise on Monday. We'd be leaving on Wednesday, and the next class would be the following Friday.

At 4:21 P.M., I opened the door to look at the thermometer. Was it still warm outside the air-conditioned coach? One hundred seven degrees. Unbelievable! Was it hot in Tucson, too? Today's paper called for a high of 81 there and a low of 42. Would Mesa turn out to be a place we'd want to return to another winter?

· 24 ·

Milestones

SOON SATURDAY BECAME Sunday, February 25th, at Valle del Oro in Mesa. I had a growing sense that we were enjoying the place—that it might be what we'd been looking for on our dream journey. But we'd only been there three full days.

Sometime after Paul and I were both out of bed, dressed, and done with breakfast and the dishes, Paul was brushing his teeth. I walked past the cleared kitchen counter and saw a loose rubber band lying there. "Where did this rubber band come from?"

"Don't throw it away. Goes on the soda box!" Paul replied in a strong but good-natured tone from the bathroom as he brushed his teeth.

"We're really keeping things shipshape, aren't we?" I noted, referring to how the cleanliness of the counter had played up the presence of the rubber band. The rubber band helped keep the tab-type lid closed on our box of baking soda when we were cruising. We had temporarily run out of toothpaste and were using baking soda to brush our teeth. Baking soda was just one of the staples we kept on board. Others included sugar, flour, salt, laundry and dishwashing supplies, first-aid supplies, bathroom tissue, paper towels, plastic utensils, trash bags, paper plates, cups, napkins, bed linens, umbrella, galoshes, rain gear, and mechanics overalls for Paul.

"Huh?"

"We're really keeping things shipshape, aren't we?"

Stepping out into the hall, still brushing his teeth, Paul affirmed, "Oh, yeah! That's great!"

As I stood beside the sofa at the front of the coach, I had a good view of its appearance. At the rear, the bed was made, with Mary and her Little Lamb resting against the pillows. Moving my eyes forward, the closet doors in the hallway were closed, the kitchen counter was clear (except for the rubber band), the dinette table was clear, and the two pillows with ducks on them were arranged neatly at one corner of the sofa. The small table across from the sofa held my laptop and printer and accessories. No clothes lay strewn around, except an extra pair of shoes for each of us that we had worn but not yet put away. (Nobody's perfect!) Overall, I felt pleased that we worked together to keep the motorhome in order. It certainly made living in a small space less frustrating. Somewhere I had read that if you can clear at least one large surface in a room, the room looks orderly. Thus, we make the bed and try to keep the dinette table and counter area free of clutter.

Another milestone for us occurred that morning as Paul and I made the bed. He said, "Let's see. Are we going to see *Driving Miss Daisy* at 5:10 and *Blaze* at 7:10 this evening?"

Wow! When we started the journey, he had been one to wait and see what the moment brought. Now he was thinking through our plans for the day. How refreshing to have some structure in the day.

"That's fine with me. What'll we do about visiting other resorts? Is Sunday a good time?" I asked, consciously seeking his input. I could have said I thought we should visit other resorts sometime today.

"Their offices probably aren't open Sundays. I think it'd be better to do that Monday and Tuesday," he responded.

I told him that was fine with me and that I planned to go to the chapel service that morning at 10:00.

"I don't think I'll go with you. I'm going to work on the car. I can't take too much of that gospel music. Tears me up."

So that was why he'd been reluctant to attend church on this trip! His emotions were sensitive; his eyes filled up and even shed tears during certain "heart" music. At home, he ran the church's sound system during worship services, but we didn't have much gospel music there. He and I both knew he was a Christian in mind and heart. He prayed throughout the day and was satisfied with his worship practices and relationship with God.

As I thought ahead about going to the movies, I asked Paul, "Okay with you if we have our large meal at noon and our sandwiches this evening?"

"Fine with me, however you want to do it. We also need to call Nancy and Jeff this afternoon."

"How about calling them around 11:30, which would be 1:30 their time?"

"Sounds good," he said. We finished making the bed. Each of us could now work on tasks knowing what the day's goals and schedules were. I liked that and I thought Paul did, too. Thank you, Lord!

When I left for the chapel shortly before 10:00, Paul was happily puttering with Patches, saying that its choke was almost stuck shut again. I walked on concrete paths past a large expanse of green lawn toward the ballroom at the office complex. Others headed in the same direction. The huge, high-ceilinged ballroom contained many rows of folding chairs facing the stage that served as a chancel for the nondenominational service. Someone played the piano. Others greeted worshipers and handed out bulletins showing the order of worship and announcements. Smiling, friendly people came in and sat down.

I sat beside a man in a brown suit and tie. His wife, wearing a cream-colored suit, sat on the other side of him. The husband told me that they were from Michigan and had been coming to Valle del Oro during the winter for 11 years. He had arthritis and the weather helped him. They stayed for five months every year. Before discovering Mesa, they had gone to Florida for five years but found that area too humid. Also, Mesa had no mosquitoes or flies to speak of.

He told me that the current winter was the coldest they had encountered there. At first, they camped in Superstition State Park. While there, they made reservations for Valle del Oro, which at the time was under construction with huge earthmovers preparing the site for the office complex and campground. They had come back every year since.

"There's something to do here all the time," he said. "We brought our trailer for about six years and then we bought a park model. So now we travel back and forth in a car. We're thinking of buying a condominium and living here year-round." A park model is a large trailer designed primarily to remain at one site rather than for touring.

During the service, the leader announced that the attendance for that day was approximately 775. The offering went to the Salvation Army and the Navajo Evangelical Lutheran Mission. The service bulletin listed times for a choir rehearsal and several Bible study meetings. Everyone was invited to a social time with coffee and cookies following the service.

Afterward, I didn't stay for the reception but walked back to the motorhome. We wanted to call Nancy and Jeff at 11:30.

Paul turned another corner that morning. As we prepared to walk to the telephones at the laundry building up the street, he changed from the greasy clothes he had worn when fixing the Toyota. "Did you notice I'm taking enough interest in my attire to be presentable? I could have gone in my dirty clothes, you know." At home he would slip into town on a quick errand wearing his soiled work outfit.

"Really appreciate that," I said as we headed for the telephones.

When Paul talked with Jeff, he learned disturbing news about Mother Beard. She had suffered congestive heart failure at 4:30 that morning. Her physician, Dr. Welliver, had seen her twice, and she had responded to additional medication. While the prognosis was uncertain, the doctor had said there was no need to hospitalize her or give her heroic efforts. We learned also that the Carroll Lutheran Village Health Care Center, where Mother lived, was under a flu quarantine. Jeff sounded concerned but was trying to be calm, Paul told me later.

As I thought about Mother's illness, I remembered a neighbor at home, in her 90s also. Her daughter-in-law told me that her mother-in-law had lived with congestive heart failure for several years. So I didn't feel as anxious about the diagnosis as the name suggested.

Since Jeff was in the middle of his lunch, we arranged to call him back in two hours to go over the mail. During that time, Paul and I ate our lunch at the dinette table in the motorhome, subdued by our concern for Mother. I pictured her smiling the way she did when we saw her that Sunday night before we left on our dream journey.

After lunch, Paul dumped the gray water. While doing so, he noticed fresh water dripping onto the ground from under the bathroom area of the coach. He kept his cool about his mother's illness and worked immediately on the leak problem, thinking and talking as he did so. "You know, I was thinking that if we have to go home in a hurry, it would take at least four days. We can't travel as fast in this as in a car," he said.

We began thinking of possibilities in the event that Mother didn't pull through this episode. Yet I didn't have any feeling of panic about it.

"It's not her pattern to do anything in a hurry."

Paul chuckled. "You know, you're right!"

We called Jeff again about 2:00. He caught us up on the mail. I had a good conversation with Nancy about her work in drafting at an electronics manufacturing firm and the computer-aided design class she took on Saturdays. I talked with Jeff about his work and his teaching a Sunday school class that day on the subject of the Holy Spirit. The telephone connection was so clear that I felt they were with us. We were all trying to stay composed about Mother Beard.

Immediately after talking with Jeff, Paul called the health care center to learn about Mother's condition. Simultaneously, his sister Hazel was on another line calling about her also. The charge nurse was with Mother in her room. Paul asked the person he was talking with to tell Mother we had called.

About ten minutes later, Paul called Hazel in Pennsylvania. She had not yet heard back from the charge nurse who was getting information together on Mother's condition. She did say, however, that earlier in the day, the doctor said he thought Mother had only a few hours or a few days to live. Paul and Hazel decided that Paul would call the next morning at 9:00 her time, 7:00 our time. Only six days after her mastectomy, Hazel said she was doing fine. Her voice sounded strong and rejoicing. Her doctor, however, advised against her going so soon after her operation to the health care center with its flu quarantine.

Paul thought that no matter what happened with Mother, the next morning was early enough for us to know. I wasn't so sure about that but said nothing. I remembered that when we had been in British Columbia on vacation, we got the word about Dad's death. Paul had wanted to leave immediately, although it was the middle of the night, saying he wouldn't be able to sleep anyway. That was before the motorhome. We had left the resort motel and had driven in our car day and night, except for one six-hour sleep in a motel. We did this to get home in time for the visitations at the funeral parlor and the service.

If we had to travel day and night to get home for Mother, Paul thought we were in a good position to do so. We could take turns driving and could stretch out on the sofa and sleep better than in the car. We had everything we needed with us and would have to stop mainly for gasoline. We tried to prepare ourselves mentally for whatever direction Mother's health took.

Paul took the front vinyl panel off the bathtub and found what he thought was causing the leak, a loose fitting. He wanted to test his repairs later, so he didn't replace the panel just then.

Susie Flock from the creative writing class came to our door—a pleasant surprise. She was going around the park delivering a pack of papers to each class member on that Sunday afternoon. She had attached a handwritten note addressed to me, as I imagined she had done with the others. I gave her my assignment in case I was unable to drop it by Wanda's park model the next morning. Her generosity and friendliness warmed me.

As I looked at the papers Susie brought, Paul said he thought that there may be a line at the movies and that we should get there early. So we got into Patches and headed for the AMC Sunvalley Plaza 10 about a half-hour away.

I began to relax and think we were as close as we would come to my Maryland vision of warm weather, creative activities, and snow-capped mountains. We could see Superstition Mountain from some places within the resort. A week ago, in Tucson, we had stood shivering in winter coats as hot-air balloons ascended in grand style. This afternoon we stood in short sleeves at the movie ticket window, carrying sweaters needed only for the air conditioning inside the theater.

As we settled into theater seats, I wondered how Mother felt and what tomorrow morning would bring.

Monday's News

I GOT UP MONDAY morning at Valle del Oro in Mesa, Arizona, feeling uncertain about what the news might be from Hazel in Pennsylvania that day.

Paul ate his usual breakfast of Raisin Bran, peanut butter, and half a banana with skim milk. He drank a cup of hot water containing a heaping teaspoon of sugar and a little skim milk. About 7:00, he walked alone up the street, a long city block, to use a telephone at the laundry area.

While he was gone, I finished my breakfast, read a chapter in the Bible, made the bed, and dressed in shorts for the aerobics session at 8:00. I stood at the kitchen sink washing the breakfast dishes when Paul pulled open the entry door.

"How are things?" I asked gently.

His lips trembled and he reached for me as I stepped over to him.

"Oh, honey, I'm sorry! So sorry! Do you want to sit down?"

Unable to answer, he stood in the stairwell, sobbing on my shoulder. With my arms around him, I moved one hand back and forth across his shoulders, trying to console him.

He couldn't do anything but stand in the stairwell, sobbing and holding onto me. I continued to stroke his shoulders, feeling his hurt.

"I'm sorry!" he said, still crying and leaning on me. "I held it all in when I talked with Hazel. I needed to write down some notes, and I had to hold it all in."

As the sobs lessened, I asked again if he wanted to sit down on the sofa.

Hardly aware that he was still standing up, he moved with me over to the sofa, where we sat close together. I continued to hold him and gently caressed his shoulders. I told him to just go ahead and cry all that he wanted, that it was so good for him.

"I knew I was going to cry like this, and I'll probably do more of this on the way back, and especially at the funeral home," Paul cautioned me. I thought only about *his* emotional trauma. Still unable to say what Hazel had told him, he pointed to a lined pad lying on the engine hump on which he had written during their telephone conversation.

"I made notes," he sobbed, motioning that I should read them.

Paul's notes were neat and organized, even though written during his emotional distress.

1. Died 2:10 A.M., 2-26; much fluid; very pleasant, smiled much Harold (brother) and Pearl (sister-in-law) there till 9:30 P.M.
2. Harold & Al (Guyer) are now bringing (her) th(ings) to Hazel's.
3. Paul G. (Paul Groff, Mother's pastor) going on vac. this week. Al may do service. Children agreeable.
4. (Memorial service) At church on Sat. 2:00 P.M. or 2:30 P.M. Julia (Hitchcock) to sing; Paul Guyer to play (organ); Bernice to speak perhaps, think about on way home.
5. Visitation on Friday at Pritts 2-4 & 7-9 P.M.

As I silently read, Paul said, "Add to that list: call Hazel along the way home."

Handkerchief in hands, Paul continued to think of Mother. "She would like to have had this happen years ago."

During the last 20 years, she had suffered daily with arthritis in both knees, hands, and feet. In the early 1980s, Dad Beard had arranged for them to buy a large apartment in the soon-to-be-built Carroll Lutheran Village, just outside Westminster. They were both octogenarians, with Dad in good health. Before they moved in, however, Dad had a severe stroke and entered the health care center at the village. With only dim hopes of Dad's being able to live in the apartment with her, Mother decided to buy a smaller two-bedroom apartment.

Moving into the apartment meant selling the two-story colonial brick home she had designed on a brown paper bag back in the '30s. She and Dad reared their family of four children in that handsome house on a hill near Westminster. They had two daughters, Hazel and Elsie, and two sons, Harold and Paul. Mother had to deal with many fond memories and many collected treasures as Hazel and Elsie helped her work through the process of sorting and distributing household items. Decision making had always been hard for her.

When she moved into the apartment at the village, she lived alone. Dad lived a short walk away in a room at the health care center. For special occasions, we brought him to the apartment in a wheelchair. His mind wandered and his head drooped, far different from the erect, distinguished-looking businessman he once was.

Then Mother had a mastectomy. She came through it well; however, she eventually got weaker. We hired professional aides to come in, but one after another left for various reasons. When we no longer could find a suitable helper, family members took turns staying at night with her. One day when alone, she fell in her kitchen. The time came when both she and the family were wearing out and she agreed reluctantly to join Dad at the health care center.

She asked to be placed in a separate room down the same hall. She knew that if she were in the room with Dad, he would think she still had her good health and would ask her to do things for him. She was unable to care for even herself. She visited Dad in her wheelchair.

Dad died at age 89. Mother, herself 90, went to the church for the funeral service, but the hot, humid weather and her frail condition precluded her going to the cemetery.

In delicate health most of her life, neither she nor her family had expected her to outlive her robust husband. She had had a steady faith in God, and she was ready to go whenever he called her. As I thought about it, she was more than ready. She must have welcomed it.

"She was a loving mother, giving us hugs and kisses," Paul remembered, as he struggled to regain his composure. "She always gave people the benefit of the doubt. She was never the one to cast the first stone. If she acknowledged a wrongdoing of someone, and that would not be publicly, she would say that he or she probably had some reason for it."

"Did she play with you as children?"

"Oh, yes, I think so. We played Rook and dominoes as kids."

We sat quietly.

"I did a lot of grieving for Dad *before* he died; with Mother I didn't," Paul continued.

"Well, you just go ahead and cry all you want. You know I will understand. I have been through this, too, with my parents."

Gradually, his sobs lessened, and he began saying what he needed to do before leaving the campsite. I started writing a to-do list for both of us.

- Bank (for cash on trip home)
- Look at map (to decide best route home)
- Refund? (Will resort refund unused portion of our week's advance payment?)
- Call hairdresser (I had scheduled a permanent in Mesa for Tuesday)
- Call Marilyn Cross (for hair appointments at home for both Paul and me)
- Jeff Beard (to let him know our plans)
- Water (drinking—get a supply for trip home)
- Mail postcards (already written)
- Garbage
- Gas for MH and Patches
- Get Sprite in small bottles (handy for setting in holders beside driver's and passenger's seats; they have screw tops)
- Unhook battery (of Patches to prepare it for towing)

Shaky, but motivated, Paul got up from the sofa, saying, "I guess one of the first things I must do is tighten the fitting that may have been causing the leak in the bath and put back the vinyl panel on the shower tub." He headed in that direction.

While Paul worked in the bathroom, I went through the motorhome getting it in shape to travel. I did whatever needed doing as I moved around the inside perimeter of the coach. Starting with the bedroom, I unplugged the electric clock, wrapped the cord around it, and put it on the floor near my nightstand. Moving along, I made sure overhead cabinet and wardrobe doors were closed. I put away anything sitting out, like the liquid soap bottle on the kitchen counter.

As I prepared the motorhome, I thought about Mother Beard. As a mother-in-law, she was one of the best. I looked to her as a model of conduct for me to follow with my own daughter-in-law. She never interfered but instead encouraged my desires and ambitions. Tedious at times because she found it difficult to decide, she more than made up for that trait with her tact, generosity, and patient noncriticism of me and others. How much I had to thank her for! Hazel told Paul that their mother had died peacefully, in her sleep. For that, I was glad.

Once Paul completed tightening the fitting on the bathroom pipe, we drove Patches to the laundry area to make telephone calls. Then we drove to the resort office. We learned that since we had paid the lower weekly rate and only two days remained in that week, we were not eligible for a refund.

Back at our campsite, our next-door neighbor offered to put our two bags of garbage out the next day. He stored them beneath the front part of his fifth wheel. It would have been unsightly for us to leave our garbage at our vacant campsite until it was picked up by the resort personnel. In addition, some other camper may be assigned our site once we left it.

As I changed into long cotton pants for the drive homeward, I marveled at how well the Lord provided and how well he worked things out. For one example, I thought of how Susie had come around to our motorhome yesterday afternoon on her adult tricycle delivering the writing class papers. Her unexpected visit had given me an opportunity to hand in my class assignment. Originally, I had planned to drop it by the teacher's campsite on my way from aerobics

Monday morning. In his sovereignty, the Lord helped us work out the details of our lives.

By 10:00, we had completed most of the items on our to-do list. We had made phone calls, checked out the refund, mailed postcards, looked at the map for the best route home, and arranged for garbage pickup. Before leaving Mesa, we would stop at a bank and a gas station. The drinking water machine at the laundry area nearest us was empty, so we decided to look for bottled water on the way home. We'd also pick up Sprite in small bottles en route. The only task left was unhooking the battery in the tow car, which we'd do when we hooked up Patches to the motorhome.

Paul slowly edged the motorhome out of our site. He pulled to the opposite side of the street. Meanwhile, I drove Patches in behind him.

As Paul hooked up the car to the motorhome, two neighboring men watched, giving suggestions. Somehow they knew about Paul's Mother's death. We'd been here only five days and already sensed the kindness and sharing of the community.

With Patches hitched in its towing position, I slid out from behind the steering wheel and into the driver's seat in the motorhome. Meanwhile, Paul walked back to the rear of the tow car and we did the lights check, making sure that the brake and turn-signal lights worked on both vehicles.

Just before Paul pulled away from the roadside, I made sure the refrigerator and freezer doors were locked, the water pump was off, the water heater was off, and the entry door was locked.

After less than a week in the warm Mesa sun, days when we had begun to relax and live the fun life, we drove through the exit of Valle del Oro, headed home. It was 10:17 A.M. I turned back in the passenger seat and took a picture of the resort's flag-adorned entrance. Then pointing the camera ahead, I photographed Superstition Mountain through the windshield. Although I couldn't see the mountain from our particular campsite, I now let its majesty fill me and my camera lens. Too soon, we turned away.

Earlier that morning, I awoke feeling uncertain about what this day would bring. Now I felt sure about two things: one was that

Mother was joyfully at peace, that her suffering was over, and the second was that Mesa had provided the sunshine and creative activities I had envisioned back in Maryland. It was indeed our Shangri-la. In a way, both Mother Beard and we had found our paradises.

Uncertainties hovered, however. Paul wondered how long it would take us to get home. I wondered how long we would drive before stopping to sleep.

· 26 ·

Using
Truck Stops

WE DROVE AWAY FROM Valle del Oro RV
Resort on Monday morning feeling the gamut of emotions. We were
regretful about leaving the warm sunshine and myriad activities that
we had at last discovered in Mesa, sorrowful about the loss of Mother
Beard, relieved that her suffering was over, sorry not to have been
with her during her last hours, glad we could picture her gentle smile
and blessing from our visit before we came west, determined to get
back in time for the visitations and service, and excited about the
challenge of the pilgrimage home.

As we headed toward the business district of Mesa, Paul leaned
forward like an eagle trying to get a bead on its prey, eyes scanning
the street ahead for a gas station.

From habit, he looked for a filling station on our side of the street
so that we didn't have to cross traffic lanes, perhaps holding up vehicles behind us. He looked also at how the station was laid out. Was
the roof over the pumps high enough for the motorhome to pass
under? Did the station provide room to maneuver to and from the gas
pump island? Were the entrance and exit of the station level enough
that the rear hitch on the motorhome would not drag on the ground?

A Mobil station in Mesa fulfilled our requirements. At 10:32
A.M., we bought 30.2 gallons of gasoline at $1.19 a gallon. I logged
our odometer reading: 19,599.

We found a bank near the Mobil station where Paul withdrew $800. He divided it with me. I looked at the watch I had bought in San Antonio—11:00 A.M. and still running.

Clutching a Mesa city map, I called out names of cross streets, which Paul repeated as we reached them. By 11:28 A.M., we found I-10 at Phoenix and headed east. Paul said we had (what else?) a headwind as we faced homeward.

Since leaving our Maryland driveway, we had traveled 3,438 miles south and west. Now we had reversed directions and would go east and north. We would take I-10 through Arizona, New Mexico, and the western part of Texas; then branch north on I-20 through the rest of Texas, Louisiana, and Mississippi; then head north on I-59 in Alabama to I-75 in Tennessee; then follow I-81 through Virginia and West Virginia; and finally take I-70 to our home area in Maryland. Paul concentrated on getting home. It was Monday; visitations at the funeral home would be Friday afternoon and evening. The funeral and burial services would be Saturday afternoon. He would rather have spare time than arrive late or have to hurry. He usually chose a conservative course, often using two nails or screws where many people would use one or choosing the longer route because it was safer than the shortcut.

Meanwhile I thought (hoped) that by traveling in the motorhome we would surely stop to sleep at night. I hoped that Paul wouldn't want to travel around the clock.

With Mesa and Phoenix behind us, Paul drove for about an hour. Suddenly he pulled over to the wide shoulder.

"I need some rest. I've been going on nervous energy. I wanted to get us out of the city and on our route home, but I'd appreciate it if you'd take over for a while."

How grateful we were that I could share the driving. Paul had been wiser than even I had thought when he encouraged me to learn to drive the motorhome. That was the second time this trip that my being able to drive had paid off. The first was when Paul had bursitis in Texas on the way out to Arizona.

Once again, I enjoyed the power of the motorhome's Chevrolet 454 engine as I steered onto the highway. Paul rested in the passenger seat briefly, then fixed a sandwich, and ate it at the dinette table. After an hour or so, he took a turn driving again.

We drove smoothly through Arizona with only occasional sprinkles of rain touching the windshield.

"Do you see that rainbow ahead?" Paul asked.

"Beautiful, isn't it, in the wonderful expanse of this western sky." As we traveled east, we saw other rainbows arcing high above the desert. To us, they symbolized God's peace for Mother Beard and comforted us.

Little whirlwinds, twisting and swirling dust like mini-tornadoes, touched down as we drove through arid areas of Arizona.

"Remember how we meandered on our way out here?" I asked. "How we kinda took our time? How we wanted to find a relaxing place to spend a couple of weeks and then go on to California and come back this way in time to visit Alice and Ray in Arkansas?"

"You can forget that!"

"Yeah, I know—but did you really think we'd fulfill all our hopes that we had when we left home?"

"Well, yes, I thought we'd do all of those things, providing, of course, something like this didn't come up."

"To me, it seemed too good to be true," I said. "I'm not used to all of this leisure; it feels more right to work. I don't mind that the trip's cut short. It's already been an adventure. I imagine Mother would mind our having to hurry home more than we do."

"I'm sure that's right. She never wanted to be a bother to anybody."

I relieved Paul at the wheel again. At 3:37 P.M., I drove into the Chevron truck stop at Willcox, Arizona, to refuel. Since truck stops stay open all night, Paul planned to use them for most of our gasoline fill-ups. Thinking ahead, he said he wanted to buy a directory that would give locations of truck stops across the country.

Paul operated the gas pump outside. Inside the motorhome, I opened the refrigerator door with one hand while holding a bottle of diet, caffeine-free Coca-Cola in the other. Before I knew what had happened, the last piece of sugar-free apple pie and a gallon jug of milk fell out. The milk jug fell to the floor but fortunately didn't spill. The pie, contrarily, landed upside down on the carpet, leaving some of its delicious contents clinging to the refrigerator. Paul had personally selected that pie in the bakery section of a Mesa grocery store. At lunch he had cut in half the last big piece, saving the remainder for later.

"I'm *very* sorry to say that your apple pie fell out of the refrigerator and landed upside down on the rug!" I reported to Paul as he stood outside waiting for the gas tank to fill.

"It *what*? My *good* apple pie!"

"Do you want me to get some kind of pastry in the store here?"

"Yeah. I'll have some later this evening as we drive along."

In the truck stop store, I selected a honey cinnamon bun, Hostess lite cupcakes, and Hostess SnoBalls (my favorite). Paul browsed until he found a directory of truck stops. I enjoyed going into stores at truck stops. They carried all kinds of merchandise that truckers (or tourists like us) might need or want—from travel logs to clothes to souvenirs, like an old-time variety store brought up to date with modern wares. And of course the adjoining restaurants usually served good food because that was especially important to people making their living on the road. Even at home, Paul and I had ferreted out a truck stop, Spangler's, about 40 minutes north of us. When we hadn't used the motorhome for a month, we would exercise it by driving there and enjoying one of their delicious home-cooked meals, usually ending with their delectable chocolate peanut butter cream pie.

By 6:34 P.M., having finished another stint of driving, I lay down on the sofa, my feet almost touching the back of the driver's seat and my head on pillows facing the front of the vehicle. "I'll try to stay rested so I can relieve you."

"Okay. That's great," Paul agreed. He turned his head sideways so I could hear him better. "I'll feel a bit more relaxed after we go the first 500 miles and see how our time's working out." We were in New Mexico, well short of Paul's first 500-mile mark.

"Do you think we'll be stopping at any campgrounds?" I ventured, thinking ahead to researching one in the *Directory*.

"No, definitely not. We'll need to find truck stops instead. I plan to drive days and well into the night. I think the wind will die down in the evening, making driving more pleasant and helping us get better gas mileage. So far we've had mostly headwinds."

I had begun thinking of a tribute for Mother Beard. Months before we had left home, Paul mentioned briefly that Hazel and Elsie might ask me to write something about Mother when the time came. I had held my breath then because, although it was an honor, it seemed a monumental responsibility. I had put it out of my mind.

Now with the actual invitation from Hazel through Paul, my brain began incubating thoughts. Those thoughts moved me to get up from the sofa, go to the dinette table, and "cluster" about her. In clustering, I wrote down everything that came to mind about her, my handwriting shaky from the vibrations of the moving coach. This would help me know what to say and to find a focus on which to build the eulogy. Already I used the creative writing lesson learned from Wanda Lund.

With the clustering paper in front of me, I called to Paul as he drove, "I hope this won't be too hurtful for you, but if you think of things about Mother that you're grateful for, would you tell them to me? I want to possibly work them into the tribute."

"Oh, okay. Since you are already interrupted, would you come up here and plug in the earplug wire to the CB?"

I slid to the end of the dinette seat cushion, lifted myself up, and wobbled forward, hands touching stabilizing places like the kitchen counter and end table. I inserted the plug wire into the hanging CB radio unit. Paul put the other end into his ear and began monitoring one of the channels.

"Where are we?"

"I don't know," Paul replied.

"Oh," I chuckled and so did he.

"I didn't mean to give you a smart answer, but I really don't know. I assume, according to the gas tank, maybe 120 or 115 miles west of El Paso," Paul added.

I settled in again at the dinette table. I tried to think of funny happenings about Mother Beard. She enjoyed humor and liked people to have fun, but she was not a laughing-out-loud kind of person.

Miles went by. My paper became so filled that I squeezed in between handwritten lines such thoughts as "Nothing was too much trouble. Projects thoroughly completed." We entered a rest area for supper; I put aside the clustering.

Paul turned on the auxiliary generator at the dash and went outside to check the tires on both vehicles. By the time he got back, I had set the table, filled the water tumblers, prepared two frozen entrees in the microwave oven, and added two individual servings of applesauce. Paul said the blessing. Eating brought a few grateful moments of normalcy and stillness.

We lost no time in getting back on I-10.

At 8:15 on this dark, windy Monday evening, we stopped for gas at a Truck Stops of America station in Las Cruces, New Mexico. With steady driving and taking turns, we had come about 400 miles since leaving Mesa this morning. I began to understand Paul's need to see how long it took to go 500 miles.

Again at the wheel, I gained access to I-10 after which Paul announced he was going to the bathroom. "If I don't come out, look for me," he shouted from midship.

"Okay," I chuckled.

We would always remember this day: Monday, February 26, the day that Mother Beard died. We'd traveled a good day's drive toward home, but where would we reach the 500 milestone, and would we camp tonight?

I continued driving on that dark Monday night. Our motorhome's headlights revealed I-10 as a four-lane highway with a median strip. Tiny reflective raised pavement markers (Botts dots) imbedded in the centerline and both edges of the two lanes came at me like comets. Red tail lights of cars faded ahead after they passed me.

Behind me in the motorhome, Paul came out of the bathroom. He looked in the top drawer of the pullout pantry for the pastries I bought earlier. He settled at the dinette table for a snack and then joined me up front, reclining in the passenger seat.

At 9:47 P.M., off exit 37 on the edge of El Paso, just inside the westernmost border of Texas, I pulled into a huge truck stop. Driving around its perimeter, I noticed several motorhomes parked for the night. My hopes for such a restful pause leaped up.

Paul motioned me past that area, however, and we parked near an enormous tractor trailer headed out of the truck stop. I yawned. "Are we going to park here for the night?"

"No, sir! I'm just stopping here to look for another one of those truck stop books!"

"How are you doing? I mean about Mother," I asked gently as he swiveled the passenger seat toward me in order to get up from it.

"Oh, better than I expected. It'll probably hit me once we get home and I have more time to think. Right now, I'm just thinking about getting home on time and hoping the weather stays okay and we don't have any unexpected problems that delay us," replied Paul hastily. He headed for the truck stop store where he would also look for the bottles of Sprite that we'd been unable to find since leaving the resort in Mesa.

As I waited for him to return, I knew I was ready to stop for a few hours. I liked being responsive to my biological clock. How heavenly it would be to join the other RV campers parked here for the night. Yet I dared not let myself stray too far from Paul's thinking; he had enough weighing on his mind and heart.

Paul returned, but without the Sprite or the second truck stop directory that he hoped would give a more detailed description of locations and services, and we moved on.

I catnapped on the sofa, trying to be ready for my next driving round. Paul, on the other hand, couldn't sleep or even rest on the sofa because he found the sofa ride too bumpy. Instead, he reclined in the passenger seat during his breaks from driving. At times, I too relaxed there.

On we went into Monday night, sometimes in silence, sometimes talking about the traffic or where we were. A little after midnight, we stopped at Van Horn, Texas, for gasoline and went from mountain time into central. This meant that we lost an hour and that the time there was 1:04 A.M. Going into the truck stop store and restaurant, we treated ourselves—a hot dog for Paul and a chili dog for me. I also bought a loaf of bread, a box of corn flakes, and a gallon of drinking water. Our odometer read 20,160; we had come 561 miles since leaving Valle del Oro in Mesa. Although we had achieved the first 500 miles, Paul didn't suggest we stop to sleep.

· 27 ·

Tuesday's Travel

LIKE NIGHT OWLS, Paul and I continued our flight toward Maryland as Monday became Tuesday. The miles passed beneath us as we cruised at 50 miles per hour instead of 55 because of decreased visibility in the darkness. We left I-10 and took I-20, a more northerly route through Texas. I carefully avoided saying so to Paul, but I continued to wonder if we would stop to get some real rest time. Although Paul was a light sleeper, he had a lot of stamina in crisis situations. I was a sound sleeper and thought I needed regular snoozing to keep up my energy, which was why I tried to rest as much as possible when I wasn't driving. Paul endured much longer turns at the wheel than I. I couldn't seem to drive much longer than an hour and a half at a stretch before my eyes and body got really fatigued.

At 4:53 A.M., Tuesday, February 27, we stopped for gasoline at Big Springs, Texas. While there, we also looked for LP gas because our tank was getting low from the refrigerator using it while we were on the road. Sure, the refrigerator also would run on electricity from the auxiliary generator, which we could turn on going down the road, but using the generator would mean that we would have to stop more often for gasoline.

"Most truck stops just don't handle LP gas—not enough calls for it, I guess," commented Paul when we found that none was available there.

"That seems unbelievable to me," I said as I reached for the *National Truck Stop Directory*. Finding propane listed as a heading, I scanned the chart to see if it was available at any truck stops on our route. It surprised me that most truck stops didn't offer it. Some states, like North Dakota, were more likely to offer it than other states, such as Texas. "So what do we do?" I asked.

"Get some at a campground. When it gets light, we'll look for a campground near the highway," said Paul.

I swiveled the passenger seat and stepped down to the sofa where I snuggled under the brown wool afghan that my grandmother had crocheted more than 20 years ago while sitting in her rocking chair in the living room at home. I dozed until Paul woke me. "The sun's coming up. You can get up now and look for a campground with LP gas."

Like a robot, I threw back the afghan, reached for my glasses on the seat of the small swivel chair, and yawned my way to the passenger seat. Neither of us had changed clothes during the night. "Where should I look?"

"Somewhere around Abilene, I'd say," Paul answered.

"Is that in Texas? I never heard of an Abilene in Texas. I've heard of Abilene, Kansas, where Eisenhower lived."

"I think you'll find it on the Texas map," Paul tenderly assured me. How did he know so much? I mused.

A KOA campground was listed in the *Trailer Life Directory* at Abilene, off I-20 on our route east. Paul drove into it and I went sluggishly into the office to ask. My legs seemed leaden but my mind was awake. Soon a man directed Paul to the LP gas area and filled our tank. With this accomplished, Paul turned the driving privileges over to me since he had driven from midnight to dawn.

After getting back on I-20, I looked for the next rest area, where we stopped for breakfast. Afterward, Paul dropped into the passenger seat, turned the seat lever, and settled into its reclining position to try to sleep.

I drove along, simply being sure to stay on I-20, Paul's only instructions. I thought about Mother Beard and the tribute, my mind automatically clustering.

The arrow on the fuel gauge crept toward the one-fourth mark. I stopped so Paul could refuel at Weatherford, near Fort Worth, Texas. It was late morning, 11:39 A.M. central time. Paul drove again.

Since Paul wanted to keep driving while he ate lunch instead of pulling into the parking area of a truck stop or a rest area, he turned on the auxiliary generator so that I could use the microwave oven to fix lunch while we moved along. That was Tuesday noon. He was making every effort to get home by Thursday (36 hours away!), and I didn't want to interfere with his efforts.

When Paul drove around Dallas, he munched on a ham and cheese sandwich. I sat at the dinette table eating an orange, having already finished my sandwich.

"Are you enjoying your lunch, Miss Daisy?" Paul asked congenially, turning his head sideways and smiling toward me as he steered.

"Oh, yes!" I giggled. We both had enjoyed *Driving Miss Daisy* at the movies on Sunday in Mesa. (He inferred that he was the chauffeur, Hoke Colburn, and I was Miss Daisy. Morgan Freeman and Jessica Tandy starred in the major roles of the award-winning film.)

After lunch, still at the dinette table, I drafted a first attempt at the tribute for Mother Beard, using my earlier clustering notes. With the vehicle going over road strips and bumps, my handwriting looked scribbled, large, and shaky. Two hours passed quickly; five handwritten pages accumulated. At 2:08 P.M., I relieved Paul from driving, surprisingly invigorated by the writing session.

By 3:45 P.M., we stopped at a National truck stop in Louisiana. After I recorded (as usual) the time, odometer reading, and gasoline purchase information in the motorhome logbook, I calculated that it had taken us about 18 hours to travel the 826 miles across Texas. No wonder we had thought we would never get out of that state on the way west!

Continuing on I-20, Paul asked from behind the wheel, "Where are we now, dear, I mean in relation to where we want to be?"

From the passenger seat as I had done many times on the trip, I reached for the U.S. map that I kept folded to the relevant section and ready to grab from on top of the dashboard. I pointed to where we were on the map. "So far we've come this far. Here is Mesa and here is home."

"Looks like we're about halfway," he commented, looking quickly between the road ahead and the map several times.

"I'd say so. Great!"

At 5:00 on that Tuesday evening, we drove into a busy 76 Unocal truck stop. We didn't need gasoline, but we did need a telephone to call Hazel and many rest areas didn't offer these. As we ate in the dinette in the motorhome, we watched people and vehicles coming and going at the large complex that provided fuel, food, and goods. For a break in driving, we visited the sizable Unocal store as if it were a museum, each pursuing our own interests. Paul and I met at the cash register. He had an electric light fixture with switch that he wanted to install in a small, dark, outside compartment of the motorhome that housed the lever he pulled when dumping, another truck stop directory, and a wood tire knocker (for hitting each tire to see if it sounded solid or whether it might be leaking air). I had found a western-style shirt for Nancy who owned a horse and pony and rode (the horse) western style.

While I took our purchases to the motorhome, Paul went to the outside telephones to call Hazel. I soon joined him.

I wondered how Hazel was handling both her mastectomy and Mother's death. In addition, she was the personal representative (the term our lawyer used for the role of executrix) for Mother Beard's estate. While Mother had been living in the health care center, Hazel was the main one who handled her financial, health care, and personal needs.

To my relief, Hazel's voice sounded strong and cheerful. She told me that Al, her minister husband, had agreed to handle the details of the service and give the sermon since Mother's regular pastor was away. I told her I would be honored to speak about Mother at the service and asked if she could give me some idea of how long it should be. She turned me over to Al, who gave a clear, precise rundown of the service. Stephen Guyer, Hazel and Al's older son, and I would each give "words of memory," as Al was calling the eulogies. He told me that all six grandchildren would participate in the service.

After giving a few more details about the times of the service, interment, and fellowship meal afterward, Al turned me back to Hazel. Having previously discussed it with Paul, I offered to have out-of-town members of the family come to a buffet supper at our house Friday between the afternoon and evening visitations at Pritts Funeral Home. Hazel sounded pleased, saying she had hoped they wouldn't have to go to a local restaurant. I asked Hazel who would be coming to supper so that I'd know how to plan.

Feeling relieved about Hazel's health and more in touch with the arrangements, I returned with Paul to the motorhome. Now that I had officially committed myself to the words of memory, my mind continued to work on them. As Paul drove, I lay propped against pillows on the sofa, with pencil and paper ready to write thoughts that came to mind. Darkness came a second night as we drove on; I used a small penlight to see as I wrote.

At 10:39 P.M. Tuesday, we stopped for gas in Vicksburg, Mississippi, and I took a shift at driving until about midnight. Then Paul drove as I slept, fully clothed, on the sofa behind him. I had laid my eyeglasses on the floor under the table across from me.

Asleep for a while, I roused as the coach slowed and then stopped. "I just can't go any farther. We're going to stop here so I can get some sleep!" Paul said.

"Do you want me to drive while you sleep?" I offered sleepily, hoping I could stay where I was on the sofa.

"No," he said, "I can't sleep with the coach moving. I'm going back to sleep on the bed."

"Where are we?"

"At a welcome center parking area in Alabama. We were lucky to get the last parking space. It's about 2:00 in the morning," Paul answered as he walked past the sofa toward the bedroom. I heard a soft crunch of metal under his foot.

"Is there anything I can get for you?" I asked, worried about how he managed to keep going.

"No, just some sleep. I'll just sleep for a little while. I'll be all right," his voice came from the bedroom.

I reached for my glasses in the dark and ran my fingers over the lenses. Not broken. When I tried them on, however, they felt cock-eyed. Too sleepy to pursue it, I told myself that, if necessary, I could wear my prescription sunglasses that lay in the glove compartment.

We both drifted off.

Barely more than an hour later, Paul came forward.

"Shall I drive for a while?" I asked again from the sofa.

"No, I'm okay now. I just needed to get some real sleep," he said.

Tuesday had been a 24-hour day of travel, bringing us better than halfway home. In spite of erratic sleep periods, we both seemed to be holding our own in energy and positive attitudes. Wednesday promised to be another long travel day. As I drifted off again on the sofa, questions filled my mind. I wondered how my glasses would fit, whether we would stop to camp anytime, how Paul was feeling about his Mother's death, and when we would get home.

Making Lists

BY 5:20 A.M. WEDNESDAY, February 28, we pulled into another truck stop, this one at Tuscaloosa, Alabama, ready for another gulp of gasoline to take us homeward. Just when we would arrive home was a mystery to me. At that point, I didn't even guess—I didn't want to disappoint myself. It would be sometime Thursday, which gave me a kind of déjà vu. I had gone through a similar mystery before we left home on this trip: knowing our departure would be Thursday but not knowing the exact time. We both concentrated on keeping up our momentum on the road and our good cheer with one another. My glasses were definitely out of alignment but wearable. Another lesson learned: put my glasses where they will not be stepped on.

It was still dark outside, but it was fun to be awake when most of the world slept. As we entered the well-lighted store of the truck stop, I felt a special camaraderie with workers and other travelers.

Truck stops provided little time-outs for truckers and travelers where they could stop and be refreshed in body and spirit. They offered a change of pace and place, a bright oasis of activity in the night. For a few moments, you could forget who you were and where you were going as you browsed among the potpourri of wares and people.

As we left, I drove while Paul reclined in the passenger seat. "Let's see. Where is that map you used to show how far we've come? Oh, yeah, here it is," he said as he leaned forward and retrieved the U.S. map. "I figure we're now about two-thirds of the way home."

"That's encouraging."

"Yeah. Sure is," he agreed, and he reclined again for some sleep.

At 9:15 A.M., with Paul now behind the wheel and me at the dinette table barely noticing scenery flashing past the motorhome, I scrawled more notes for the words of memory. I put in more than I needed, knowing that I would edit and shorten the eulogy later.

Besides working on the tribute, I began a to-do list for when we got home. I knew I might get rattled by the emotional and social activities once we got home, so I wrote down items that came to me.

- Call Jeff/Nancy (to let them know we are home)
- Call Jane, Jean, and Alice (my sisters to let them know about Mother Beard's death)
- Call supermarket—order platters of meat, vegetables, and fruit
- Call Pritts—private visit to funeral home
- Prepare tribute on computer
- Clean house
- Set dining room table (for Friday evening's buffet guests)
- Shop for groceries
- Fix eyeglasses

I made a separate list with the heading "Buffet Supper—Friday"

- 16 people possible
- 16 at dining room table
- Breakfast table for buffet food
- Paper plates—dinner size
- Plastic knives, forks, & spoons—large
- Paper cups—hot and cold
- Napkins—dinner size
- Deli—veg. platter for 16-20
- Fruit platter for 16-20
- Meat platter for 16-20
- Small hamburger rolls
- Stick margarine
- Mustard

- Coffee
- Block ice cream & paper plates
- Cookies—soft sugar
- Choc. chip
- Ice
- Sodas—Root Beer
- Sprite
- Coke

At the bottom of the list, I added everyday items, such as milk and cereal, that we would need to restock our refrigerator and pantry at home.

I felt much more organized by 11:23 A.M. Wednesday as we stopped at an Exxon station between Chattanooga and Dayton, Tennessee, on I-75. We "lost" another hour, having driven through central into eastern time.

As we drove away, I said excitedly to Paul from the passenger seat, "Guess what that last gas mileage was?"

"I don't know. We've had more winds at night than I expected. That was one reason I wanted to drive at night—to gain more mileage because I thought the wind would have died down."

"Well, wind or no, it was 7.207!" Our first mileage on this dream journey had been only 5.55 miles per gallon.

"Terrific! They said we should get better mileage after the coach is broken in, so I guess we can expect better mileage."

Keeping the motorhome log helped me keep track of the days and dates. That was Wednesday, February 28, 11:49 A.M. eastern time. It was about 55 degrees and partly sunny.

Soon we stopped at a rest area to eat lunch. As we sat at the dinette table, Paul said he felt better about our progress toward home. I asked gently if he wanted to talk about how he was feeling about his mother's passing.

"Overall, good. I know it's the best thing that could happen to her. You have the initial feeling of shock, but then you look at it as a real blessing. I don't see how you can look at it any other way. I'm not angry at anybody, including God," Paul said.

I told him I was glad he felt that way and gave an inward sigh of relief. Driving home day and night was stress enough without also carrying a heavy burden of sorrow.

He had had only two or three catnaps of an hour or so each in the reclining passenger seat and a brief time of "real" sleep when he stretched out on the bed once. I didn't see how he continued physically. I had driven a lot, but not as much as he had. I could fall sleep easily and promptly on the sofa even as we traveled over roads with potholes and bumps. Usually when I got up from such a nap, I felt refreshed. But Paul had always been a light sleeper, often finding it difficult to get to sleep and then rousing easily.

"As we ride along, I have been reliving some past experiences involving Mother, going over various memories of things that happened with her in my lifetime," Paul added.

"I like to do that with memories of my parents. It's a healing connection for me," I commented.

"But I'm still not sure how I will react when I see the body," Paul cautioned.

After lunch, I splashed my face with cold water and applied makeup according to my usual custom when getting up in the morning (now it was noon and I was off schedule). On Monday night, I hadn't washed my face, showered, or changed clothes. On Tuesday night, I brushed my teeth during one stop and basin-washed during another, changing clothes. Since my face hadn't been made up since its wash on Tuesday night, it was ready for a cold splash and cosmetics.

I drove the next leg. Now that I knew how Paul felt about his mother's death, had talked with Hazel and Al about the funeral service, was getting a handle on the tribute to Mother, and had made the to-do lists, I felt more in control, more focused. Paul estimated we would be home sometime the next morning.

As we traveled, Paul and I recalled things we had seen on that same route in late January when we drove south. So far, we had not had any rainy or bad weather as we hurried home, for which I thanked God.

By 4:06 P.M., we were in Bristol, Tennessee, getting gasoline again. Normally, we avoided buying snacks as we traveled. On this homeward trek, for a change of activity and scene, we both went into the stores at truck stops and came out with our favorite pastries. At that stop, I found two packs of Hostess SnoBalls, a rarity on this trip. Finding them was fun, like a treasure hunt; they must be a hot item.

More gas went into our tank at 9:11 P.M., north of Lexington, Virginia. As Paul drove, I wrote more notes for Mother's tribute. I thought of her patience in living with painful arthritis and an aging body. Yet she had smiled, made wry comments, and apologized when she needed assistance. "I never thought I would have a hearing problem and be so crippled up," I remembered her saying. Her keen, intelligent mind and excellent memory were disciplined by education. Although very much a presence among us, she never interfered and didn't try to run our lives.

The calendar turned to Thursday, March 1. Shortly after midnight, we arrived at the Panhandle 76 Auto-Truck Stop (Unocal) in Martinsburg, West Virginia—almost home! After getting gasoline, we celebrated having come this far by eating a meal in the restaurant.

We chose a booth inside the brightly lit dining area, a distinct contrast to the black velvet night outside. We ordered a full, hot dinner, strange for us at this middle-of-the-night hour.

"Can you believe we're almost home?" I exclaimed to Paul.

"Well, we have a way to go yet."

"How many miles?

"Oh, I'd say about seventy. We should be home by dawn."

"Dawn? Before that I would think."

"Well, it depends on weather and traffic and nothing happening to the vehicles."

"Can you believe the difference between the bad weather we had going to Mesa and how we haven't run into any rain or snow on the way back? I'm so thankful. I feel like the Lord is very much with us."

"Yep. I'd say so. We've had much more wind than I expected but no rain or fog so far."

I looked around the restaurant.

"I wonder what brings other people in here at this hour. Maybe some of them are traveling home on a mission like ours. I didn't realize so much activity went on at night in these truck stops," I rambled.

"I'm not surprised. The trucking industry is quite large. Truckers can make good time traveling at night."

We finished our meal and returned to the motorhome. "Do you want me to drive?" I asked, feeling tired and not sure I was up to the task but wondering how Paul could be either.

"No, I think I can manage." Then I realized that probably only severe pain could have kept Paul from piloting us home on the last portion of our flight.

In darkness, the miles flew by. My eyelids kept closing. I wondered how Paul could keep going but was thankful that he did. We reached Frederick, then Taneytown, about ten miles from home. In Taneytown, Paul drove into the huge parking lot at the shopping center on the east edge of town. Its bright yellow lights provided illumination to unhook the tow car. No other vehicles or people moved about. The unhooking done, in cold, sleep-chasing air, I managed to doggedly drive Patches the last lap of the trip as Paul followed in the motorhome.

At 3:45 A.M., Thursday, March 1, after traveling day and night from Mesa, Arizona, I steered Patches into the main driveway, and Paul guided the motorhome into its driveway. As at the beginning of our dream journey, it was just the two of us in our own time, at our own pace. We had traveled 2,506 miles since leaving Valle del Oro RV Resort 65½ hours ago. Of the $800 cash Paul had withdrawn at the bank in Mesa, we had spent $610 on the way home, of which $468.16 was for gasoline alone.

Feeling like a swimmer rising wet and heavy out of water, yet momentarily revived by the excitement of being home, I walked slowly through the garage and into the hallway. "Hello, house. We're home!" I continued into the dining room, looked into the living room, and surveyed the kitchen. How neat everything looked. Had some-

"I steered Patches into the main driveway, and Paul guided the motorhome into its driveway."

one been through and cleaned? How would the house look in daylight? It seemed big, unmoving.

When Paul entered, I asked,

"Are you going to take a shower?"

"No, sir! I'm going straight to bed," he announced, heading for our room at the front part of the house. That decided it for me, too.

As my body settled itself for sleep, my mind moved to God. I thanked him for safe travel in the comfort of the motorhome from midmorning Monday in Mesa to this early Thursday morning in Maryland. I prayed for his help today too.

· 29 ·

Reflecting

AROUND NOON on Thursday, with sunshine turning the opaque pleated shades to ivory, I woke up in our bedroom at home. Stillness. As I walked toward the bathroom, my posture upright, I missed the sway of the motorhome. I still had my "sea legs" I guess.

We were home at least three weeks earlier than we had expected. I postponed reflecting on our journey—whether it was a dream come true or whether the unsettling questions that I had just before leaving home had been warranted. Paul's and my thoughts centered on Mother Beard, her death, and the visitations and services to come.

The to-do lists made on the way home helped to focus my activities. Even before eating, I called my supermarket's delicatessen to order food for the next day's buffet supper.

The part that Paul had dreaded most in Mesa—seeing his mother's lifeless body—turned into a tranquil moment in Maryland. About 5:00, we stepped to the front door of the handsome, colonial-style funeral mansion in Westminster. It was locked. Paul pressed the bell. Ms. Pritts, daughter of the owners, invited us inside.

We walked slowly with her toward a softly lighted arena in the far alcove of an enormous room. Banks of beautiful flowers silhouetted the open, satin-lined lid of the casket. Paul first saw his mother as he was talking quietly with Ms. Pritts. They discussed questions that he and Hazel had talked about on the telephone. The flowers, the satin, and the quiet conversation softened the harsh reality for Paul.

I could tell that he liked the way she looked—peaceful, smiling, in beautiful pink chiffon, a color that Dad had liked her to wear. She had worn a pink sweater the last time we saw her in the health care center before our journey.

We left the funeral home realizing Paul had dealt with the moment without tears, surprising himself. At home, I worked on keying the Words of Memory into the computer and printing them.

The next morning, Friday, I prepared the house for the buffet supper. Because I had thoroughly cleaned the house just before we left and since no one had used it in the meantime, I had only light cleaning to do. Paul and I picked up large platters of fruit, meats and cheeses, and vegetables with dip from the supermarket in Westminster, thankfully at the time they promised.

At the afternoon viewing, I found a few quiet moments when Al, Hazel, and Stephen could read my Words of Memory for any changes they might suggest.

On Saturday afternoon, Paul and I walked solemnly with the family from the library entrance into the sanctuary of the Westminster Church of the Brethren for the Celebration of the Life of Anna Marie Engler Beard. As a group, we sat in the front two rows, feeling the support of a host of loving friends and family already gathered.

Paul Guyer, a grandson of Mother Beard's and an organist, was playing the prelude. He chimed the hour from the console.

Al Guyer, minister and son-in-law, already seated in the chancel, stepped to the pulpit and led the Affirmation of Life memorial service. Our son, Jeff, gave his invocation from the lectern. Susan Lowry Hare and Sharon Lowry Lally, granddaughters, each read a meaningful passage from the Old Testament. A family friend and accomplished soprano, Julia Hitchcock, sang "In My Father's House Are Many Mansions."

Next it was my turn. I spoke about Mother Beard's patience and understanding as she and Dad Beard reared four children, her activities in church and community groups, and her caring for her mother and others in her home. I illustrated her sense of humor and told about her last birthday party with streamers and balloons and presents. I said she was patient, smiling, dependable, accepting, forgiving, understanding, generous, even-tempered, strong, and dignified—all those things and so much more. I ended by saying that she was our touchstone for high moral values and Christian virtues.

Stephen Guyer followed me at the pulpit. In his tribute, he said that he thought of his grandmother's intangible gifts to him when he needed to remind himself that there was dignity, tolerance, and patience in this world and that kindness didn't need to be difficult.

Cameron Lowry, completing the participation of the grandchildren, read 1 Corinthians 15:39–46.

Al's sermon, "Assurances from Unlikely Sources," comforted us. With his usual humorous touch, he helped us place the moment in context with Mother's wishes. He referred to her sensitive spirit, strong faith in her church, hospitality, acceptance of others, patience, and her love and commitment to Christ.

Following prayers, a congregational hymn, and the benediction, Paul Guyer played the postlude.

The funeral procession led to Pipe Creek Cemetery, near Uniontown, Maryland, about 15 minutes away. There, Mother Beard's body was interred beside her husband, John P. W. Beard. They had been married 69 years before his death three years earlier.

We returned to the church for the fellowship meal and social time with family and friends. Paul held up well, sustained I'm sure by all the words of comfort and sympathy. Later, Paul and I joined the aunts, uncles, and cousins (all of whom lived out of town) at Nancy and Jeff's new house in the country, where we began to refocus our lives by exploring their home and looking at or riding the horse and pony.

By the following Wednesday, March 7, I wrote in my journal.

I'm finding that the same discipline I learned to use in the motorhome, that is, forcing myself to do whatever was necessary, works well here at home. I have watched very little television and have concentrated on priorities. At first, those tasks dealt with Mother Beard's funeral. The following Monday, they included getting a permanent at the hairdresser's and taking many rolls of slides to the camera shop. After lunch and a nap, I carried in notebooks, files, and summer clothes from the motorhome.

The week following our return rushed by. Paul drove the motorhome to a local dumping station and emptied the gray and black water holding tanks. I brought into the house more items from the motorhome, including all the food except sugar and salt. Flour tended to quickly taste old so I brought it into the house to use and started out the next trip with fresh foods. But paper products, laundry powder, cleaning products, and nonperishables stayed in the motorhome. My last armload included my grandmother's brown afghan, hand towels, tea towels and dishcloths from the kitchen, and the red umbrella that Paul tilted over himself as he hooked up the tow car on the rainy morning that we had left town.

Our trip log revealed that we had driven 5,939 miles in the motorhome, from Maryland to Louisiana to Arizona and back to Maryland. It took 36 days, averaging 164.9 miles a day. We spent $2,656.55 cash, or about $73.79 per day. The cost of gasoline was $1,128.07, or an average of $1.1469 per gallon, and our motorhome averaged 6.04 miles per gallon.

I thought of all those questions that had raced through my mind before we left home. I needn't have worried. For as we traveled, I continued to feel a part of our Maryland community through telephone calls to Jeff, sending postcards to family and friends at home, and the FMCA message service. No one even hinted that we had run away from community service. In fact, people commented on how sorry they were that we had to make such a hurried trip home. We all agreed that that's just the way it is.

I didn't get homesick. In the role of tourist, meeting new people came naturally. The mail arrangements worked well, with Jeff discussing anything important with us by telephone each week. Even my ivy plant did fine in the limited sunshine of the basement.

I learned to use the laptop computer as we rode along and also to find stretches of time when I could be alone to write.

An unexpected benefit had come from our trip in the motorhome. Paul and I grew closer after 41 years of marriage; our love deepened. We became more alert to and respectful of the feelings, desires, likes, and dislikes of one another. In addition, Paul learned to plan, and I learned to share with him what before I had thought was either too private or too unimportant for him.

I had wondered if we would really like traveling in a motorhome. Without question, we both loved it. As for driving with a car in tow, I hardly knew the vehicle was behind me.

In the end, we did indeed find the sunny paradise we had sought, although our stay in Mesa, Arizona, was short-lived.

I had looked forward to many things on this trip: time on the road in our motorhome, just the two of us, without the demands of returning to a job; new scenes to see as we traveled; the freedom of being away from schedules at home; adventure; warmer weather than in Maryland; a good time; and inviting campgrounds. And they all were realized. In addition, the motorhome itself responded well, even during its marathon trip home.

It is hard to describe the affinity I feel for that traveling machine. I just know that when I step up into it, worries and anxieties leave, and in their place comes excitement about being in it and on the road again.

During our dream journey, Mother Beard's health concerned us, but we would have had that at home as well. I continue to sense her engaging spirit. In my mind's eye, I see her smile at us encouragingly, with a bit of excitement in her voice, as she says, "And where will you go next?"

Where, indeed? Already, we're dreaming of future adventures.

Epilogue

THE WRIST WATCH that I bought for $4.99 at the KOA store in San Antonio, Texas, worked faithfully. I replaced it a few years later only when the face became filled with dust, making the digits illegible.

An optician tried to straighten the frames on my eyeglasses, which Paul had stepped on accidentally en route home when I had foolishly laid them on the floor, but they never really fit well again. The next time I had to change lenses, I bought new frames as well. It kept me up to date with frame fashions.

A year after our trip, the *Trailer Life Campground/RV Park & Services Directory* added a third category to its rating system for campgrounds. Besides completeness of facilities and cleanliness and physical characteristics of rest rooms and showers, it added scenic and environmental quality.

As the technology became available, the Family Motor Coach Association completely automated its message service. Using the automated service, my family may call a toll-free number and leave me a message (as many as 31 per month), and I may call the toll-free number and listen to their message (as many as 31 times per month).

My most difficult questions to answer about owning a motor-home were those I had at the national park in Virginia when Paul and I were trying out a rented vehicle before buying one. After owning one for several years, I've found most of the answers.

1. Would a motorhome bring its own problems, like a swimming pool may draw "friends" you never knew you had? It turned out that after the initial excitement of showing our new vehicle to people, nobody asked to borrow it or travel with us, and we did not invite anyone. No one else has used our motorhome. When we had a houseful of wedding guests or vacationers, *we* stayed in the motorhome. It came in handy to transport bridesmaids gowns when our son got married and to chauffeur more friends than a car would hold.

   To some owners, maintenance may be a problem. To Paul, the motorhome is his hobby. He enjoys maintaining it, doing most of the regular maintenance of changing the oil and filters himself. He has a close working rapport with Thom Beckley, of Endless Summer RV's near Frederick, Maryland, who provides maintenance that requires shop attention. He also feels free to call the manufacturer of our coach, Holiday Rambler, in Wakarusa, Indiana. They have always been friendly and accommodating in both information and service. Paul sees each problem as a challenging opportunity to learn more about the vehicle. In addition, he invariably has a customizing project on the go, such as installing wall switches so that we don't have to reach up to a ceiling light to turn it on.

2. Where would we park a motorhome? We made a second driveway with a concrete pad for the motorhome. This new driveway lies on the opposite side of our house from the regular driveway. The motorhome is convenient yet out of our normal traffic pattern.

3. Are we foolish to consider an expenditure of this size—perhaps $60,000–$80,000? After examining our income and assets, I could see that spending this amount on a motorhome would not be foolhardy for us.

4. Later in our retirement, would the motorhome be an outdated monster and cause us painful financial loss? It's too soon to answer this question because we continue to travel in and enjoy

the motorhome. We have had it eight years now, continually customizing it, and don't plan to sell or upgrade anytime soon.

Unlike a home property that appreciates, however, a motorhome rapidly depreciates. Nevertheless, I'm rationalizing depreciation as part of the cost of travel in this comfortable manner. Right now, far from being a white elephant during our retirement, the motorhome is a white knight in shining armor as it adds zest to our everyday lives, saving us from a stay-at-home, mundane existence. I feel its special appeal every time I step up into it, an appeal that makes me smile inside and out. That's worth a lot!

5. Is it a sin to spend money on a second home when some people are homeless and starving? This question gnawed at me for a long time. I have concluded, however, that one cannot hold dollar bills in one's hand and think: Shall I buy a motorhome or shall I give this money to a homeless, starving person? The question is not that simple. It involves looking at one's total income and deciding what percentage to give to charity and what percentage to

"We continue to travel in and enjoy the motorhome."

keep for savings, food, clothes, utilities, maintenance, and recreation.

A long time ago, I decided to give at least 10 percent of my income to charity, which includes homeless, starving people. After giving to charity and handling other budget expenses, I am free to spend the amount I can afford on recreation. After all, recreation is vital to one's well-being.

Today's economy needs our purchases of recreational equipment to create jobs and a living for others. Indeed, our purchase of an RV helps prevent persons from being homeless and starving because our money helps pay their salaries.

Dollarwise, we motorhome owners pay a hefty price for recreational travel, but that money is well spent in human returns. We have met numerous wonderful people in our travels and have participated in service projects from helping buy stained glass windows for a church in Mexico to making apple butter with our local camping group as a fund-raiser for a church camp.

So one cannot think simplistically about this fifth and last question. The answer goes well beyond its seemingly right or wrong, good or bad answer.

Since our journey to Arizona, Paul and I have enjoyed ten trips in our motorhome. The most extensive was a 44-day expedition to Alaska with a recreational vehicle tour group. We also attended the FMCA national conventions in North Dakota and Indiana, the Holiday Rambler Recreational Vehicle Club convention in Missouri, and an annual conference of the Church of the Brethren in Oregon. We visited AmeriFlora in Ohio and relatives in Canada and California; enjoyed Branson, Missouri; spent two winter months in Florida; and toured the beautiful state of Colorado. Between trips, we have camped on weekends with the Westminster Church of the Brethren camping group. We have not yet returned to Mesa, mostly because of going on other long trips, but when we settle down for the winter, Valle del Oro will be at the top of our list.

If I were to list the pros and cons of motorhoming, I would say that the former outnumbers the latter. A benefit that I especially enjoy comes when we visit friends or relatives overnight or for a few days and sleep at night in our own motorhome bed. It saves our hosts the trouble of putting us up while we remain comfortable, and each family has its privacy at night.

To the uninitiated motorhomer, loading and unloading the vehicle, finding one's way, looking for campgrounds, and not having tour guides may seem like drawbacks. However, the veteran motorhomer willingly takes these seeming obstacles in stride. Equipping the RV, navigating, getting lost, and seeking out campgrounds are all part of the adventure, just as gleaning travel information from tour books, other travelers, and tourist centers are part of the pleasant sociability connected with camping. If a person is willing to tackle these challenges, he or she will be rewarded with the joys of this style of travel and recreation.

As I think about traveling in our motorhome, I recognize its tremendous influence on molding my spouse and me into a team. It has helped us talk in its intimate interior, bringing us closer together as we looked at maps, discussed routes, found campgrounds, and shared the peace and sights of the countryside. I cannot help feeling that the motorhome has been and is a special blessing from God.

Our motorhome has brought us into the camping group at church, where we have learned to know and to love camping friends whom we might never have known otherwise. When camping on Sunday mornings, our group either attends a worship service presented by the campground or provides its own. Children and youth as well as the adults take part. In the casual outdoor atmosphere, we've found that we feel less intimidated and freer to pray aloud and read and talk in front of a group; it's a training opportunity for all of us.

Campers everywhere usually turn out to be genuine, down-to-earth people of great value with a common bond of enjoying the outdoors and RV travel.

I eased into motorhoming because of Paul's desire; I am finding it personally life-enhancing and a form of recreation that my husband and I both enjoy. By reading, traveling, observing, asking questions, and experimenting, the mystery of motorhoming unraveled for us. Only its magic remains.

Until we meet again, perhaps on the road when you're traveling *your* way in your motorhome, at your own pace, I wish you well!

Appendix

FOR ADDITIONAL INFORMATION on motorhoming you will find the following in this appendix:
—Questions for Traveling *Your* Way
—What's the Difference?
—RV Types & Terms
—RV and Camping Shows
—Clubs for Campers
—RV Trade Associations
—Directories for Campgrounds
—Publications
—Guides for Buying and Using an RV

Questions for Traveling *Your* Way

Whether you want to see Elvis's Graceland, the Truman or Eisenhower Presidential Libraries, or the Grand Canyon, you can stay in your motorhome in a nearby campground. You have just read how Paul and I traveled our way in our motorhome at our own pace. Following are questions to help you decide if you should do it *your* way in your motorhome at your own pace.

Your Congeniality Factor

- Do you *want* to make traveling with someone else in a motorhome work? Are you willing to work at it?
- Are you willing to be patient, flexible, cheerful, understanding, and complimentary with your traveling companion in the small area of the motorhome?
- Would you like to join a local camping group, one that camps together perhaps once a month during the normal camping season in your area, and thereby come to enjoy and appreciate being a part of it as you make new, congenial friends?
- Are you willing to accept the unspoken tradition that others in your camping group or caravan will not necessarily do the same things that you do at the same time; that camping is freedom to relax, shop, sightsee, work on your vehicle, or whatever; or that

you can invite others but they may just want to keep to themselves or may have already planned to go somewhere with someone else?

Your Comfort Zone

- Are you willing to travel with accommodations that are luxurious compared to a tent?
- Are you claustrophobic to the point that you would be uncomfortable sleeping in a motorhome even though, in addition to the entry doors, it has exit windows at the front and rear and a ceiling vent or fan in the bathroom through which you could see the outdoors?
- Do you get carsick?
- Do you expect everything to be perfect when you travel?
- If you are on a trip of a month or longer, would you want to cover a lot of territory and stay in a different campground every night, which can be exhausting, or would you plan to stay in the same campground two or more nights each week?
- Do you like to stop and sightsee whenever you wish rather than be part of a commercial bus, plane, train, or cruise tour group for the whole trip?
- Are you willing to relax in the same coach at night in which you've been riding all day?
- Are you willing to occupy a smaller space than you have at home?
- Would you enjoy pulling into a rest area and having lunch in your motorhome rather than eating in a restaurant somewhere?
- Would you enjoy conversing and swapping experiences about camping and motorhomes with strangers as if you've known them for 20 years?
- Could you accept that what you choose as your motorhome is right for you and just as satisfying as the vehicle that someone else has chosen?
- Do you believe that you are just as good as the next person, no matter what RV that person has or what you have?
- Are you comfortable or willing to learn more about reading maps and finding your way?

Your Flexibility

- Do you like to take long, lingering showers or would you be amenable to shortening them to save water and gray water holding tank space when camping without hookups to water and sewer?
- Are you willing to be flexible about the amount of space you have to move around in, the campground you choose, or finding your way on your own?
- Do you enjoy meeting other RV travelers and being friendly with them?
- Are you willing to learn through travel books and information centers how to take city or other tours according to your interests?
- Are you flexible enough when riding as the passenger to come out of your reverie and turn off the pump or heater without feeling like a martyr?
- Would you take in stride doing the following:
  - —Loading and unloading food, clothes, and other items?
  - —Traveling in all kinds of weather—rain, snow, tornado warnings, and others?
  - —Traveling through road construction areas?
  - —Preparing meals and/or eating out?
  - —Giving up the luxury of a motel each night?
  - —Shopping for groceries en route?
  - —Hooking and unhooking from water and electricity, and dumping?
  - —Not knowing where you will be staying from one night to the next?
  - —Realizing that no trip will ever be totally perfect in your view and instead enjoying its high moments and seeing its humor?
  - —Adjusting your normal home routine to traveling on the road?

Your Bathroom

- Are you or is someone who will travel in your motorhome a "two-hours-in-the-bathroom" person who would tie up that area when someone else wants to use it?
- Would you like a split bath (with a toilet in one part and a shower/tub in another across the aisle) or would you like them all in one area?
- Would you like faucets that have mixer valves so that you can easily adjust the temperature of the water?

Your Bedroom

- What kind of bed are you comfortable in—twin, double, or queen size?
- Would you be able to cope with making a bed that was against the wall at the head and one side or would you find it easier to make an island bed where you could walk around its two sides and end?
- Do you want to sleep with a window above your head that may allow a draft to flow down on you?
- Would you like a side or central aisle that leads from the living area to the bedroom?
- Would you like a separate bedroom area so that at the end of the day you do not have to make up the bed but it is already waiting?

Your Kitchen/Dinette

- Do you use a lot of ice cubes so that you would want an automatic icemaker that would be separate from the freezer?
- Do you drink hot beverages so that you would want an automatic coffee maker installed in the kitchen or dining area?
- Do you enjoy toast with your meals and therefore would like a toaster oven installed in the kitchen or dining area?
- Is the dinette area large enough for the number of people you plan to travel with?
- Would you like slide-out shelves in the pantry or a slide-out pantry so that you can easily see and select food?

- Would you like (1) one air conditioner in the front of the coach, (2) two air conditioners—one in the front and one in the bedroom, or (3) central air conditioning?
- Would you like a ceiling fan that automatically draws in outside air when the coach gets too warm and shuts off when it rains?

Your Storage Space

- Do you enjoy wearing a lot of different clothes and would therefore require a lot of wardrobe space, including both short and full-length closets?
- Would you like to have a space for file folders and office supplies and for a computer and printer?
- Would you like outside storage space for items such as baby strollers, highchairs, golf gear, lawn chairs, tools, toys, and other items too large for storing inside or not normally used inside the motorhome?
- Do you require a clean towel every day, which would take up a lot of storage space for which you would need to plan?
- Would you like to take enough clothes along on a two- or three-week trip so that you would not have to do laundry and would therefore require adequate storage space?

Choosing Your Options

- Would you use the vacuum cleaner from your house or buy one to keep in the motorhome, or would you opt for a central vacuum cleaner with attachments that store in the motorhome?
- Would you be satisfied with side view mirrors that are manually adjusted or would you like automatic, heated side view mirrors that you can control from the driver's seat?
- Would you like hydraulic jacks to level the motorhome instead of having to manually level it with blocks of wood or other objects?
- Would you prefer a rear view mirror or a rear view monitor?
- Would you like electric seats for both driver and passenger so that either person can automatically adjust the chair's position up or down, forward or backward?
- Would you like reclining seats for both driver and passenger?

- Would you like a television, video cassette recorder, or stereo installed in your unit?
- What amenities would you like in your motorhome—microwave oven, dishwasher, washer and dryer?
- Would you like a set of docking lights in addition to the backup lights that come with the motorhome for those times when you must park in a campsite at night and could use extra lighting?

Decor and Layout of Your Motorhome

- What colors and fabrics would be pleasing to you in the interior of the motorhome?
- Would you like a lot of light so that you can easily read, write, or do close-up work at night?
- Would it be more natural to you to have the kitchen on the street side or on the curbside?
- Would you find it comfortable to have a separate living area in which to unwind, read, watch television, or listen to music at the end of the travel day?
- Would you like a Class C (see Type C on page 247) with a sleeping or storage area over the driver and passenger seats?
- Would you like a slide-out extension in the bedroom, living room, dining room, or kitchen areas so that when you are parked you can enlarge the size of the motorhome?

Exterior Features of Your Motorhome

- Would you prefer corrugated siding that is less expensive but more difficult to wash and wax or a smooth vinyl or aluminum finish that is easier to wash and wax?
- Would you like your vehicle to have the largest gray water holding tank available for that model so that when camping without a sewer hookup you would not have to temporarily leave the campsite and drive to the campground's central dumping station to dump water from the sinks and shower?

Your Economic Thoughts

- Are you willing to get anywhere from 5 or 6 to 12 or 13 miles per gallon of gasoline for your vehicle?

- Are you willing to spend $30 (sometimes more) for a campsite per day?
- Can you afford payments on a vehicle costing $30,000 plus, depending on the size of the motorhome?

When You Browse for Motorhomes

- Have you *ever* been inside of a motorhome or seen one *lately*?
- Do you think or feel that you would enjoy traveling in a motorhome?
- Would you enjoy going to RV shows and dealerships until you come across the motorhome that speaks to your heart and pocketbook?
- Are you willing to temporarily leave family and friends and go off on your own adventure in a motorhome?
- What length of motorhome seems right for your living requirements and to accommodate your supplies?
- At this time in your life, would a Class B, or van type, (see Type B on page 247) meet your requirements for brief trips either overnight or for a few days?
- Are you planning to spend a month or two at a time, perhaps at one location, in the motorhome and would therefore like a longer vehicle with perhaps a slide-out extension?
- Would a specific motorhome light up your life, make you feel excited about traveling, and reach you at your "gut" level?

As You Buy Your Motorhome

- Are you willing to talk with dealers and take test rides to ascertain which motorhome has the most comfortable ride since some chassis have less sway from side to side and front to back than others?
- Are you willing to consider a repossessed or pre-owned motorhome (which often provides a significant cost savings)?
- Are you willing to compare prices at various dealerships?
- Are you aware that dealers often give price reductions on motorhomes that are on the floor of an RV show?

Maintaining Your Motorhome

- Are you willing to be prepared to work out any "bugs" in your new motorhome during its warranty period?
- Are you willing to keep the motorhome washed and waxed and in good running condition?
- Are you willing to maintain the "motor" part of your motor-home—oil changes, filters, and so forth?
- Are you willing to either work on any mechanical and motorhome body problems yourself or contact an RV service center for consultation and/or repair?
- Are you willing to give the vehicle the care and respect it needs and deserves to keep it in good running condition?

Your Courtesy on the Road

- Do you know and practice driver courtesy on the road, such as staying calm and collected when another driver pulls out in front of you?
- Are you willing to observe the following courtesies:
    - —*Never* dump except at a dump station or at a sewer connection at a campsite?
    - —When three or more vehicles are backed up behind you, and road conditions permit, pull onto the shoulder to let traffic pass?
    - —Drive with the flow of traffic unless it is above the posted speed limit or you have a mechanical problem?
    - —*Never* tailgate?

Your Communication with Others

- Are you willing to have your mail either forwarded to you for long trips or, for shorter trips, forwarded to someone else with whom you would be in contact by telephone, or held at the post office while you travel?
- If it is important to you to keep in touch with family and friends while you are away, are you willing to do so by telephone, a national motorhome association message service, or mail?

- Would you like to join a local, regional, or national camping group so that you can swap information and enjoy good times together?

Your Motorhome Education

- Between you and your traveling companion, are you willing to learn how to use the microwave/convection oven, refrigerator/freezer, and other appliances in the motorhome?
- Are you willing to acquaint yourself with the instruction books enough to know where to find answers and to safely operate the vehicle and fill out warranty cards?
- Are you willing to learn the basics of how to operate and travel in a motorhome, such as the following:
  - —Operate the water heater, water pump, auxiliary generator?
  - —Hook up to water, electricity, and sewer?
  - —Using directories, find and register at campgrounds?
- Would you enjoy continuing to learn about motorhomes from dealers, RV service people, RV publications, camping friends, and seminars at rallies and conventions?

Your Trip Satisfaction

- Do you have an overall focus for your trip so that you know where you're going yet have the excitement of not knowing what adventure lies ahead?
- Does seeing the natural landscape with its wide vistas, lakes, and big sky intrigue or interest you and give you a sense of fulfillment?
- Would you like to feel the power of sitting up high in the front seat of a motorhome and being able to see farther ahead and on each side than when in your automobile?
- Would you enjoy the following advantages of traveling in a motorhome:
  - —Having more space in which to move about en route than in a car?
  - —Being able to get snacks, go to the bathroom, rest, or sleep en route?
  - —Always having your home with you?

—Being able to hang up clothes?

—Having no suitcases to pack and unpack each day?

—Not carrying suitcases in and out of motels?

—Going to different places rather than having a set place to go on vacation?

—Experiencing a casual lifestyle?

—Getting up and on the road on your own schedule?

—Spending 50 percent less than on car/hotel vacations, 60 percent less than bus/hotel vacations, 70 percent less than air/hotel vacations, and two-thirds less than budget cruise getaways, according to a recent study by PKF Consultants?

• Lastly, would you like the satisfaction of having traveled *your* way in your motorhome at your own pace?

What's the Difference?

Trailer? Motorhome? Mobile home? Yes, there's a decided difference—in definition, cost, looks, and even whether or not it is considered an RV. I recently found an excellent booklet that answered clearly and graphically all of these questions from the Recreation Vehicle Industry Association (P.O. Box 2999, Reston, VA 20195-0999). The following is excerpted from *RVIA Information Sources for Camping & the RV Lifestyle*, May 1996.

RV Types & Terms

Recreation Vehicle/RV (AR'-Vee) n. — A recreation vehicle, or RV, is a motorized or towable vehicle that combines transportation and temporary living quarters for travel, recreation, and camping. RVs do not include mobile homes, off-road vehicles, or snowmobiles. Following are descriptions of specific types of RVs and their average retail price.

Motorized

A recreational camping and travel vehicle built on or as an integral part of a self-propelled motor vehicle chassis. It may provide kitchen, sleeping, and bathroom facilities and be equipped with the ability to store and carry fresh water and sewage.

$82,000
Motorhome (Type A)

The living unit has been entirely constructed on a bare, specially designed motor vehicle chassis to include temporary living amenities including kitchen, living and bath areas, fresh water holding tanks, waste water holding tanks, electrical hookups and city water hookups.

$40,110
Van Camper (Type B)

A panel type truck to which the RV manufacturer adds, at a minimum, any two of the following conveniences: sleeping, kitchen, and toilet facilities. Also must add 120-volt hookup, fresh water storage, and city water hookup.

$41,800
Motorhome (Type C)

This unit is built on an automotive manufactured van frame with an attached cab section. The RV manufacturer completes the body section containing the living area and attaches it to the cab section.

$29,347
Conversion Vehicles

Vans, trucks, and sport utility vehicles manufactured by an automaker then modified for transportation and recreation use by a company specializing in customized vehicles. These changes may include windows, carpeting, paneling, seats, sofas, and accessories.

Towables

An RV designed to be towed by a motorized vehicle (auto, van, or pickup truck) and of such size and weight as not to require a special highway movement permit. It is designed to provide temporary living quarters for recreational, camping, or travel use, does not require permanent on-site hookup and may provide kitchen, sleeping, and bathroom facilities and be equipped with the ability to store and carry fresh water and sewage.

$12,979
Conventional Travel Trailer

A hard-sided towable unit mounted on wheels, which is transported by means of a bumper or frame hitch attached to the towing vehicle.

$20,694
Fifth-Wheel Travel Trailer

This unit can be equipped the same as the conventional travel trailer but is constructed with a raised forward section that creates a bi-level floor plan.

This style is designed to be towed by a vehicle equipped with a fifth-wheel hitch affixed to the bed of a truck.

$4,752
Folding Camping Trailer

A recreational camping unit that is mounted on wheels and has partial solid walls connected with collapsible sidewalls that fold for towing by a motorized vehicle.

$9,994
Truck Camper

A hard-sided portable unit designed to be loaded onto the bed or chassis of a truck.

RV and Camping Shows

These huge displays give you hands-on experience with the hundreds of RVs available today. They usually charge an admission fee but sometimes send out discount coupons for admission. You can roam all day among the vehicles, asking questions of dealers, their representatives, and other showgoers. They're like living museums of modern RV technology.

A good way to get a listing of shows all over the United States is to call or write an RV trade association such as the RVIA, Dept. SL. You can watch in the media for announcements of forthcoming shows. In the past, shows have been held in cities in more than 30 states.

Clubs for Campers

National camping clubs and brand-name clubs spend thousands of dollars staying in touch with RVers by getting them together for national and regional rallies, educating them, and keeping them up to date with maintenance and other information.

Listed below are some national camping clubs:

Escapees RV Club
100 Rainbow Drive
Livingston, TX 77351
(409) 327-8873

Family Campers and Rvers
4804 Transit Road, Bldg. 2
Depew, NY 14043
(716) 668-6242

Family Motor Coach Association
(Motorhome owners only)
8291 Clough Pike
Cincinnati, OH 45244
(513) 474-3622

The Good Sam Club
P.O. Box 11097
Des Moines, IA 50381-1097
(800) 234-3450

The International Family Recreation Association
P.O. Box 520
Gonzalez, FL 32560-0520
(904) 477-7992

Loners on Wheels
P.O. Box 1355
Poplar Bluff, MO 63902
FAX: (573) 686-9342

The National RV Owners Club
P.O. Drawer 17148
Pensacola, FL 32522-7148
(904) 477-7992

RV Elderhostel
75 Federal Street
Boston, MA 02110-1941
(617) 426-7788

RVing Women
P.O. Box 1940
Apache Junction, AZ 85217
(602) 983-4678

S*M*A*R*T
Special Military Active Retired Travel Club Inc.
600 University Office Blvd., Suite 1A
Pensacola, FL 32504
(904) 478-1986

Wandering Individual Network (WIN)
P.O. Box 2010, Dept B
Sparks, NV 89432-2010

Brand-name clubs include

- Alpenlite Travel Club
- American Clipper Owners Club
- Avion Travelcade Club
- Barth Ranger Club
- Beaver Ambassador Club
- Bounders United Inc.
- Carriage Travel Club, Inc.
- Cortez National Motorhome Club
- Country Coach International
- El Dorado Caravan Club
- Firan Owners Association
- Fireball Caravaners, Inc.
- Foretravel Motorcade Club
- Georgie Boy Owners Club
- Gulf Streamers International RV Club
- Hitch Hiker of America International (NuWa)
- Holiday Rambler RV Club
- International Coachmen Caravan Club
- International Skamper Camper Club
- Jayco Jafari International Travel Club
- Lazy Daze Caravan Club
- National Collins RV Club
- Newmar Kountry Klub
- SOI Club
- Starcraft Camper Club
- Supreme Travel Club
- Wally Byam Caravan Club International (Airstream)
- Wings RV Club
- Winnebago Itasca-Travelers

RV Trade Associations

One of the basic purposes of these associations is representing their industry to the public. They invite your inquiries.

Canadian Recreational Vehicle Association
    670 Bloor St. West, Suite 200
    Toronto, Ontario CANADA
    M6G 1L2
    (416) 533-7800
    FAX: (416) 533-4795

Canadian Recreation Vehicle Dealers Association
    #209 - 20353 - 64th Avenue
    Langley, British Columbia CANADA
    V2Y 1N5
    (604) 533-4010
    FAX: (604) 533-0795

Recreation Vehicle Dealers Association (RVDA)
RV Rental Association (RVRA)
RV Aftermarket Association (RVAM)
    3930 University Drive
    Fairfax, VA 22030

Recreation Vehicle Industry Association (RVIA)
    1896 Preston White Drive
    P.O. Box 2999
    Reston, VA 20195-0999

Directories for Campgrounds

Every RV traveler at one time or another needs a directory that shows where campgrounds are located. We carry one with us in the motorhome all the time. A list of such directories is provided below.

AAA Campbooks
    Available to members only through your local AAA office

Anderson's Campground Directory
    Drawer 467
    Lewisburg, WV 24901
    (304) 645-1897

Camping Guides

Woodall Publications Corp.
13975 W. Polo Trail Drive
Lake Forest, IL 60045
(847) 362-6700

KOA Directory/Road Atlas/Camping Guide
Kampgrounds of America, Inc.
P.O. Box 30558
Billings, MT 59114-0558
(Free at any KOA campground in North America)

"Plan It—Pack It—Go" Camping Guide
Woodall Publications Corp.
13975 W. Polo Trail Drive
Lake Forest, IL 60045
(847) 362-6700

Trailer Life Campground/RV Park & Services Directory
T.L. Enterprises, Inc.
2575 Vista Del Mar Drive
Ventura, CA 93001-2575
(800) 234-3450
(805) 667-4100

Wheelers Recreational Vehicle Resort & Campground Guide
Print Media Services
1310 Jarvis Avenue
Elk Grove Village, IL 60007

Woodall's Campground Directories

Woodall Publications Corp.
13975 W. Polo Trail Drive
Lake Forest, IL 60045
(847) 362-6700
(North American, Eastern, and Western Editions)

Yogi Bear's Jellystone Park Campground Directory (Free)
Leisure Systems, Inc.
6201 Kellogg Avenue
Cincinnati, OH 45230

Publications

Magazines play an important role in educating me about RV travel. Following are some whose mission is directed toward RVers:

Camperways
Camp-orama
RV Traveler
Southern RV
    Woodall Publications Corp.
    13975 W. Polo Trail Drive
    Lake Forest, IL 60045
    (847) 362-6700

Camping and RV Magazine
    P.O. Box 458
    Washburn, WI 54891
    (715) 373-5556

The Caretaker Gazette
    23800 NE Ellis Way, Suite C-16
    Pullman, WA 99163-5303
    (509) 332-0806

Chevy Outdoors
    P.O. Box 2063
    Warren, MI 48090-2063
    (810) 574-9100

Disabled Outdoors
    HC 80, Box 395
    Grand Marais, MN 55604
    (218) 387-9100

Family Motor Coaching
    8291 Clough Pike
    Cincinnati, OH 45244
    (513) 474-3622

Highways
Motorhome
Trailer Life
    T.L. Enterprises, Inc.
    2575 Vista Del Mar Drive
    Ventura, CA 93001-2575
    (805) 667-4100
    (800) 234-3450

Midwest Outdoors
    111 Shore Drive
    Burr Ridge, IL 60521-5885
    (708) 887-7722

Northeast Outdoors
  70 Edwin Avenue
  Box 2180
  Waterbury, CT 06722
  (203) 755-0158

The Recreation Advisor
  Recreation World Services, Inc.
  P.O. Box 520
  Gonzalez, FL 32560-0520
  (904) 477-7992

RV West
  4125 Mohr Avenue, Suite E
  Pleasanton, CA 94566
  (510) 426-3200
  (800) 700-6962

Trailblazer
  Thousand Trails, Inc.
  2711 LBJ Freeway, Suite 200
  Dallas, TX 75234
  (214) 488-5021
  (800) 328-6226

Travelin'
  P.O. Box 23005
  Eugene, OR 97402-0424
  (503) 485-8533

Western RV News
  56405 Cascade View Lane
  Warren, OR 97053-9736
  (503) 222-1255

Workamper News
  201 Hiram Road
  Heber Springs, AR 72543-8747
  (501) 362-2637

Guides for Buying and Using an RV

Want to consult a guidebook before buying your RV or have one on hand when using your unit? The following are available:

King of the Road: The Beginner's Guide to RV Travel by Ted Pollard
Remington Press, Ltd.
Box 8327
Radnor, PA 19087
(610) 293-0202

Rental Directory
Recreation Vehicle Rental Association
3930 University Drive
Fairfax, VA 22030

RV Buyers Guide
RV Repair and Maintenance Manual
T.L. Enterprises, Inc.
2575 Vista Del Mar Drive
Ventura, CA 93001-2575
(800) 234-3450
(805) 667-4100

RV Lifestyle Publications Catalog (Free)
Recreation Vehicle Industry Association
Dept. POF
P.O. Box 2999
Reston, VA 20195-0999

Woodall's Go & Rent...Rent & Go
Woodall's RV Buyer's Guide
Woodall's RV Owner's Handbook (Three volumes)
Woodall Publications Corp.
13975 W. Polo Trail Drive
Lake Forest, IL 60045
(847) 362-6700

Index

ORDER FORM

If you know someone who would like his or her own copy of *At Your Own Pace: Traveling Your Way in Your Motorhome*, you can order more copies of this book by filling out the following information.

Please send _____ copies of *At Your Own Pace: Traveling Your Way in Your Motorhome* to

(Please Print)

Name_____

Address_____

City _____ State _____Zip _____

Telephone (_____)_____

Fax (_____)_____

Cost: Single copy $16.95	$_____	
Maryland residents add 5% sales tax	$_____	
Shipping (add $3.00 for the first book, $1.50 for each additional book)	$_____	
TOTAL ENCLOSED	$_____	

Please send check or money order to

Arbor House Publishing
332 One Forty Village Rd., Suite 6-197
Westminster, MD 21157
Telephone (410) 857-4146
Fax: (410) 857-3835